MEDIEVAL
MORALITY PLAYS
AND
INTERLUDES

EDITED BY

VINCENT F. HOPPER

and

GERALD B. LAHEY

New York University

BARRON'S EDUCATIONAL SERIES, INC.

Woodbury, New York • London • Toronto • Sydney

Medieval Mystery Plays

ABRAHAM AND ISAAC

NOAH'S FLOOD

THE SECOND SHEPHERDS' PLAY

Morality Plays

THE CASTLE OF PERSEVERANCE

EVERYMAN

AND

Interludes

JOHAN, THE HUSBAND

THE FOUR PP.

All inquiries should be addressed to
Barron's Educational Series, Inc.
113 Crossways Park Drive
Woodbury, New York 11797

PRINTED IN THE UNITED STATES OF AMERICA

Library of Congress Catalog Card Number: 61-18362

4567   510   17 16 15 14 13 12 11

THEATRE CLASSICS FOR THE
MODERN READER

To reproduce the values and effects of the theatre on the printed page is the ambitious aim of this series of the classics of the stage. Although good plays have always been read as well as acted, few playwrights before the era of Ibsen and Shaw have ever written with any public other than the theatre audience sharply in their minds. In consequence, the reader of older plays is usually required to supply his own visualizing of the staging and his own interpretation of stage action and even the manner of the delivery of the lines themselves. Frequently he is also required to put up with abbreviations and other space-saving printing devices.

This modern reader's edition of theatre classics vitalizes the outstanding plays of the past with the kind of eye-pleasing text and the kinds of reading and acting guides to which today's reader is accustomed in good published editions of twentieth century dramas. The text itself has not been altered except for occasional modernizations of spelling and punctuation (common to all modern editions of earlier works) and the rare use of italics for emphasis when the reading of a line is not immediately clear. Essentially, that is, the author's text is as he wrote it. Added to it are descriptions of scenes and costumes, indications of expression and action, and explanation of words and references not readily comprehensible.

The illustrations should aid immeasurably in visualizing the play. A description of the original staging, stage conditions, and stage techniques is provided partly as still another aid to visualization but principally to show how the playwright adapted his materials to suit the particular stage conventions of his time. Companioning each play are also a sketch of the author's life, an analysis of the play, and a selective bibliography to make this as much an all-in-one edition as possible.

CONTENTS

Introduction

THE BEGINNING

In respect to the political and dramatic developments of medieval England, there were in the beginning not one but two Words: *Magna Carta* for the former and *Quem Quaeritis* for the latter. Just as the significance of Magna Carta lay in general implications to be wrought out by history, so the significance of the little liturgical playlet or trope known as the *Quem Quaeritis* resided not in itself but in what is so minutely prefigured for the centuries to come.

The term *trope* designates an unofficial literary addition in dramatic form to the ordinary Church service or liturgy, the latter not having been so finally determined in medieval times as now. The trope is different from the Church service in that the latter is a purely symbolic commemorative ritual (viewed externally) whereas the trope invites dramatic impersonation and scenic setting. The term *tropes* in the plural often indicates the totality of these dramatic additions to the ordinary Catholic liturgy, developments which occurred widely and rapidly beginning around the tenth century.

Since it is now almost an unwritten law that no discussion of Medieval Drama can be undertaken without examples of the trope, two very early ones are given. Although tropes originated in both the Christmas and Easter services, along with other festivals of the Church, the Easter tropes are the earlier. They dramatize and celebrate the triumphant event in the Christian scheme of the redemption: the Resurrection. The subject of both of the following very early and simple tropes is the visit of the Marys to the empty sepulchre of Christ for the purpose of annointing with aromatic spices the body supposedly there. Since the Gospel narratives themselves vary in assigning the number of Marys visiting the tomb and the number of angels present, different manuscripts give different numbers of actors. There are two or more Marys, one or more angels, depending on the manuscript consulted. The trope immediately following is from a manuscript of the monastery of St. Gall of the tenth century, one of the simplest extant specimens. Obviously the "Interrogatio" introduces the angel or angels; the "Responsio," the Marys:

Interrogatio: Quem quaeritis in sepulchro, O Christicolae?
(Whom do you seek in the sepulchre, O Christian women?)

Responsio: Iesum Nazarenum crucifixum, o caelocolae.
(Jesus of Nazareth, who was crucified, O Heavenly Ones.)

Angeli: Non est hic, surrexit sicut predixerat; ite, nuntiate quia surrexit de sepulchro.
(He is not here; He is risen just as He foretold. Go, announce that He is risen from the sepulchre.)

The second illustration is taken from the *Regularis Concordia* of St. Ethelwold, who was Abbot of Abingdon in 954 and then became Bishop of Winchester in 963. The *Concordia* was an appendix to the Rule of St. Benedict drawn up by Ethelwold, the Bishop, at the Cathedral. This trope had been transferred from the Easter Mass and placed to follow the third lesson at Matins. The Latin words within the parentheses are expansions of the original as set down in the *Concordia,* where oftentimes merely introductory words were written, the lines being already known by the performer.

Quem quaeritis (in sepulchro, O Christicolae?)
(Whom do you seek in the tomb, O Christian women?)

Ihesum Nazarenum (crucifixum, O Coelicola.)
(Jesus of Nazareth, who was crucified, O Heavenly
One.)

Non est hic; surrexit sicut praedixerat. Ite, nuntiate
quia resurrexit a mortuis.
(He is not here; He is risen just as He foretold. Go,
announce that He is risen from the dead.)

Alleluia, resurrexit Dominus, (hodie resurrexit leo
fortis, Christus, filius Dei.)
(Alleluia, the Lord is risen, today He has risen, the
strong lion, Christ, the Son of God.)

Venite et videte (ubi positus erat Dominus, alleluia.)
(Come and see the place where the Lord was laid,
Alleluia.)

Surrexit Dominus de sepulchro, (qui pro nobis per-
pendit in ligno, alleluia.)
(The Lord is arisen from the sepulchre, who hung
upon the cross for us, Alleluia.)

Te Deum laudamus.
(We praise Thee, O God.)

One of the fullest records of the background and
actual context of the performance of a trope is given
in the *Regularis Concordia* of St. Ethelwold, a document in Latin reprinted in many publications concerning the development of medieval drama and
liturgy. The *Concordia* answers in some ways to a
"script" with directions for production. Before presenting the *Quem Quaeritis,* the *Concordia* discusses a
Good Friday ceremony to which the *Quem Quaeritis*
is in some ways the Easter morning sequel. The Good
Friday ceremony is the *Depositio Crucis,* or burial of
the Cross. The manuscript speaks didactically of using

the trope "to the strengthening of the faith in the unlettered vulgar and in neophytes."

To that end, the document directs that "a likeness of the sepulchre be made in a vacant part of the altar and a veil stretched on a ring," the latter to hang until the ceremony of the "adoration of the cross" has been completed. Thereafter the deacons who previously carried the cross are told to "come and wrap it in a shroud in the place where it was adored." Afterwards, singing antiphons, they are to carry it back "until they come to the place of the monument and there, having put down the cross as if it were the buried body of our Lord Jesus Christ, let them sing an antiphon."

Then, St. Ethelwold, apparently anticipating strong popular interest, warns that the buried cross, which is symbolic of the buried body of Christ, "be guarded with all reverence" up to the night of the Resurrection of the Lord. Giving flexible directions to be observed according as the crowd is large or small, he concludes this portion of his comment: "At night especially let two brothers or three—or as many as the size of the congregation shall require—be appointed who may keep faithful watch singing psalms."

At this point there follows a description of the activities which took place either in the monastery or cathedral in the dim light of Easter morning:

> While the third lesson is being sung, let four of the brethren vest themselves, one of whom, vested in an alb, is to enter as if to participate in the service. But let him unnoticed go to the place of the sepulchre, and there sit quietly holding a palm in his hand. While the third responsory is being celebrated, let the remaining three follow, and be vested in copes, and bear in their hands thuribles with incense, and advancing tentatively as though uncertainly seeking for something, let them come before the place of the sepulchre. These things are enacted in imitation of the angel seated in the monument and of the women coming with spices to anoint the body of Jesus.
>
> When he who is seated by the tomb sees how these three

approach him like wanderers seeking after something, he should begin to sing softly and sweetly, *Quem quaeritis:* when he has sung this to the end, the other three must answer him in unison: *Ihesum Nazarenum.* To whom the first one replies: *Non est hic: surrexit, sicut praedixerat. Ite nuntiate quia surrexit a mortuis.* At the word of this bidding, let the three turn to the choir saying *Alleluia: resurrexit dominus.* After these words have been uttered, let the former, seating himself and as if recalling them, sing the antiphon *Venite et videte locum.* While saying this, let him rise and lift the veil to show them the place stripped of the cross, with nought but the winding sheets remaining with which the cross had been wrapped. When they have seen this, let them set down their thuribles which they have carried into that very sepulchre and let them take up the shroud and spread it out before the clergy; and as if to make manifest that the Lord has risen and is no longer wrapped within it, let them sing this antiphon: *Surrexit dominus de sepulchro,* and let them place the shroud upon the altar. When the antiphon is concluded, let the Prior, sharing in their jubilation at the triumph of our King, who in conquering death rose again, begin the hymn *Te Deum laudamus.* After this has begun, let all the bells be rung together.

The candle-lighted ceremony in the heart of the cloister in the dawn of an Easter morning stood in a long perspective: the theatre of Dionysus at Athens at one end; the spacious imaginative world of the Globe just outside of London at the other. Thus in taking the earliest liturgical addition, the Visitation-of-the-Sepulchre trope as our vantage point for beginning a discussion of medieval drama, we are looking at a small fire in the wide and long canyon of dramatic history. The author of the *Concordia* could only with great imaginative effort have applied to his own historical moment the words of the visionary hero of Tennyson's *Locksley Hall:*

When the centuries behind me like a fruitful land reposed;
When I clung to all the present for the promise that it closed.

It was still many years ahead to the great medieval mystery (or miracle) cycles of the fourteenth and fifteenth centuries, those of Chester, York, Wakefield, and Coventry, with their secular theatrical tradition and spoken vernacular. Viewed from the year 970, the fruitful land of the past, which had withered with the decay of the Roman theatre, was a ghostly thing of legend and scandal.

THE PAST

By the year 568 A.D., the Roman theatre of the plays and the *spectacula* (all public entertainment) had been obliterated. It is needless to mention more than a detail or two of its decline and fall. The performers in Rome were slaves. Despite the fame of a Roscius, the social status of the actor was much debased. The incursion of the barbarians from the north had brought only incomprehension and indifference to the old theatre. The only element of the older tradition that survived was that of the *mimi,* or mimes—those who formerly were of the incidental or subordinate *intermezzi* now became the sole and central survivors. They themselves were the descendants of the more ancient Greek *phylakes,* Walpurgis-night spirits of the antique world who portrayed life without taboo or inhibition, satiric and anti-heroic, not to say, on occasion, lascivious and indecent in word, song, and gesture.

The surviving mimes or *histriones* of the older Rome were disdainful of and reciprocally despised by the priests of the lingering paganism and the Fathers of the early Church. To the mimes both were dubious and incredible. Because the new Christian religion puzzled them and bewildered them, they gave burlesque performances of such sacramental rites as baptism. The latter was crudely ridiculed by the introduction of a drunken candidate for the ceremony, and the rite turned into a general "dunking" party. It is not surprising that eventually the Christians refused even to baptize an actor. By the year 200 Tertullian, a Latin Father writing in *de Spectaculum* could promise Christians compensation for ignoring the theatre here by the anticipation of the greatest of revelations—that of Judgment Day. Then the Christians could rejoice at the tragedians whose "lamentations will be more poignant because of their own pain" and laugh more delightedly at the comedians who would "turn and twist . . . nimbler . . . by the sting of the fire that is never quenched!" On the other hand, later Latin Fathers, such as St. Augustine, though opposed to much of the theatre, critically discriminated between the good and the bad. It should be remembered that the better Romans denounced what was coarse and depraved in the Roman theatre.

At any rate, across the "dark ages" the decrees of Councils and Synods, the voices of saints, doctors, and confessors, of bishops and abbots mingle in denunciation of the theatre as the armory and forge of the weapons of the great Adversary, the arch-enemy Satan. From the Council of Nicea in 325 in which St. Athanasius condemns Arius by association with the theatre to the Council of Paris in 829, the theatre, its pomp, and its players are deplored and reprobated. The voices of eminent ecclesiastical worthies boom across the centuries like the subdued thunder-roll of distant artillery: Tertullian, Cyprian, Chrysostom, Augustine, Jerome are ranged against the ancient institution. Thinkers like Alcuin warn that it is better to serve God than the players. Even an occasional pope, an Innocent III, condemns the entertainment of the players.

For all of that—indeed, in the light of that—some sort of itinerant, migratory tradition of the mimes persisted. Otherwise protests, prohibitions, and warnings would not have been sounded so regularly. In the seventh century, Isidore of Seville bears truculent witness to the fact of a vanished theatre but of a surviving tradition of jongleurs, histriones, tellers of tales, puppet-masters, musical instrumentalists. Thomas de Cab-

ham, a clerical official of Salisbury (d.1313) gives, like
Isidore, at a later date but in more detail an account
of the continuance of the mimes. He carefully classifies
them as to moral status. Besides the indecent and
licentious in dance and gesture who perform in public
houses is a second class of satirists and parodists who
perform at the courts and in the halls of the great and
the affluent. They satirize shamefully and scandalously
absent faces and names. A third class, more respectable,
are the singers of saintly lives and the deeds of heroic
princes. Despite the saving remnant of the third class,
a Bishop of Lindisfarne protests in an official document
that it is better to feed paupers at the monastery gates
than to play host to actors within. He thus indicates
that the clergy themselves found the players diverting.

All in all then, there is a scattered but continuous
evidence of a tradition of nomadic entertainers and
jongleurs, wandering troupes of the successors of the
mimes, comparable to scops, gleemen, troubadours.
They are itinerant actors and satirical *goliardi;* comedians, dancers, instrumentalists, tellers of tales, clowns
and fools who move in the shadowy twilight of the
dark ages along the trade and pilgrim routes, the busy
highways, at the cross-roads, in castle and court, in
tavern and public house. Their entertainment is endlessly varied: the jokes, gaiety, burlesque songs and
stories of the song-and-dance man. Yet they range from
the indecent dance and story to moving tales of heroic
deeds and accomplishments. It is not difficult to see
their tradition stretching to that of the full-blown medieval drama—to Abraham and Isaac, the Shepherds,
Noah's wife, the bewilderment of Joseph at the Annunciation, the roaring and raging Herods, the furious an-
tics of demons and devils.

Still, the tradition of the mimes, conjectural as it is,
almost certainly did not flow directly into that of the
medieval mysteries, miracles, and moralities. Such, at
any rate, is the conventional view of the standard historians. It is a fact that the secular drama of the Middle

Ages developed from the liturgical drama, and that the latter in turn is the expansion of the tropes. An accepted fact, also, is that the tropes issued from the Church services, or at least appeared in conjunction with them at first. The question is historically how to bridge the gap, the distance between the liturgical and the secular drama. Before commenting briefly on the latter, a word or two on the terms used to describe the components of medieval drama.

In discussions of medieval drama, the student constantly encounters the terms *mystery, miracle,* and *morality* as words descriptive of distinct types of plays. This verbal distinction between *mystery* and *miracle* was little known during the centuries in which medieval drama flourished. It appears to have been introduced in the middle of the eighteenth century to formally distinguish between religious plays based on Biblical stories and factual narratives (the *mystery*) and plays based upon the lives and legends of the saints (the *miracle*). Originally most writers used the word *miracle* to refer to any medieval play, the word deriving from *miraculum.* That word was not originally limited to a specific kind of supernatural "intervention" in the course of "nature." It meant anything of a religious character in general. At the present time, some writers use *miracle* to refer to any vernacular religious play acted outside the Church, thus excluding from its scope the liturgical drama.

Notwithstanding, there was in France some evidence of a tradition of calling Biblical plays *mystery plays.* The French *mystère* derived neither from the Greek *mysterion,* referring to secret or clandestine religious ceremonies, nor was it related to the English term *mystery* as descriptive of a specialized trade or craft. It is supposedly derived from the late Latin *ministerium,* referring to Church service. Whatever be the truth of the matter, the distinction observed is convenient. As is the term *morality* convenient to describe plays based upon the conflict of abstractions and ideas, virtues and vices, personified. They, in the main, do not turn upon historical events, Biblical or hagiographical, but are imaginatively constructed to illustrate ethical issues bearing upon conduct and salvation.

The reader should not regard these terms and their ideas as something medieval and academic, something "esoteric." If Macaulay's prophetic vision of a future New Zealander arriving in England to survey its ruins were to materialize, the visitor, something of an amateur archeologist, might, in unearthing the ruins of Ayot St. Lawrence, come to the conclusion that a medieval writer once lived there, despite some chronological evidence to the contrary. The visitor, acquainted with medieval drama and conceiving its forms to be merely period ones, would point to surviving manuscripts (themselves supposedly extant plays from a larger lost cycle) to illustrate that the versatile writer did all types of medieval play: the mystery play (*Back to Methuselah*), the morality play (*Man and Superman*), and a remarkably clever miracle play (*St. Joan*). Conscious of the Wakefield Master, the visitor would dub the unknown author "the St. Lawrence Master," noting that he shared with the original a curious mingling of the religious-imaginative and the realistic. The point is that in one way or another the terms loosely but adequately describe a good deal of drama this side of the middle ages.

THE MYSTERY CYCLES

There exists a number of great sequences of individual dramas variously known collectively as Mystery Cycles, or Biblical Pageants or Cyclic Pageants, or, finally, as Corpus Christi Plays or Pageants. The term *pageant,* equivalent to the Biblical or mystery play, is used to draw attention to the fact of its being a part of the total Cycle, an episode comparable to the "Book" of one of the great epics. That is, the term *pageant* emphasizes the continuous unified structure of a Cycle, the parts of which were successively played before the

same audience either on a single day from dawn to
dusk, or on two or three successive days, according
to local custom. In this impressive epic sequence, the
guild pageants or Biblical mysteries presented the econ-
omy of salvation, the redemptive scheme of God for
man in a succession of mystery plays. Mystery dramas,
although centering mainly on the dramatization of
Gospel events, nevertheless include within their range
episodes and characters from the Old Testament as
well. A Cycle, for example, would begin with a play
about the Fall of Lucifer, proceed to plays of the
Creation and Fall of Man, and then—among others—
present a drama of Noah, one of Cain and Abel, one
of Abraham and Isaac, then a group of Nativity plays,
an Annunciation perhaps with scenes of Joseph's
troubled response to the news, then episodes from the
life of Christ, the Passion and the Resurrection (including a *Quem Quaeritis* buried in the center). These,
together with many others, would terminate fittingly in
a Day of Doom play or *Judicium*. Thus within the interval of a day or several days, the medieval townsfolk
would witness an historical panorama comprising events
before and after the history of mankind on this earth,
a generous range of interest.

There are several well-known and deservedly celebrated Cycles, only a portion of a much larger original
mass now presumable lost. We do not have the orig-
inals of any Cycle, the manuscripts surviving being
transcripts of endless revisions and of discreet inter-
borrowings. The York, Chester, Wakefield, and N. town
Cycles are the principal collections.

The Wakefield Cycle is sometimes referred to as the
Towneley Cycle because it was once in the possession of
the Towneley family of Burnley, Lancashire. The manuscripts are now in the Huntington Library, San Marino,
California. Presumably the Wakefield craft and trade
guilds presented them, although it is not certain that
they owned them. They may possibly have been the
property of a near-by Abbey. There are now in the

manuscript collection thirty plays or "pageants." Not all are complete, however. These manuscripts are possibly a transcript or copy of what was originally an official text of the Cycle. Five or six of these plays are attributed to a hypothetical single author known as the Wakefield Master. The ascription is based upon numerous local allusions, highly individual stanza forms, and individuality of style and idiom. From a literary standpoint, they are the most valued plays in the collection. The Cycle in general is closely related to the York Cycle, which is a little earlier than the Wakefield. The York Cycle dates from 1340-1350, the manuscripts from about 1430. Both the York and Wakefield Cycles were ordinarily given processionally on a single day, beginning at 4:30 or 5:00 A.M. and continuing until nightfall.

The N. town Cycle is a collection of forty-two pageants surviving in a late fifteenth century manuscript. Because of the designation *Ludus Coventriae* appearing in the course of it, it was once believed to embody the Corpus Christi or Mystery Cycle of Coventry. Actually, it has nothing to do with Coventry—the real or true Coventry collection consisting only of two surviving pageants, the better known being an Annunciation mystery once performed by the Shearmen and Tailors of Coventry. Notwithstanding, some writers still refer to the N. town Cycle as the "Coventry" Cycle. Others, because they believe the pageants to have been in the possession of one Robert Hegge, refer to them as the Hegge Cycle. The dissatisfaction with the name of Coventry arises from the fact that the plays probably do not belong to Coventry but to the East Midlands, the Eastern counties. The term *N. town* is derived from an insert in a prologue to one of the plays:

> A Sunday next, yf that we may,
> At six of the belle, we gynne our play
> In N——— towne. . . .

The verse points to a company of strolling players and provides a basis for inference that these plays were given on stationary platforms and not in the more common processional manner. The N————, of course, is for *Nomen,* the name of the town to be supplied by the wandering banner-bearers or vexillatores, who as "advance publicity men" proclaimed the coming of the play at a given town. Their function and manner is illustrated in the *Castle of Perseverance.* Dating from the second half of the fifteenth century, the N———— town plays are considered to be the most soberly didactic and least dramatic of any of the Cycles. The other three Cycles, at least, were presented under the auspices of local town and municipal guilds, religious confraternities, or civic bodies.

The Chester plays are the oldest Cycle, and in the opinion of some critics the most perfect in form and spirit, taken as a whole. Their humor is more reserved, their religious tone higher, and their didacticism is felt to be less obtrusive. Although there is no extant manuscript earlier than 1591, it is thought that the plays are based on a text originating near the beginning of the fifteenth century. The original composition of them is assigned to a period perhaps fifty years prior to that— around the middle of the fourteenth century. The Chester plays comprise a total of twenty-five separate plays or pageants. Mode of production and weather conditions made it possible to present Christmas plays, etc. in correlation with the appropriate time of the year. In 1264 Pope Urban had instituted the Feast of the Corpus Christi, a festival with processions in honor of the Holy Sacrament, coming about eight weeks after Easter. The decree was more effectively re-enacted by Clement V in 1311. The Chester Cycle appears to have been first given at this season of the year, the late May or early June weather having been propitious for out-of-doors performance. Because of the coincidence of the performance and the Festival, the great Cycles are, as

has been noted, occasionally referred to as Corpus
Christi Cycles. Many of the municipal corporations and
guilds of the towns adopted this season for dramatic and
other festivals. Some critics, to make the matter more
complicated, reserve the term "Corpus Christi play" to
refer only to Passion or Resurrection plays. At this
festival period the twenty-five Chester plays were given,
spread fairly evenly over three days.

MODE OF PRODUCTION

As has been already indicated, the development of medieval drama led to its removal from within
the sacred precincts of the Church to an out-of-door,
open-air performance in meadows, public greens, in
highways, and in streets of market and cathedral towns.
Religious fraternities, the great municipal corporations,
the trade and craft guilds (uniting economics and religion and the laity) sponsored and effected the presentation of the Cycles. It might be noted in passing
that medieval trade and craft guilds were not the
equivalent of modern trade unions. In the former, what
would now be regarded as executives and managers
were members as well as craftsmen and workers. Naturally, the passing of the drama from the hands of the
clergy to the laity led to the use of the spoken vernacular, to the introduction of a more worldly, comic,
often farcical tone but without displacing the essentially serious and reverent intention of the earlier
liturgical playlets.

There were two methods of production: (1) the stationary and (2) the ambulatory or processional, the
latter generally preferred by the great guild Cycles. In
the former, a meadow with a ditch, wall, or fence
enclosure provided a theatre-in-the-round. There could,
of course, be a number of them, and spectators could
wander from one to the other. According to the second
method, the more usual one, the medieval townsfolk
assembled at festival time at a series of stations along
a main route. The plays were then successively brought

forward to them, a production *seriatim*—by pageant wagons or "floats." No. 1 play or pageant-wagon stopped at No. 1 station, gave its performance (*The Fall of Lucifer*, say) and then made way for the No. 2 pageant-wagon to take its place at the first station to present the *Creation of Adam and Eve*, etc. Thus the Cycle of plays proceeded from Creation to Judgment Day, during one or several days. The emerging destiny of mankind was progressively displayed before the eyes of the spectators. Anyone having seen or read Marc Connelly's *Green Pastures* will have experienced a much abbreviated but comparable dramatic panorama.

A well-known account of the processional type of performance is that of one Archdeacon Rogers who witnessed one of the last performances of the Chester plays in the last decade of the sixteenth century:

> Every company has his pagiant, or parte, which pagiants weare a high scafolde with two rowmes, a higher and a lower, upon four wheeles. In the lower they apparelled them selves, and in the higher rowme they played, beinge all open on the tope, that all behoulders mighte heare and see them. They places where they played them was in every streete. They begane first at the abay gates, and when the firste pagiante was played it was wheeled to the highe crosse before the mayor, and so to every streete; and soe every streete had a pagiant playinge before them at one time, till all the pagiantes for the days appoynted weare played: and then when one pagiant was neere ended, worde was broughte from streete to streete, that soe they mighte come in place thereof exceding orderlye, and all the streetes have theire pagiantes afore them all at one time playeinge togeather; to se which playes was great resorte, and also scafoldes and stages made in the streetes in those places where they determined to playe theire pagiantes.

The two-level pageant-wagons referred to were apparently big and cumbrous vehicles appropriate for such a huge municipal enterprise. The stage-platforms are often referred to as *lius* (*lieux*), *estals, sedes, sieges,* etc. As the account indicates, there was a dressing or

tiring room on the first or lower level, a curtained area.
The open stage was on the second or upper level, thus
permitting greater visibility to the large audiences. The
street in front of and just around the pageant-wagon
was "neutral" or stage-ground. There, of course, Herod
raved and raged, and devils and demons fired their
squibs, obscenities, and blasphemies as occasion de-
manded or improvisation suggested.

There was some effort towards realistic scenery and
stage effects and properties. We often note smoke, fire-
works, the tumultuous rattling of pots, kettles, and pans
in connection with devils and hell. Devils appeared in
black leather, complete with horns, hoofs, tail, and
wooden fork. God wore white leather, white hair and
beard in venerable style, and shone with a gilded countenance. Paradise scenes for the temptation and fall of
man were curtained, Adam and Eve being visible from
the shoulders up. If not curtained, then the original
pair were clothed in tight white-leather to simulate
nudity. The primeval Garden was hung with silks,
fruits, fragrant flowers and blossoms, together with leafy
boughs. Burning altars and bladders of blood served for
melodramatic moments. Linen sometimes served for
white clouds. In scenes of the Magi, for example, rich
costume, gold, censors, costly vessels were to be seen. In
the *Castle of Perseverance* and presumably other plays
there was a color symbolism (in which the liturgy and
rubrics of the Church were so rich): white for mercy,
red for righteousness; truth was apparelled in "sad
grene," and the spectator saw "Pes all in blake." There
is frequent record of varying payments to actors for
the performance of different roles and the acquisition
of suitable properties.

A picturesque aspect of the guild production of the
performances is the often quaint correlation between
scene and guild-trade. The following guilds, for example, produced the following scenes in one Cycle:
The Shipwrights—Noah's Ark, the Bakers—the Last
Supper, The Vintners—The Miracle at Cana, The

Goldsmiths—the scene of the Magi, the Plumbers—the Woman taken in Adultery, the Carpenters—the Resurrection scene, the Butchers—the Crucifixion, the Cardmakers—the Creation of Adam and Eve.

SOME MODERN VIEWS

We originally noted that political liberty and medieval drama began with two Latin words each. It is evident that each case presents an impressive gap between what the two words distantly prefigure and the historical realization. It is a long reach from the self-aggrandizing, feudal, baronial *Magna Carta* of early June of 1215 to the American *Declaration of Independence* and the French Declaration of the Rights of Man. Yet the historical tradition that asserts a causal relation is probably right.

Likewise there is an immense historical gap to be filled in between the modest little *Quem Quaeritis* of the tenth century and the great Cycles and innumerable lesser individual dramas being written and performed all over England in the fourteenth, fifteenth, and sixteenth centuries. The central question is what fertilizing and expansive energies transformed the Latin chanted by clergymen within the cloistered precincts of the Church into the vast secular enterprise it became. A possession of the laity, acted and managed by them, and by their guilds and corporations; performed in the tumultuous, thronging streets; embodied in a lively, humorful, mirthful, spoken vernacular. Again, the historical instinct is vaguely right which asserts a direct line of relationship between the secular medieval drama of the later centuries and the tiny liturgical drama of the tenth. Yet there are decisively important tributary channels flowing into and swelling the main stream in both instances.

A number of modern critics reject as quite inadequate and unreal the view that a mere didactic impulse, an ecclesiastical interest in instruction and edification, was the sole or even central energizing force behind the development. The distance between a minuscule Christmas trope of Limoges of the eleventh century, or of a little liturgical Christmas drama the *Pastores* of Rouen of the eleventh century and *The Second Shepherds' Play* is psychologically too great for such an explanation, they insist. Neither can they tolerate with great patience what is the more direct, certainly the simpler, hypothesis: the theory of the "spontaneous outburst" school of interpretation. The following is a fairly typical specimen taken from a highly reputable work on medieval drama, touching on the *Quem Quaeritis*:

> This visitation of the Sepulchre, the earliest liturgical play, was a spontaneous outburst of the dramatic instinct in the heart of the cloister; the inevitable overflow of the pent-up emotions of Passion Week in commemorative action, ending with the Te Deum and the triumphant peal of bells. For hundreds of years this theme, with variations and additions, was presented in 'he monastic and cathedral churches of Western Europe. . . . In the twelfth century manuscripts of Fleury we have a complete mystery play of the Resurrection, still retaining at its core the Quem quaeritis trope from which it had sprung.

Most theories explain something; no one explains everything. "Sprung," "outburst," "overflow," "instinct" —these terms sometimes merely assume what they purport to explain. When they do so, they mask the real problem by dwelling on the surface expression as though a development *sui generis*. As if to trace the origin of language to something called "voice" or to an "upwelling" of articulateness or as the spontaneous outburst of high feeling into grammar and syntax.

Medieval physicians knew for centuries that certain visitations, the Black Plague, for instance, rapidly took on epidemic proportions. It could have been explained as the spontaneous outburst of long pent-up "maleficient factors." The hypothesis would not have been wrong. Merely verbal. Until a Pasteur explained by the germ theory specifically how disease was developed and transmitted, nothing was really understood. Afterwards, at

least one tangible link between health and epidemic
disease was provided.

The same kind of theorizing about the development
of medieval drama is dubiously reinforced by appeals
to history, particularly the supposed analogy of the
ancient world. Writers on medieval drama inherit a
tradition that the religion and rites of Dionysus gave
rise to Greek drama and the Greek theatre. But that
sequence of events is little more than a huge *post hoc
ergo propter hoc*. A gap of centuries intervenes, the
interspaces of which are vacant of specific evidence and
data. Whence arose the view: religion spontaneously
produces drama. We have now reached the point where
writers on the history of Greek drama appeal to medieval drama in illustration of their theory of spontaneous
generation. Reciprocally, writers on medieval drama appeal to the history of Greek drama with the same fra-
ternal confidence. In each case an enigma is summoned
in support of a riddle. Writers on medieval drama have
even less grounds for using the analogy. What re-
semblance is there between the Dionysian frenzy, its
orgiastic dances and primitive ecstasies, and the contemplative reminiscence, the cloistered monastic calm
of the sequestered trope? The aestheticism of the monastery or cathedral would be naturally hostile to the
violent excitement supposedly the origin of the Greek
drama. How do opposite causes produce the same phe-
nomenon? There is no "outburst," no "overflow" in
the *Quem Quaeritis*. There is a gentle elegiac sigh;
a nostalgic tear of happiness.

Unless and until we know *how,* can present some
tangible step in the mutation, we really know little or
nothing about the development of medieval drama.
There are in English, German, French, and Italian massive two-volume documentations of tropes, liturgical
dramas, catalogues of medieval manuscripts and their
plays, their conjectured origins, dates, ownership, history of possession, manner of presentation, linguistic
peculiarities, and local allusions, etc., fully equipped

with specimens and glossaries. There are lengthy and learned discussions of the Greek and Roman theatres, of life in the Middle Ages, religious and folk customs. But as for explaining development, exhibiting the specific milieu wherein the trope became *The Castle of Perseverance*, these splendid tomes of learning are magnificent museums wherein the erudite and the arid are locked in still and sterile embrace.

To further worry the "outburst" theory, Europe had been Christianized for many centuries prior to the tenth. Why did emotions "pent up" during these long centuries not "overflow" long before they did? Had they not been just as intense for many centuries before? Was any great "impulse" or "instinct" required to produce the minute drama of the trope, multiply and distribute texts and variations to the monasteries of Europe? If the Mass itself, the elaborate and formal ceremonies of Holy Week—all of them a large "commemorative action"—did not in earlier centuries stimulate the dramatic imagination, why did the cumulative action of the centuries produce but the brief and delicate *Quem Quaeritis?*

More specifically: the really dramatic elements of the Holy Week commemoration were those connected with the Passion. If one looks today for any special expression of the "pent-up" emotions of Holy Week, he finds them, for example, in the Catholic Church in the devotional practice of the Stations of the Cross. These do commemorate the most dramatic elements of the Passion. What more appropriate materials for the embodiment of feeling in dramatic form than the events preceding the Passion: the Last Supper, the betrayal by Judas, the ordeal and trial of Jesus, the prophetic warning of St. Peter's denial and its fulfillment, etc? Here is the real stuff of drama: suspense, suffering, villains, deserting friends. Why the pretty charm and quaint simplicity of the *Quem Quaeritis* as the expression of such dark and prolonged agony? Wordsworth's "overflow" theory of the origin of his own poetry may possibly be used to explain the poetry of other individuals. But it is not suitable for the slow, silent labor of centuries. It recalls the now venerable attempt to describe the Renaissance as a leap into light from the "Dark Ages."

These simple observations serve as a prelude to little more than a cursory mention of the new school of critics now intruding into the dust of the stately precincts of the history of medieval drama. The new types of criticism may be illustrated by *The Origin of the Theatre* by B. Hunningher and *Medieval English Poetry, the Non-Chaucerian Tradition* by John Speirs, as two specimens among many. Besides literary sophistication, the critics of the new school embody an amphibian strain: part historian of dramatic performance and entertainment, part amateur anthropologist. They thus employ twin weapons of analysis: one utilizing a very definite type of evidence from which fairly large inferences are made, the other a highly conjectural, speculative approach to medieval drama, together with a disposition to elicit, at times, possibly arbitrary significance from details of specific dramas.

The latter type of analysis lays much stress on ancient heathen, pre-Christian fertility and rebirth rites supposed to have survived in symbolically disguised forms: seasonal ceremonies annually enacted in the spring of the year, the spring-rites of folk-play and village fertility ceremony, folk dances, games, and contests. The view is the belated fruit of *The Golden Bough* of Sir James Frazer. Any postulated "overflow" or "outburst" proceeds along channels formed by the archetypal patterns of Dr. Jung's collective unconscious. Indeed they tend to turn the venerable history of medieval drama into an *Emperor Jones* monograph which discloses beneath the rational surface-sophistication of the dramatic action a strong irrational substratum, to find the conscious drama of art imbedded in the ritual drama of primitive fecundity rites.

From the point of view of ritual drama, such rites

serve to produce not merely "imitation," but to animate, revive, re-awaken feeling and life. Hence one William Newhall in the mid-sixteenth century could say of the Chester plays that they were not only for "increase of the holy and catholick faith of our Savyour, Jhu' Crist, and to exort the mynds of the co'mon people to good devotion and holsome doctryne thereof, but also for the co'mon Welth and prosperitie of this Citie . . . plaies . . . devised to the honour of God . . ." They provided mana as well as manna.

To take first the newer historical view. It begins by dismissing sharply the still surviving hypothesis of the romantic school of the nineteenth century—already commented upon—that religion automatically produces drama. In so doing, the new criticism expounds fully all the points we have just summarized so briefly in relation to the Dionysian analogy and the spontaneous generation theories.

Next, this critical attitude is emphatic in its rejection of the idea that there was any theatrical vacuum for some centuries before the rise of the tropes. They emphasize the flourishing tradition of actors and performers in Byzantium and the fact that no "iron curtain" hung at that time between East and West. Rather they note active communication. Early plays are cited and analyzed to demonstrate that an acting and performing tradition must be presupposed to account for them reasonably.

A particular stress is laid upon the very facts that have often heretofore been used to prove the obliteration of the mime-tradition. Mindful of the axiom that action and re-action are equal and opposite, they note that the mounting opposition of the Church was but a reflection of the tenacity of the mime and *histriones* tradition, the survival of the actors. The newer critics note that "The century in which the Church issued its anti-mimic edicts was the century in which the trope came into fashion." Then the Church, it is contended, did what it had done heretofore in earlier analogous instances: assimilated the mime-tradition and transmuted it to the service of the Christian community. Just as the Church in the fourth century fixed Christ's birthday on the twenty-fifth of December to absorb the heathen sun festival, so the Easter tropes were encouraged to coincide with pagan rites on the eve of the old spring fertility-festival which celebrated the burial and triumphant resurrection of Nature, the dead year. Thus was the heathen vigil both imitated and sanctified.

But more particularly, they assert, it was a definite living tradition of the mimes, the trouvères, the jongleurs that was a part of the historical current that, flowing into the monasteries, picked up the trope and helped to float it and its successors into the thronging secular harbor of the guild mystery-cycles, the individual dramas. Specific manuscript evidence from the Bibliothèque Nationale of Paris is cited, dating from the tenth century. The manuscripts cited are taken from the alleged center of the production of tropes at that moment, the Abbey of St. Martial at Limoges. Richly illuminated miniatures portray the mimes and the *histriones* as acting, dancing, and accompanying themselves on musical instruments. The artists (so the argument runs) unquestioningly took them for granted as part of the trope performance and tradition. Otherwise he would not have dared so casually and naturally to glorify mimes and trouvères if they had been other than chief performers of the tropes. Still less ignore the clergy and substitute for them the "enemies" of the Church. The medieval mimes are then compared with their distant predecessors portrayed on Greek vases and other antiquities to show how little the mimes had changed from the days of antiquity. As well as how closely connected in the tenth century with the tropes. What the Church had not succeeded in suppressing, she then in the tenth century adopted and tolerated insofar as it served her own purpose.

Finally, the presence of the mimes explains how the element of impersonation was restored in contrast to the purely symbolic "commemorative action" of Church services. The mimes, called on first to perform, then to elaborate and develop tropes and dramas, naturally brought to their activity that which was their particular skill and their professional interest: performance and impersonation. "So," concludes B. Hunningher, "it happened that theater was not reborn in the Church, but was adopted and taken in by her however great the distance originally had been that separated . . ."

The second approach of more recent criticism picks up and expands what is merely incidental and marginal to the first. It begins not as formerly with Dionysus and the Greek theatre but with the Egyptian deities, their death-rebirth rites, a ceremony designed to bring restoration and fecundity to the earth after the death of winter; to ensure the mysterious restoration and renewal of universal life in flock and field, woodland and orchard, the family itself. In their copious review of seasonal rites to replenish the earth, the exponents of the second school take us back to ancient vegetation-rites, follow these as they pass into the Egyptian king-dramas, the ancient year-gods and year-priests of Syrians and Babylonians, the Osiris-Adonis rites.

Next, this recent stress on the continuity of dramatic performance emphasizes another type of semi-dramatic phenomena in the suburbs and outskirts of the high centers of formal achievement. Our attention is directed to specimens of the winter-spring battles and symbolic contests of folk in village and countryside, to games and ceremonial dramas which are the medieval descendants of the ancient fertility ceremonials. It is curious that long before these present theories connected medieval religious dramas and folk games and ceremonies, Goethe had anticipated it in the early scenes of his *Faust*. In his scene on the eve of Easter, he re-stages with choir and church-bells the *Quem Quaeritis*. Then immediately in a succeeding scene he consciously blends with the Marys' discovery of the

Resurrection the folk-ceremonies which celebrated the fact of how

> From icy bondage streams and brooks are freed
> By Spring's life-giving, lovely light;
> In the valleys hope and happiness swelling the seed,
> While weak old Winter, creeping out of sight . . .

Of particular interest to the anthropological critics who see the continuity under many forms of the ancient rebirth rite is the resurrection story according to St. John. There the crucifixion takes place in or near a garden; burial is in a new sepulchre in the garden. At the resurrection, Mary Magdalen mistakes the risen Christ for a gardener. Added to this is the peculiar "Touch me not," warning issued to Mary by the risen Christ, suggesting the *taboo* period of withdrawal and seclusion used so widely in primitive initiation rites. These latter also simulated dramatically death and rebirth. Finally, there is a running race or "contest" between two of the disciples, which may be regarded as a carry-over of the spring-games contest.

Liturgical dramas of the type of the *Sepulchrum*, taken from a thirteenth century manuscript from Orléans, France, embody this Gospel version. The play is to be found in J. Q. Adams' *Chief Pre-Shakespearean Dramas*. All of these events are dramatized. But the Christ is not merely mistaken for a gardener. The directions explicitly say, "Let one prepared before hand in the likeness of a gardener . . ." The risen Christ also wears a robe of dazzling white. Altogether, it can be taken as a ceremonial drama of light and life arising out of winter darkness and death. Naturally, much or little can be made of such materials—depending upon the interpretative mood of the critic. The anthropological temperament makes much of such details.

Needless to say, the anthropological critics hold the magnifying lens of the amateur over the palimpsest of medieval drama. Like the scrutinizing art connoisseur with the X-ray vision, he sees a double layer of representation on his canvass. Under the shiny, late surface-figures, he discovers cloudy outlines and filmy shapes of earlier and more primitive drawings. Here and there the old lines faintly coincide with the recent and brightly superimposed ones. Thus the old lines of the ancient ritual drama of the folk run into and blend with the more conscious drama of art. Medieval drama is thus presented as standing mid-way between conscious art and "the irrational borderland of experience," where the supernatural and the unconscious interpenetrate.

Looking at our Easter Sunday parades on Fifth Avenue at the crowded hour of the high-fashion noon-day Services, our critics would recall that the term Easter (suggesting the East and the rising sun) derives from the name of the Teutonic goddess of the spring. That the colorful new hats and dresses, with flowers and accessories, with the further decorative symbols of numerous rabbits and Easter eggs—that all are decorative embellishments charged with sexual and fertility connotation. That for all of its sophistication, it probably reaches back to ancient fertility ceremonies. But whereas this situation is obvious and visible to the untrained eye, the connection between primitively inspired medieval folk-drama and the conscious drama of art is for them a special "detective" work in the restoration of the original.

From this point of view, the great Mystery cycles, enacted on successive days in the spring and festival time of the year are invested with an aura of the old ritual drama. The critics see no mere chronicle play or mere panoramic staging of world-history tableaus. The Pilate of the Mystery plays is not the Pilate of history. He is a "ritual antagonist." Herod is also a "ritual" king. Like the old king in endless folk-tales and performances, he is determined to destroy the prophesied challenger who is to overthrow him. Hence he is much more than the Herod of history. Christ's antagonists, such as Pilate and Herod, are ritual opponents much as was Captain Slasher, the Turkish Knight, the dragon in opposition to St. George. All are symbolic re-enactments (among other things) of winter-spring death and rebirth combats, a part of the endless cycle of ceremonies celebrating the death and rebirth combats of the royal hero-god. The darkness at the Crucifixion and the triumphant Easter morning resurrection prefigure the emergence of the spring sun, scattering with light the demons of darkness, and renewing life.

In approaching the Mystery cycles of the guilds, the anthropological critics put a primary emphasis on their total pattern or structure. These critics note that in the Cycles ranging from Creation to Judgment, the events of central and major significance are birth, death, resurrection. Such for them are the *Quem Quaeritis*, the Nativity plays; plays such as the Noah plays, the Abraham and Isaac, and Sacrifice of Isaac plays (son and father sacrifice, nearness of slayer and slain, man's death and rebirth and return into hope and life again: the king is dead, long live the king, etc.). Performed at the same time of year as the ancient fertility rites, they are presented to us as embodying the same underlying idea. Just as the line of the minstrels, trouvères, and mimes is supposed to reach to the first Tudor actors, so is medieval drama in the process of becoming the drama of art. The anthropological critics claim that it is on the borderline. They disclaim any desire to absorb the religious and the secular into the primitive but merely to see a blending.

In ritual drama, the actors and participants are not quite so detached and separated into actors and audience, active and passive. The latter are present in a spirit of active worship as well as diversion. In ritual drama there is a total disregard of anachronism. The world is presented in a timeless present. The pre-historical, the temporal, the eschatological are all one. For example, *The Second Shepherds' Play* presents characters saturated with the idiom, ideas, religious customs of medieval Christianity although the Shepherds who are so thoroughly Christianized are (in the play) yet to ceremonially welcome the founder and first Christian in the crib at Bethlehem. The ritual element consists in this—that history is "annually re-made or renewed for the well-being of each and all of the community." The past had to be re-made in order that the future, for that year, might be made propitious. Past and Future are mutually present in the Mystery Cycle; indeed, the Cycle regularly ends with what we regard as a future event, the Last Judgment. "The Cycle then was seen by the medieval towns-folk as an annual renewal of the world, an unfolding ritual of ever present life from Creation to Doomsday."

Within such a framework of interpretation, the Noah plays are emphasized as seasonal Nature rituals, the darkness and the flood, the obliteration of life and light. Then the re-emergence of sun and green earth, followed by reverent gratitude. In *The Second Shepherds' Play*, Mak's charmed circle magic spell upon the sleeping shepherds, their awakening, followed by two nativity scenes and ending in light and hope and birth after darkness and death—all this variety turns upon one central axis: unconscious reminiscence of the death-rebirth cycle.

In such a scheme of interpretation, minor elements take on sudden symbolic magnitude. The sprig of cherries in the Shepherds' play is a mid-winter darkness fertility symbol; the "hornyd lad" in the cradle is an unconscious representation of the ancient heathen worship of a deity incarnated in goat or sheep, bull or stag. The old satyrs and sileni, ancient fertility and vegetation deities, are now demons and devils raging and ranting in the medieval streets. The ceremonies are regarded in somewhat the same light in which the faithful regard the Church which preserved them: ever ancient and ever new.

Such an approach naturally negates the older view that Church drama and folk drama divided into two

streams on encountering the medieval Church—not
again united and intermingled until the emergence of
the Elizabethan drama of Shakespeare and his contemporaries. For all of this speculation, nothing could
be more modest or timely than the closing remarks of
B. Hunningher's work: "All this is conjecture, of
course." For those who may be disquieted or troubled
by so much that is conjectural, a suitable antidote will
be found in a recent book by Professor Hardin Craig,
English Religious Drama. The ritual-performance mode
of interpretation of medieval and modern drama must
be employed discreetly; like a piquant sauce, it may
overwhelm the original rather than elicit its particular
flavor. If Mr. Eliot's "Hippopotamus" were to survive
a world catastrophe and fall into the hands of an ex-
uberantly ambitious anthropological critic, it might
quickly lose its critical flavor as a twentieth century
commentary on the Church. It might issue from the
filter of the new interpretation as a religious-ritual
poem, presenting, through the medium of an Egyptian
water-deity, the ancient death-rebirth theme.

Abraham and Isaac

There are at least five extant medieval plays
upon this subject, obviously a favorite one. The Chester
Cycle contains a *Sacrifice of Isaac* which in form and
language strikingly resembles the play in this volume—
known as the Brome version. A source relationship between the Chester and the Brome versions is assumed
because of verbal parallelisms too extended to be explained merely by a common tradition of treatment.
Either there is an X-original common to both or they
are in some other way directly related. The Brome
version takes its name from a manuscript found in
Brome Manor, Suffolk. The manuscript supposedly
dates from about 1470-80 but is a transcript of an
original which may have been as early as the fourteenth
century. The Brome version of the story differs from

the others in its more subtle and less bald treatment, especially in its quite conscious interest in eliciting the pathos inherent in the artless innocence of Isaac. Special emphasis is placed on his affectionate sweetness of disposition, his simple, unpretentious fortitude, on his being the favorite child of the aging but tenderly affectionate patriarch.

Taken superficially, the plot of the play is the trial and ordeal, the testing of Abraham. But in spirit and handling it is totally unlike Job, the great prototype of the ordeal play. In the Brome version there are four characters, not counting the expositor or "Doctor" who appears in a sort of epilogue at the end to make even more explicit the teaching of the play: God's will is the highest of values; man's obedience, the noblest possible conduct. The character of God differs from the Biblical original in that He at no time speaks directly to Abraham but only through an intermediary.

Viewed traditionally, Abraham is the type of the obedient and loyal servant of the Lord. Isaac in the role of the willing "victim" is traditionally regarded as an Old Testament type or prefigurement of Christ. Such facts impose limitations upon the handling of the characters. Abraham must obey without rebellion. Isaac must not resist his role as "victim." Rather he must accept it heroically and magnanimously. The dramatist, however, goes beyond this traditional picture of them as mere types and successfully humanizes them. Although their wills are in essential harmony, the author delicately manages to create a dramatic tension between them. That tension cannot be, as already noted, one of an ancient conflict between Father and Son. Yet a tension is skillfully evoked. And ironically. For although Abraham and the audience are aware of the mounting tension, Isaac is not equally so. Since the story, like the plots of the Greek dramas, is known to the audience, there is a general irony investing the plot. God and the audience know all; Abraham a part; Isaac least of all. We derive from it the pleasurable irony of reading history: noting the contrast between what we know and what contemporaries believed they knew.

A special dramatic tension is derived from Isaac's instinctive shrinking from the physical pain of the sacrifice and his consequent plea to the Father for several boons—two not directly related to the tension; a third very much so. The first two are that the Father use his sacrificial knife skillfully; second, that Isaac's face be not merely covered but turned downwards away from the stroke of the blade. But the third request creates the tension. Isaac would have the sacrifice performed at once to be released from the agony of the suspense. Abraham, on the other hand, in a long series of "asides" not heard by Isaac, displays his mounting reluctance to act. In order to postpone the agony of the slaying, Abraham would delay the event Isaac would hasten.

Another dramatic factor is subtly handled. There is just a touch of *hubris* about Abraham. He assumes that the performance of his duty in the concrete can be as readily accomplished as his assent in the abstract. When first commanded to sacrifice his son, he responds promptly and without any apparent disabling conflict:

> Welcome to me be my Lord's command,
> And his behest I will not withstand

To the Angel's applauding his ready response to the Divine Will, Abraham again replies most easily, mentioning among his motives love of God along with awe and dread of Him:

> Nay, nay, forsooth, I hold me well paid
> To please my God the best that I may.

But as his "asides" reveal, when brought to the task, Abraham reiterates his anguish in variations of the following:

> Ah, Lord, my heart resisteth thee again;
> I may not find it in my heart to smite.

Perhaps it is not too far-fetched to be reminded by Abraham's reluctance to slay his "fair sweet son" of Othello's different yet equally poignant conflict in the slaying of Desdemona. Abraham says,

> I love my child as my life,
> But yet I love my God much more.

Othello says,

> It is the cause, it is the cause, my soul
> . . .
> Thou cunning'st pattern of excelling nature.

Curiously, the Chester text of the same play uses language reminiscent of Othello's when Abraham exclaims,

> O! comelye creature, but I thee kille,
> I greve my God, and that full ylle.

For both it is "the cause, the cause" that alone compels what so makes against the heart. Thus, for all of his early confidence does Abraham the dutiful patriarch modulate into the sorely tried and afflicted father.

The author is interested in strong dramatic effects as well as in gently pathetic ones. He manages a most vivid dramatic moment in the "revelation" scene, the climactic and culminating moment as Isaac moves from wonderment to surmise, then to suspicion, then to knowledge of his destiny. Abraham, now at last no longer evasive and equivocal, presents the situation to Isaac with the dramatic suddenness of a pistol shot shattering the most solemn moment of a church service. There is no obscure hinting, no mitigating euphemism of language. Rather the poignantly direct:

> Ah, Isaac, Isaac, I must kill thee.

It is reminiscent of Beatrice's startling reply to Benedict, who has likewise been asking for her mind: "Kill Claudio."

As for Isaac, after his first moment of dismay and

shock, he (necessarily as a prefigurement of the Christ) accepts it most willingly and promptly. Then his role passes quickly from that of the "victim" to that of the sensitive and thoughtful comforter of the hesitating and hapless father. It is now Isaac who encourages Abraham to go about his duty, who sustains him emotionally in the task. Indeed so all-compassionating is Isaac that he himself suffers to see his father suffer at the prospect of his own (Isaac's) suffering. A rather involved double-suffering.

Ironically, Isaac's cheerfully heroic submission to his fate, together with his sympathetically helpful response, makes the task more difficult for Abraham. For the latter only glimpses the more clearly in Isaac's behavior the excellence and sweetness of a child whom he already loves too dearly:

> Ah, Lord, my heart breaketh in twain
> This child's words, they be so tender

In portraying Isaac's ingenuous and simple sweetness of nature, the author is so consciously intent upon an almost sentimental pathos as to bring the play momentarily within sight of the gaslight era of Victorian domestic melodrama. Isaac's reiterated reference to "mother, dear mother" hints at this calamity. Notwithstanding, the author is too delicate and skillful to allow the sentiment to become cloying or obtrusive. Or to obscure the essentially stark, spare, noble dignity of the little drama.

In conclusion, it is interesting to compare this summons to death and the ensuing response with that of the hero of *Everyman*. In the latter play, portraying a much later historical time, all attention is focused upon securing the best possible terms with the next world by addressing oneself to available sacramental rites and priestly aid before the departure from this world. Everyman is intensely self-preoccupied. His moral vision is explicitly one of belated reverence qualified by prudence and the taking of all sound measures for the future.

Everyman is focused upon the next world, the after-life, and a suitable approach to it. The *Abraham and Isaac* in its here-and-now has an almost Greek austerity in its lack of consoling visions of reunion and happiness together in eternity. Isaac, as a parting rite, only kneels in simple dignity to ask his father's blessing. Their only consolation is the formal embrace of separation. Isaac even attempts to assuage Abraham's pain by dwelling upon the severely temporal nature of life:

> For, be I once dead, and from you gone,
> I shall be soon out of your mind.

It is their unfaltering obedience to an inscrutable, transcendental will that alone gives a stark yet gentle and lofty dignity to their predicament. Hence it is that the seizure of the blade at the moment of its descent by the Angel *ex machina* bestows a special poignancy upon their restoration to each other. Their future reward is to be of this world. Abraham is to be the begetter of a great dynasty. From the point of view of the audience, of course, this is to culminate in the Christ, prefigured in Isaac.

The Noah Play

It is not surprising that an event so calamitous as a universal deluge should have appealed to the medieval imagination. Even by St. Luke's time, the stories of Noah and of Lot were regarded as foreshadowing the coming of Christ. St. Luke's view is that of a dooms-day eschatalogist. As flood and universal disaster in the time of Noah, fire and brimstone in the day of Lot, "Even thus shall it be in the day when the Son of Man is revealed," he prophesies in the seventeenth chapter of his Gospel.

It was but to be expected that a narrative so capable of impressing religious susceptibility should have appeared in all of the great medieval Cycles as a highly popular pageant. Not only is it found in much the same form in the York and Towneley as in the Chester Cycle but fragments of it have survived as mementos of other Cycles. That it should have been assigned to water-drawers and carriers for staging and performance reveals a touch of whimsical humor. In other manuscript collections the Noah play was assigned to somewhat more impressive occupational groups, such as master mariners and pilots. The ship-wrights might also have put in a formidable claim. However, there is more water in the play than timber or navigation.

Like *The Second Shepherds' Play*, the Noah play combines the lofty and the ludicrous. It is a representation of God's struggle with sinful man, an exhibition of His indignation and punitive wrath. Also His reconcilement to the continuation of so wild and wayward a species because of the righteous Noah. Along with the exalted figure of Noah is the exasperating one of *Uxor eius*, perverse, willful, and stubborn. She is, of course, in the main stream of the farcical tradition of the termagant wife. Hence she introduces an element of folk revelry into a serious play, somewhat after the manner of Gyll of *The Second Shepherds' Play*. She is often compared with Chaucer's Wife of Bath as a specimen of the aggressively self-willed spouse. Chaucer had Noah's wife in mind in his *Miller's Tale*, wherein his deceiving clerk Nicholas mentions the character of the troublesome wife.

The two themes, the serious and the comic, are run together in a sort of medieval blending of their own contemporary versions of the old man and the sea, and the taming of the shrew. Except, of course, that the shrew is already a wife of impressive longevity. No negligible part of the comedy to medieval folks, with their implicit belief in Biblical chronology, may have been the fact of Noah's being six hundred years old at the time of the penal flood. That interval of endurance would have indeed marked him both as a heroically patient man and a thoroughly hen-pecked husband. Noah is a serious version of Chauntecleer of Chaucer's

Nun's Priest's Tale as is his wife a farcical version of Dame Pertelote. Both husbands were possessed of a prophetic vision of disaster to come, the one impeded, the other disabled in making the response to his knowledge by an uncooperative and nagging wife.

Noah *Uxor* has had a history somewhat larger than that of the medieval pageants. The wife is somewhat in the situation of a film actress who changed from ideal roles in the silent films to raffish ones in the "talkies." In the Old Testament, the wife is not a speaking character. Neither is she by hint or otherwise an obstinate wife. In the course of the development of the Old Testament typology, Noah *Uxor* took both of the two possible routes of development. She could be related to an earlier figure, such as Eve, the erring wife susceptible to the lures of Satan, or she could be regarded as a prototype of the mild and submissive Mary, Mother of God. From the latter point of view, she reinforces the significance of Noah as the righteous man. Very early medieval writers wrote: "Noah signifies Christ, his wife the blessed Mary." Considering the almost anonymous role of *uxor eius* in Genesis, it is surprising that so much dignity was accorded her. Not even President Coolidge made so much out of silence.

If the interpreter instead stole a backward glance, as already suggested, he would relate Noah's wife to Eve. In the learned world of early patristic controversy, Noah's wife is referred to in the Gnostic writings of the fourth century. Both here and later on in early medieval folk-tale elaborations and in the representations of numerous Church murals, Noah *Uxor* is either herself an incendiary or in active collusion with Satan. The object is to set the Ark on fire and so disrupt or delay the plan of salvation. In some stories, she was so successful as to delay the building of the Ark for one hundred years before her tactics were finally defeated. By the time of the present Cycles, she was a much subdued delinquent.

The Second Shepherds' Play

There are at least six extant medieval plays treating of the Adoration of the Holy Child by the Shepherds. A single play acted by the Shearmen and Taylors of Coventry, possibly a part of a lost Cycle; one each in the existing Cycles of York, Chester, and N. town. Included in the Wakefield Cycle among those attributed to "the Master" are—as the Latin explicitly states (*Secunda Pastorum*)—two Shepherds' plays. It might be more convenient, following the practice of some critics, to refer to the play included in this volume as *The Shepherds' Play—No. 2.* At any rate, it is the second of alternative treatments of the visit to the manger and the Adoration. A few critics speculate that the *Prima Pastorum* or *First Shepherds' Play* is really a first draft or rough copy of the *Secunda,* which is the mature and ripened masterpiece. The entire episode of Mak and Gyll, of the sheep-stealing, etc. belongs to the second version only.

In all of the plays, the shepherds are rough-spoken rustics, needy and hungry, blunt in talk and manner but simple and devout. In the present play, the character of Mak and his prank is possibly a folk-tale borrowing. A further inference is made by the seasonal-myth and folk-rite interpreters to the effect that Mak's magic spell represents the mysterious winter sleep and ensuing spring awakening—to blend with the new-birth jubilation at the end. They likewise lay stress on the sprig of cherries blooming in December as a fertility-rite symbol. Regardless, Mak is quite explicitly a mischievous sprite in his own right.

As for the shepherds, their somewhat individualized and distinct characterizations need no special emphasis. It has been the common topic of praise among the critics, especially since it harmonizes with our modern preoccupation with "realism" in drama, as elsewhere, and the peculiar prestige accorded to it. As a result, there is an increasing predilection for seeing *The Second Shepherds' Play* as a realistic comedy of rustic manners, including even a touch of verbal realism, the feigned southern accent of Mak. This view in turn fits into the view that the secularization of the medieval drama comes in its terminal development as it moves to a distance from its religious origin.

Moreover, insofar as any interpretation of its author can be made from the five or six plays attributed to him, the Wakefield Master is uniformly considered to be a man of sharp contemporary observation. He was formally, perhaps clerically educated, as his Latin and music, his Biblical and patristic lore indicate. He is, still, celebrated mainly for his quick sympathy for the oppressed and forgotten man, his sharp eye for character, a ready ear for colloquial, vernacular turns of speech, and a humor alternately rude and boisterous, coarse and happy. Hence despite his conscious artistry, as manifest in his feeling for intricate metrical and stanza forms, he is looked upon as a kind of medieval Steinbeck, indignantly angry at, uncompromisingly and even brutally realistic in presenting, the plight of the agricultural poor.

Thus taking the play and the author together, it is now fairly conventional to regard the former as a kind of ultimate point in the secularization of the medieval drama. Hence much emphasis on it as depicting realistically humble manners and pastoral life in the bleak hills of the West Riding of Yorkshire on a typically cold night of December 24th. After what are often regarded as almost "documentaries" given in the three successive monologues of the three shepherds, critics go on to affirm that the realism is then intensified into a burlesque mock-treatment of the Nativity. Finally as a sort of epilogue or after-thought in deference to the Biblical origin of the materials, the play slides back into an atavistic mood of early innocent reverence. Actually, as we shall see, the final scene is not only the culminating and climactic scene but perhaps the *raison d'être* of the introductory "realism."

There is much on the surface of the present play to support the conventional view of its mood of secular realism. All the same, the "realism" of the Wakefield Master is of a paradoxical turn. His wide knowledge of people as well as books indicates no cloistered contemplative but one in close relation to his times. Still, that life was after all a predominantly religious one, a time which never neglected the belief that man was a rebellious and sinful creature in need of redemption. So deeply (one can hardly say "naively" of so sophisticated a writer) and implicitly religious is the Master that he is less able (or less willing) to present actual history realistically than is the author of the Brome *Abraham and Isaac*. His historical sense is even less realistic than that of Chaucer who just a few years before had done for his own time "costume romances," such as *The Knight's Tale, Troilus and Cressida,* etc. Moreover, Chaucer had the excuse of highly romantic materials for taking liberties with history.

In contrast, the Wakefield Master, presenting a trio of Shepherds in the dark reaches of distant northern England in the last hours of the epoch B.C., gives us nothing at all like the remote sheep-tenders of a dark, pre-Christian period, sunk in primeval superstition. Rather his shepherds introduce their conversations with "Bless me," swear by the Cross, take the name of Christ profanely, invoke easily the name of the Virgin Mary or Our Lady, refer familiarly to the New Testament, to St. James, to St. Stephen, and St. Nicholas. They give humorously deformed Latin quotations from the Apostles' Creed and display knowledge of the customs of funeral masses. Yet these same Shepherds are to thrill with astonishment and wonderment at the coming of the infant Savior who is to overthrow the dominance of Satan and thus found the Christian epoch. If anachronisms are the solecisms of the unrealistic historian, the Master is as reckless as Mrs. Malaprop.

Of course, like Sheridan, the Master knew what he was doing. But perhaps we should emphasize a little less the realistic "individualizing" of the three Shepherds and their private grievances. For the depiction of their ills and privations is more than an unconscious exercise in medieval "local color." To the contrary, despite some individualization, the shepherds voice a common misery. Moreover, they appear to be selected so as to represent the full life-span. The first is perhaps the oldest man. The Second Shepherd ("Late in life it still amazes me") is also mature. The third, referred to as "boy" is obviously youthful. Thus their common voice is expressive of life for their class—one of depressed and inferior status. And that was the condition of most of humanity in that period. The First Shepherd dwells on the social and economic ills of life: the arrogant rich and the oppressive landowners exploiting the impoverished toilers. The Second Shepherd dwells more expressly on the disappointments of domestic life. The fireside which should be a haven from the struggle for existence is the arena for the battle of the sexes. The Third Shepherd gives voice to the fact that the elements themselves conspire to plague and torment the hapless worker. Hostile floods and storms, wind and cold rains intensify the already bitter existence. There is nothing "personal" and "private" in that gloomy vision.

Hence it is questionable to assert that the Shepherds are presented mainly as comic specimens of mere chronic whiners, routine complainers, sour-tempered watchers of their flocks. Actually they voice a basic common woe, not so much in the interest of local realism as to present a generalized and universal mood of desolation. They jointly testify to a fallen world, to a dark kingdom where the spirit and feelings of mankind are in a state of alienation from all bliss. By means of the first and last scenes the author fuses his moral vision into a presentation of the dark end of the spectrum of history before the news of the new-born King and

Redeemer: then the luminous end of that perspective after the news. The emphasis on the poverty, hardship, and oppressed status of the Shepherds is pointed towards the fact that the Savior-King shares their humble place in the world by selecting the abode of animals for His first home. What in the pre-Nativity world was their curse and their burden is in the new spiritual order the condition of the Shepherds' privilege:

> Prophets and patriarch of old were torn
> With yearning to behold this Child now born.

That is, even the best men sought restlessly, yet hopelessly, for the deliverance not yet come. But now in the ripeness of time the marvel is that

> To men as poor as we He will appear;
> We'll find Him first, His messenger said clear.

The introductory picture of the shepherds' existence is that of life in a spiritual dungeon of inner darkness and despair before the release into light and freedom. The visit to the manger and the Holy Child is not merely a "turning point" in history, certainly not from the standpoint of a medieval audience. It is the event that transfigured life itself, that transformed it from a sullen, painful struggle without purpose to a vision of hope and joy. The Shepherds of the final scene are men whose inward life is now illuminated and irradiated with a new glory. A world and a play that began in sorrow, pining, and loud lament are transformed into song and rejoicing.

There is also in the final scene of the Adoration an idealization. Although the Shepherds remain humble rustics and bring their charming but simple gifts to the manger, their inward perceptions are in contrast to their outward lowliness. They are now Doctors of the Church. Together they affirm directly and unhesitatingly mysterious doctrines that were to take centuries of bitter struggle before their acceptance. They assert the mysteries of the Redemption and the

Incarnation in a manner to edify St. Athanasius. They affirm the doctrine of the Virgin Birth with a readiness that might have perplexed St. Bernard.

This basically reverent moral vision the author has skillfully diversified with light farcical entertainment: the stealing of the sheep, the search of the home of Gyll and Mak, the maneuvers and suspense incidental to the attempted concealment, and the final exposure of Mak. The boisterous episode should not be read as though a gratuitous interpolation of Tony Lumpkin-ish fun and merriment, a heavy joke obtruded into a play which begins with protestation and gloom, and ends with glory and Adoration. Actually, it is functionally related to what precedes and what follows. The author has a single vision such that the middle episode or "movement" picks up significant "motifs" of the opening scenes to reinforce them. Likewise it anticipates negatively, by the contrasting mood of farcicality, points that are prominent in the final scene.

Retrospectively, it presents Gyll as the visible embodiment of that termagant Uxor of comic tradition already dwelt on by the Second Shepherd. More especially does Mak voice all of the ills of the three Shepherds. He recapitulates their dismal disgruntlement. Mak himself is a sort of proto-Malthusian prophet, burdened with a consciousness of the "population explosion." He complains with sardonic vehemence of a wife who endlessly consumes more food than he can afford to supply as a preliminary to producing more hungry mouths for the already depleted supply of bones and crusts. But if he shares with the Shepherds their squalid poverty, he is not in sympathy with them ethically. He is the clever, imaginative rascal, a pastoral-picaresque and prankish figure of feints and dodges. He would out-wit and out-maneuver the drab, hard-working world which they inherit.

Somewhat obviously the cradle trick for concealing the sheep foreshadows the Nativity scene: the stolen lamb of Mak, the Lamb of God. Gyll as the mother of the preternatural birth is in all things the negative anticipation of the gracious Virgin of Bethlehem. Again Mak's impersonation at his entry into the play, his jocose feigning to be one of the King's officers, a herald of the royal coming, as it were, anticipates the appearance of the Herald-angel. Yet Mak as royal herald would not bring good news. Rather he would be the forerunner of "purveyance," that is, the requisitioning of provisions and services at a nominal fee. To the contrary, the Herald-angel proclaims a King who comes not to take the means of sustenance but to give freely redemption and salvation. It is notable that the First Shepherd is made to respond promptly both to Mak's imposture and to the Herald-angel with the same term:

Why make ye it so qwaynt? Mak, ye do wrang.

and to the genuine royal Herald:

This was a qwaynt stevyn that euer yit I hard.

Further, Mak is in some way intended to be associated with the Devil. It is evident that the Shepherds associate him with the word and the idea three times in brief compass after his appearance. Nor do they otherwise refer to Satan until the final scene. Especially definite, among their many anticipations of trouble from him is the statement, "Seldom lies the devil dead by the gate." We of course know that it is when he pretends to be asleep that Mak makes off with the sheep. Moreover, Mak's magic spells by a waning moon, his charmed circles whereby he puts to sleep those he would rob vaguely invest Mak with an aura of demonic enchantment. Like a devil, he mocks at holy forms and invokes in place of the true Lord, the medieval lord of irresponsibility "Pontius Pilate." When the First Shepherd awakes from his troubled sleep and in fractured Latin recites "Judas carnas dominus" as a distortion, possibly, of *laudes canas domino,* his unconscious mind reveals that he associates Mak and Judas, the latter a type of the devil. It is further notable that the first comment the Shepherds make upon their appearance before the Infant Redeemer and King is that he has undermined the dominance of Satan in the affairs of mankind:

Hail, Maker, I believe, of a Maiden so mild.
Thou has cursed, I conceive, the devil so wild:
The false harmful Beguiler, himself now beguiled.

Thus does Mak, the false beguiler and worker of evil, go beguiled. He is not summoned or permitted to take the journey to the manger in Bethlehem. He belongs to the "waning moon," not the blazing star. Like Falstaff (that old "white-bearded Satan") much as he has amused us in the old order, Mak has been debarred by his conduct from a privileged role in the new order.

The Castle of Perseverance

Polonius: This is too long.
Hamlet: It shall to the barber's with your
beard . . .

The date of origin of the play is probably the first quarter of the fifteenth century, although the scribal hand of the extant manuscript is assigned to the second quarter of the same century. It is in the speech of Norfolk or of Lincolnshire, sprinkled with allusions to France and odds and ends of French phrase. Because the extant manuscript of the play (along with two other medieval plays) was once owned by the Rev. Cox Macro, an English clergyman who flourished in the first half of the eighteenth century, *The Castle* and its companion pieces are sometimes referred to as the Macro Moralities. It is one of the earliest extant morality plays. Unlike the *Everyman, The Castle* does represent the essence of the morality piece: the struggle—in the present instance that of the seven moral virtues and the seven deadly sins, together with their respective alliances.

Even the most admiring critics have not been reluctant to point out a second struggle, that of the reader with a text that is no friend to brevity. Slightly more than 3500 lines in length, it is longer than most Elizabethan plays. A compressed summary, however, and a generous selection of significant passages which keep the proportions of the original plot will bring the play within the limits of tolerance of most readers.

Determined to move only with all deliberate speed, the author is logically uninterested in the *in medias res* handling of plot narrative. He begins literally at the naked beginning. *Human Genus* or Mankind appears directly after birth. Innocent and helpless, in his first inexperienced brush with reality, he is equally guided and misguided by a good and a bad angel. Mankind is a creature of bafflement, perplexity, and uncertain groping, as yet outside of the Castle. He is in the center of a circular "place" or stage, around the periphery of which are located the "scaffolds," "stations," or platforms of the Princes of evil and their courtier-attendants. In order of their appearance, they are the World, the Devil, and the Flesh.

The first Prince is served by a somewhat extensive court, as becomes his dominant role in the play. World is served not only by Lust-liking and Folly but by a malignant Boy, together with two other important figures. One is a drifting itinerant, Backbiter by name (perhaps an early forerunner of Sir Benjamin Backbite of *The School for Scandal*). Even more significant is Sir Covetyse, a kind of personal secretary or junior partner of the World. His special importance is signalized by his having a platform of his own. The Devil (also called Belial or Satanus) is served by Pride, Envy, and Wrath. The attendants of Flesh are Gluttony, Sloth, and Lechery (the only female among the sins).

Mankind early decides without great internal struggle that the servants of the Princes of evil, the seven deadly sins, have in their possession the most lively and vital gifts. Consequently, he capitulates quickly to the blandishments of Vanity Fair. Mankind rejects the advice and appeals of the good angel and in the company of the bad angel (his Mephistopheles) takes up his residence amid the sinful pleasures of the world.

Next, Penance and Shrift take the field against the seven deadly sins. Penance punctures Mankind's pride, thus opening his heart to contrition. Shrift thereafter takes quick advantage and absolves Mankind from the bondage of his sins. He now has, it appears, another start in life. Shrift advises him to take immediate and permanent refuge in the Castle of Perseverance, whose heraldic and heroic motto is "He that shall endure unto the end, the same shall be saved." Mankind, like Fielding's Tom Jones and Byron's Don Juan is lacking in internal moral resource and is therefore inherently prone to temptation. The Castle's motto of service is perhaps somewhat too exalted for such a man. However, the Castle is guarded by the valiant Seven Sisters, the principal moral virtues.

Once Mankind is securely established in his new defense, Backbiter on a reconnaissance mission discovers his refuge. His report enrages the Princes of evil, who not only beat their own servants for their negligence in letting slip so choice a victim but then drive them to storm the Castle. There are three waves of assault as each Prince's henchmen successively attack. The deadly sins encounter their respective virtues, e.g., Pride, Meekness; Patience, Anger; Chastity, Lechery; etc. Since by Christ's passion and death, God the Father was reconciled to sinful man, the ordeal of the Cross is the chief instrument in repulsing the World, the Devil, and the Flesh. That ordeal, the Atonement, is symbolically represented by roses, the flowers of the Passion. Hence the seven sisters cast roses at the seven deadly sins in repulsing them. If the deadly sins do not because of

quick effluvia darting thro' the brain
Die of a rose in aromatic pain,

they do nonetheless retreat in disorder and dismay.

Despite this heroic defense, Mankind soon after succumbs to the lures and persuasions of Sir Covetyse, a subversion by "propaganda" after assault has failed. As Mankind is now past his prime of life, he is susceptible to the infirmities and uncertainties of old age. Sir Covetyse seduces him to desert the Castle by stressing the need for an economic basis for old-age security. Mankind is reminded that in his age he will suffer acutely from neglect, want, and desolation if without property and goods. He capitulates to Sir Covetyse.

After an appropriate interval, Death enters to claim Mankind. Mankind dies lamenting that he has forsaken the Castle and its guardians. He warns—profusely—his auditors against the insinuating lures of the World. He dies in sin, yet not without some stirrings of heart and compunctions of conscience.

The play does not end here. There is a kind of epilogue in the form of a disputation or court scene. Mankind is again the somewhat passive (and this time also silent) prize of contending forces. As in the best of earthly so in heavenly families, there are divisions. The Four Daughters of God are evenly and strenuously divided as to the ultimate disposition of Mankind. The prosecuting sisters, Truth and Righteousness, appear at times to be as stern-hearted as Goneril and Regan. They are far too fierce to be compared to the relatively innocent and restrained Shylock. Mercy, however, among the Daughters is a Portia figure, and her speeches at times remind one quite forcibly of Portia's quality-of-mercy appeal. Truth, on the other hand, insists that Mankind be burned in hell. Righteousness exults that "The righteous shall rejoice when he seeth the vengeance." Here we are reminded of old Tertullian's anticipated delight at the spectacle of the writhing and twisting of the actors doomed to the inferno.

Mercy and Peace, however, plead not only Mankind's death-bed contrition and the blood of the Lamb but dwell upon the quality of Mercy as the especially Divine attribute. "Pity runneth soon in noble heart" was the burden of the *Knight's Tale*. The heavenly

Father forgives and is reconciled. He places Mankind beside Him at His right hand. Is that generosity the reason that the Court is not composed of the Trinity—as we were led verbally to expect? Otherwise the figure at the right hand would have been the Son.

The Castle is, in a sense, a pilgrim play. It covers the life of its hero from birth to old age. Presumably the plot confronts Mankind with the full range of temptations, those of the World, the Devil, and the Flesh. Actually the encounter is rhetorical rather than dramatic. The deadly sins present their quality verbally. Actual conflict between the virtues and the vices is presented ritualistically. Personally, Mankind is susceptible to the appeal of the World and Sir Covetyse—to property and security, to creature-comforts. Mankind has bourgeois tastes but lacks bourgeois enterprise.

Hence as a pilgrim, Mankind lacks variety and liveliness. He is a victim neither of pride nor of passion in any special dramatic form. Indifferent to the more picturesque vices, he is the passive hero—both in this world and in the next. The Castle exaltation of heroic stoical endurance would have better suited a warrior in *Beowulf* or a tragic hero in a play by Webster. Mankind's lack of dynamic vice makes of him a kind of modern suburban "company" man: he seeks mainly economic abundance and old-age security. The author is a medieval Ben Jonson. He is chastising, none too violently, the acquisitive man—perhaps already apparent in the fifteenth century. At least, the play and the character lend themselves to such an interpretation.

One wonders somewhat at the absence of appeal to priest and Church in the play, to the lack of a strong emphasis on a visible intermediary system as the main channel of grace and salvation. Indeed, in his first crucial conflict, Mankind speaks in what looks like the idiom of a seventeenth century Puritan. He stands somewhat alone between God and the Bible:

Now, so God me helpe, and the holy boke,
I not wyche I may have!

Also the whole medieval concept of the importance of "good works" seems scanted. There is almost a kind of Divine election, if not predestination. Mankind is saved ultimately because it is God's will that he be saved. Still it is highly questionable that there is a shadow of Reformation doctrine upon the play. It is only when compared with the *Everyman* that *The Castle* seems neglectful of Church ordinances, despite the fact that Shrift and Penance are briefly victorious. For the *Everyman* is consciously a didactic parable exalting the role of the priest and the sacraments. The author of *The Castle* is focused upon the morality-play formula: the conflict of moral and mental abstractions, of virtues and vices personified, of good and bad angels.

Everyman

In some respects, *Everyman* is both in form and content a surprisingly modern play. In form it is transparently allegorical. But so far from that being a form confined to medieval drama, it peeks out frequently from the wings of the modern stage. In the "Epistle Dedicatory" to his *Man and Superman,* Shaw exults in the discovery that the author of *Everyman* was "no mere artist, but an artist-philosopher;" the kind that alone could be taken "quite seriously." Shaw attributes to the medieval *Everyman* the inspiration for his own creation of Ann Whitefield, the pursuer of John Tanner–Don Juan and the Doña Aña of the dream-interlude of the play. Shaw wrote:

Ann was suggested to me by the fifteenth century Dutch morality called *Everyman,* which Mr. William Poel has lately resuscitated so triumphantly. I trust he will work that vein further, and recognize that Elizabethan Renaissance fustian is no more bearable after medieval poesy than Scribe after Ibsen. As I sat watching *Everyman* at the Charterhouse, I said to myself, Why not Everywoman? Ann was the result: every woman is not Ann; but Ann is Everywoman.

Shaw's reference to Ibsen serves to remind us that one of the latter's most grimly humorous comedies *The Enemy of the People* was frankly allegorical. Still more modern writers, such as Elmer Rice and Eugene O'Neill have embodied some of their most fantastic visions in the form of allegory. When Rice wished to present his version of the modern Everyman, he gave us the arid waste of a society oriented towards mass-production and what he saw as its corollary—the mass-man. Hence *The Adding Machine* and its "hero" Mr. Zero, that dry, withered chip of humanity, who unlike medieval Everyman cannot attain to salvation. When O'Neill presented his version of the contemporary Everyman seeking to recover from the lost myth of his own significance, he gave us the allegory of *The Hairy Ape*. O'Neill again chose allegory when he presented still another aspect of his modern Everyman: the surface costume of rationality of *Emperor Jones* barely concealing an irremediably irrational nature which reverts under stress to the abjectly superstitious. The allegorical form is irresistible to those whose purpose is more didactic than dramatic.

Like *Everyman,* these modern allegories are constructed as a succession of episodes or scenes, not as the conventional five-act structure. In all of them, dramatic effect is produced by the progressive disillusionment of the main character, who becomes continuously more baffled and distraught. But the fever-chart of Everyman records not a steeply rising line ending in an abject death. Rather its pyramidal form indicates a fever arrested and a spiritual cure effected. Contrary to modern pessimism, *Everyman* is optimistic. Its spiritual triumph over death is so facile that this fact may constitute something of a barrier to modern sympathy. In the modern allegories of Everyman by O'Neill and Rice, the hero is rigorously denied any slightest crust of salvation with which to sustain himself.

Shaw no doubt rejoiced in the splendidly dignified figure that Knowledge cut in the Charterhouse production of *Everyman* around the turn of the century. The photographs show us that Knowledge (the sacramental and moral means of salvation, of course) was royally and magnificently robed. In queenly majesty, she wore the regal crown and carried the jewelled insignia of sacerdotal authority. Naturally, in Shaw's creation, the medieval significance of Knowledge suffers a sea-change. In the Don Juan of the dream-interlude, it becomes the mystical intelligence that prophesies the one far-off, divine event towards which idealistic nineteenth century evolution moved. The Good Deeds of our *Everyman* becomes in the person of Doña Aña the vehicle of a mystical vitalism that wills the superman. With Shaw, the purified intelligence and the perfected will are no longer merely the means of salvation. They are at once the means and the goal of human striving. Church theology has been supplanted by Life-Force biology, the supernatural by the superman. The two parables reflect admirably the enormous human and spiritual distance Europe has traveled between these two related dramatic events. They indicate the effort the modern imagination must make to recover the emotional and intellectual climate of medieval Everyman. Perhaps the only remaining link for numerous modern readers is that described by Wordsworth:

> Those mysteries of being which have made
> And shall continue evermore to make
> Of the whole human race one brotherhood.

As for the content of this poetic play about death, a generation brought up on the nineteenth century romantics will not find it totally foreign to the preoccupations of *Adonais* or *In Memoriam*, which explore the hidden significance of death, its mysteries and uncertainties. The subject should also be acceptable to a generation familiar with Existentialism, the expositors of which are so sympathetic to stories of Hemingway, such as "A Clean, Well-Lighted Room" or "The Snows of Kilimanjaro." Or more especially Tolstoy's "Death of Ivan Ilych." The first story treats of death as a fever of anxiety in the bone, a subtle, all-pervading fear. The latter two stress the physical horror of death—death as a grotesque, ironic, Harlequin-like (yet malicious and evil) joke upon life. Upon life—the decorous, the pleasant, the innocent and trusting.

In the medieval *Everyman*, these elements, though present, are only intimated or lightly stressed. The central focus is death the Summoner, death the subpoena which hails one into court. Death is the spiritual income-tax collector who wants a full explanation of income, spiritual and temporal, and a full accounting of how it has been used.

To recur to the dramatic form. As allegory, the play moves around the central image of the "pilgrimage" or the "journey" to be undertaken by Everyman. The latter, like Ivan Ilych, embodies our disposition to repress or ignore the universal predicament—our inevitable and ever approaching mortality. The respective gifts of Fortune and of Nature are presented to us in two separate groups: first, the external gifts of Fortune: Fellowship, Kindred, Goods, etc; then the more interior or personal gifts of Nature: Strength, Discretion, Five Wits, etc.

The action takes place along parallel lines. There is progressive disillusionment as to the cherished values of Fortune. Then at almost the half-way mark in the play, there is an illumination of Everyman attendant upon the entry of Knowledge. Thereafter a growing awareness of the value of good works, sacraments, etc. Simultaneous with increasing hope and comfort, there is a secondary development of disillusionment in terms of the gifts of Nature. This latter runs a risk of being an anti-climax: first, as repeating with diminished effectiveness the experience of Everyman with the gifts of Fortune; second, as overshadowed by the growing confidence instilled by the gifts of Knowledge.

Hence the mode of the play is more liturgical than dramatic. Actually, it is a ritualistic unfolding through the catechizing method of question-and-answer of man's true relation to the deceptive shadow-world of the senses and his proper preparation, through the appointed channels of grace, for confronting the real world beyond. In the course of the action, there is a tiny interlude celebrating the power and glory of the priesthood.

In our play, it is the idea, not the action, which is dramatic. In Chaucer's *Pardoner's Tale*, for example, we see a dramatic conflict between the figure of Death and a worldly humanity in which riches incite to and fellowship conspires in crime and murder. In *Everyman* Fellowship vaingloriously proclaims:

> But and thou will murder, or any man kill,
> In that I will help thee with a good will.

Goods also mockingly declares:

> My condition is man's soul to kill:
> If I save one, a thousand do I spill.

Despite these avowals, there is no "intrigue"; Goods does not plot nor does Fellowship conspire. The plot moves along rigidly foreordained grooves. Hence, in many productions its controlling spirit of mortal fatality is symbolized by an hour-glass which is placed conspicuously in the center-rear of the stage. It is so regulated that the last sands run out as Everyman follows Death into the bleak outer darkness. It is a much quieter counterpart to the fatal tom-tom beat that pervades the action of the *Emperor Jones*.

Hence *Everyman* is a less typical morality play than *The Castle of Perseverance*, in which the ancient, mischievous triumvirate—the World, the Flesh, and the Devil—are presented in vigorous conflict with Mankind. In *Everyman* Fellowship and Goods (aided and abetted by Strength and Beauty) are in a sense the World and the Flesh. Yet there is no dramatic struggle. The author of *Everyman* is not a medieval Father Ibsen writing *The Pillars of Salvation*. In Ibsen's *Pillars of Society*, the worldly, prosperous, pretentious males are shown up in action to be flashy, hollow, and false. The obscure, apparently insignificant females are brought forward as figures of loyalty and integrity, of wisdom. At a glance, this disposition of characters appears to fit *Everyman*: Fellowship and Goods, the pompous, fraudulent worldly males; Knowledge and Good Deeds, the unexpectedly resourceful females, who turn out to be the true pillars of salvation (rather than Ibsen's "truth and freedom"). But where Ibsen contrives intricate dramatic action to bring out the irony of appearance and reality, the author of *Everyman* is content with a tissue of conferences through which Everyman learns that his friends are hollow.

Nor is the apparent touch of Ibsenite realism towards the end of the play quite that. After Five Wits exalts the priestly office above all earthly dignities, Knowledge, the more loyal and discerning of the two characters, replies:

> If priests be good, it is so, surely.
> But . . .
> Sinful priests giveth the sinners example bad;
> Their children sitteth by other men's fires, I have
>   heard;
> And some haunteth women's company
> With unclean life, as lusts of lechery:
> These be with sin made blind.

Yet these words are not uttered in the sensational *exposé* spirit of modern realism. Ingratiating in their frankness rather than leering in their disclosure of rumored misgivings, the lines merely announce that erring incumbents of the sacerdotal office do not always avoid profaning it.

If Fellowship and Goods as false pillars are not really the villains of the play, neither is Death, who has none of the shadowy, sinister spirit of the equivocal figure in Chaucer's *Pardoner's Tale*. He is merely the grim official messenger of the Royal Will, the fell sergeant death who is swift in his arrest. Nor is the idea exploited emotionally as in Tolstoy's *Death of Ivan Ilych*.

Still less is it presented in the manner of Joyce's *Portrait of the Artist*, wherein the anvils of Stephen Dedalus's retreat-master flash and glower with the angry rhetoric of terror. The sermon of Joyce's retreat-master is not so much medieval as counter-Reformation in its tense over-wrought morbidity of mood so foreign to the urbane author of *Everyman*. In the latter play, only once, briefly at the end, does the author introduce the Scholar to give us a glimpse of the penalty or misery of the damned.

It is this complete absence of any of the melodramatic elements of medieval drama (or even the boisterous farcicality of the *Second Shepherds' Play*) that justifies critics in wondering whether the play was not originally designed for the cloister rather than the popular theatre. It moves with the urbane, solemn, formal elegance of Gray's "Elegy." Yet *elegance* is not the word here. That particular tone and color has been overshadowed by an official sobriety. In this it reminds one of Shaw's remark in his discussion of The Rhine Gold in *The Perfect Wagnerite*. There Shaw observes:

> . . . do not forget that an allegory is never quite consistent except when it is written by someone without dramatic faculty, in which case it is unreadable.

Unreadable—*Everyman* certainly is not; but dramatic— only insofar as Death's appearance is abrupt and unexpected; only insofar as the behavior of the gifts of Fortune and Nature surprise and disconcert the rather naive and innocent Everyman.

Even the attitude of God toward mankind is notable for its mildness and benignity. Far from Jehovah thundering out of Zion, His voice is more like that of Matthew Arnold reproving the Philistines. God's purposes in sending Death are gently remedial, not vindictive or vengeful:

> For, and I leave the people thus alone
> In their life and wicked tempests,
> Verily they will become much worse than beasts;

Indeed, there is a touch in His attitude of what we now call "social conscience"; again with that civilized urbanity with which Arnold sought to reclaim from anarchy to culture his noisy, clamorous, materialistic middle-classes:

> For now one would by envy another up eat;
> Charity they do all clean forget . . .

This mood is remote from the Spanish-militarist-autocratic mood of the Sermon on Death in Joyce's *Portrait*. Indeed, the author of *Everyman* is much closer to the calm, logical lucidity of Francis Bacon, who in his essay "On Death" wrote:

> Certainly the contemplation of death, as the wages of sin and passage to another world, is holy and religious, but the fear of it, as a tribute due unto nature, is weak. Yet in religious meditations there is sometimes mixture of vanity and of superstition.

The author of *Everyman* avoids all of the perils.

If there be difficulty about *Everyman*, it is this. Its modulated and measured dignity, its temperate tone bring it within hailing distance of monotony. As a result of this sobriety of tone, together with an interest in vivid theatre, the version of *Everyman* that has had considerable stage-success is the *Jedermann*, adaptation of Hugo Hofmannsthal, produced by Max Reinhardt, who in turn is remembered for two rather different productions. They are (1) the Summer *Festspiel* given at Salzburg, and (2) that given at the Century Theatre, New York City, opening in November of 1927.

The Salzburg production was presented on a wooden platform-stage before the portal of the Cathedral and thus against a background of august, ancient, and imposing majesty. In the immediate background were the massive carved doors of the Cathedral and the heroic Cathedral-scale effigies of the Prince-Bishops, which faced the audience from behind the stage and at either side of it. They were enthroned in stony and beatific

calm, having no doubt presided magisterially over the
destinies of many an Everyman over the past centuries.
There could be no more appropriate setting for the
play, for the Church was the great force of awe and
inspiration at the time of Everyman's birth. The cos-
tuming was unobtrusively rich, and banquet tables,
iron-clad money chests, numerous well-appareled guests
—including ladies, richly jeweled and bare-shouldered
in inviting decolletés—emphasized an atmosphere of
solid gold worldliness. Everyman himself wore a Rem-
brandt-style studio beret-cum-feather, a short, knee-
length robe, richly trimmed at collar and cuffs with
ermine. A silk shirt delicately embroidered down the
center showed through the carelessly opened short cloak.
A fine-leather money-pouch hung from his belt. Everyman's person was notable for a gold neck-chain adorned
with jeweled pendant. Clearly it was a play of Death
Calls for The Opulent Citizen, the latter a younger and
more fashionable version of Chaucer's Franklin, for
example, transplanted to cathedral-town, county-seat
life.

But the production, alternately decried as vulgar and
garish and acclaimed as creative and poetic, was that
of the flamboyant '20's, a decade restrained in nothing.
It was a production that fully expressed the "Doctor"
in Dr. Max Reinhardt. Given at the Century Theatre,
it was a lavish production of the *Jedermann*, aspiring
towards the spectacle-film manner. Done in a "super-
cathedral" style, it was an affair of pageantry ending
before the densely Hollywooded setting of a palatial
tomb, fully equipped with golden angels. It was solemn
with liturgical music and fanfare: the orchestra (oc-
cupying the second balcony of the theatre) was supple-
mented by bells and an organ. Antiphonal choruses
reciprocated from opposite boxes in the theatre. It was
a carnival, semi-musical-comedy version in which Death
claimed the Plutocratic Epicure. It was deplored by
hostile critics as a thing of banshee wailings in which
the opulently dying voluptuary finally obeys the sum-

mons of Death in a theatre submerged in sub-twilight mists, here and there pierced by eerie shafts of light, through all of which sounded muted drums and trumpets.

The possible justification for so prodigious a production of the Very Rich Man and Death appears to hinge upon the fact that Everyman offers Death a bribe of £1,000 cash to delay the sentence of execution for a dozen years. It was indeed a large sum of money for any medieval man to have had in pocket, as it were.

But the more academic critics have preferred not the cathedral style *Jedermann* of von Hofmannsthal and Reinhardt but the older wayside shrine manner of the traditional *Everyman*, that of noble, dignified, austere simplicity. This original Everyman is played as a bare, stark figure of doom, one blithe and youthful to begin with—perhaps a little insolent, defiant, even rakish— but at the end, pensive and penitent. At the conclusion, he is earnest, agonized, resigned, and submissive. The play ends on a note of bleak, penitential austerity.

Of the *Everyman* play, four different texts are extant: two complete, one imperfect, and one fragmentary copy. The two complete texts were printed by Skot and the remaining texts by Pynson. All four texts, containing numerous, minute variants, are conjectured to have been printed between 1508 and 1537. The text now in most general use is that reprinted in 1904 by W. W. Greg (later Sir Walter), the eminent British bibliographer, who used the edition of John Skot preserved at Britwell Court, England. It is known as the Britwell copy because, although once a part of the library of Lincoln Cathedral, it passed after much wandering to the Britwell collection. A perfect copy of another edition printed by Skot is in the British Museum. Of the Pynson editions, the fragmentary copy is in the Douce collection at the Bodleian, Oxford. The imperfect copy reposes in the British Museum.

All of the foregoing texts were reprinted by Greg between 1904 and 1910 for inclusion in the successively

appearing volumes of the *Materialien zur Kunde des
älteren Englischen Dramas* (Uystpruyst, Louvain). Besides the reprints, Greg included in the 1910 volume of
the series extensive tables for comparing the variants of
the four editions. These reprints, together with his comments, comprise a fairly ample bibliographical and
textual commentary on the *Everyman*. Dismissing any
attempt to establish a "correct" text, Greg adopted the
Britwell copy as his master text. He considered it most
free from editorial alterations and most consistent in
the use of grammatical and linguistic forms. A con-
sistency, by the bye, which Greg knew better than most
hinted at editorial standardization.

The Britwell copy is a small, thin, quarto volume
whose title-page contains the long familiar wood-cut of
Everyman: the one in which he wears the small round
hat with the saucily protruding feather, the short open
cape with the wide lapels. Everyman is depicted with
his hands held up deprecatingly, the palms outward, his
head turned disconcertedly towards the gaunt, spectral
figure of Death, who is grimly summoning the jauntily
dressed figure. Behind Death are what appear to be
graveyard crosses. Death carries what looks like an
enormous scroll, presumably the list of those to be
summarily called. The wood-cut is the perfect expression of the passage from the *Imitation of Christ* by
Thomas à Kempis:

> Quickly must thou be gone from hence, see then how
> matters stand with thee. Ah, fool—learn now to die to the
> world that thou mayst begin to live with Christ! . . .
> "Because at what hour you know not the Son of Man will
> come!"

As in all the other plays reprinted in this volume, the
present edition embodies modern spelling and punctuation, together with expansion of the original contrac-
tions. Like other editors, the present ones have taken
the liberty of adopting, wherever desirable, a variant
reading from one of the three reprints other than the

Britwell. The original spelling preserved what might with a trace of affectation be regarded as the quaint air of an antique, innocent day. It may be curious to see a character designated as "v. wyttes," or odd to note such casual mention of sacred matters as "The blessyd sacramentes, vii." References to deity might seem more picturesque in the original: "the hye Juge adonay," "Before Myssyas of Iherusalem kynge," or "Before the hyest Iupyter of all," or "Gracyous sacramentes of hye deuyuyte," etc. But easier reading is gained by modernization. And modernity is nothing if not the search for the shortest intellectual route to the rich Indies of the mind.

A word about what the older school of literary historians called the Dutch play *Elckerlijk* and what the more modern critics call the Flemish play *Elckerlyc*. It was first printed in 1495. In its relation to the English *Everyman* there were three views which aim to account for the extensive parallels between the two texts. One set of critics regards it as a sure thing that the English *Everyman* is a free translation into English of the Dutch (or Flemish) play. A second school of critics holds that *Everyman* is the prior play and its counterpart a translation or imitation of the English play. Judgment turns in part on which play a given critic considers to be the better one, the standard of excellence being based upon religious or theological orthodoxy, evenness and regularity in use of metre and metrical forms, etc. It is assumed, a little arbitrarily, that the better one is the earlier. Although the Flemish play is of an earlier printing than any extant English version, we neither know the date of the first publication of the English play nor do we know the date of composition. It is generally conjectured that *Everyman* was composed before the close of the fifteenth century. Finally, a third and small corps of diplomatic critics suggest that there may well have been a source common to both plays to account for the similarities. At any rate, to a Europe whose school-

master was the Church, the main heads of teaching
were universally familiar.

Johan, the Husband

Goneril: An interlude!

John Heywood was born in 1497 and died on
the continent in the last quarter of the sixteenth century, a religious exile from the Elizabethan religious
settlement. In his day he was a man of note: singer,
musician, wit, and dramatist. Socially and economically,
he was a man of standing, a "gentleman" of impressive
if not attractive person.

In his early days, he was possibly a student at Oxford,
residing at an ancient hostel in the parish of St. Al-
date's. The hostel, the Broadgate, later became the
present foundation Pembroke College. But, says the
chronicler Anthony à Wood of Heywood's presumed
attendance, "the crabbedness of logic not suiting with
his airy genie, he retired . . . and became noted to all
witty men, especially to Sir Thomas More."

Heywood was employed as Court musician from 1519
to 1528 and at subsequent intervals thereafter. He was
master of an organization of singing boys, possibly those
of St. Paul's cathedral. Heywood's marriage around 1523
to Joan, daughter of John Rastell, connected him
closely with the brilliant circle of Sir Thomas More.
His father-in-law was himself a noted writer of interludes. Socially and economically, Heywood prospered,
becoming eventually a landowner and city business
man, with many legal friends at the Inns of Court as
well as those at the royal Court.

Notwithstanding, his career was broken and uneven.
His fortunes fluctuated with the shifts and jars of the
Tudor religious struggles. During the reign of Henry
VIII, Heywood became implicated in an attack on the
Reformer Cranmer, an attempt which recoiled upon

the instigators. Heywood was condemned to death with forfeiture of his goods and estate, but obtained at length a pardon, apparently in 1544. A later author, Harrington, was to write of this episode, "What think you by Haywood that escaped hanging with his mirth?" During the reigns of Edward VI and Mary especially, Heywood was again in Court favor. But at length the Elizabethan religious settlement drove both him and his friends abroad and into exile. Heywood did not return, spending his last days in uneasy transit between Malines and Cologne, outliving most of his friends and acquaintances who went into exile with him.

Some of his surviving letters to England during this period reflect his neediness and distress, especially those to Lord Burleigh and his wife. Heywood's high and happy reputation of the early and middle years, contrasted with the fall of his fortunes in latter days, exerts irresistible pressure on the conventional moralist and vanity-fair biographer. Heywood was originally admired as the man "who for the myrth and quicknesse of his conceite more than for any good learning was in him came to be well benefitted by the king." He was celebrated as the "mad merry wit" who made "many mad plays." But alas, poor Yorick. In exile at the end, impoverished and neglected, Heywood wrote of his distresses to Lord Burleigh, seeking help and comfort. In 1575, shortly before his death, he writes of living "at this great pynche" and under conditions which "hath made my purse bare." Along with the fall of his external fortunes, the "airy genie" of the interludes can now only murmur, "My hearing begynneth to fayle me, and my myrrth decayeth with age, and my bodie is weake." The gay writer of the lively interludes ended pathetically appending footnotes to the book of Ecclesiastes.

In 1533, *A Play of Love, The Pardoner and the Frere, The Play of the Wether,* and *Johan, the Husband* were all published. The title-page of the first and third assigned them to John Heywood. The second and fourth were printed without title-page. Contemporary tradition and internal evidence serve as a basis for assigning them also to Heywood. The last named is also referred to as *The Play between Johan Johan the husband, Tyb his wife*, etc., *The Play between Johan and his Wife, Johan Johan*, etc.

As used derisively by Lear's daughter, the term *interlude* signifies a bit of farcical entertainment or nonsense. Some critics have taken the term to mean a play enacted between the pauses or courses of a banquet, or at least an entertainment interpolated into a larger social context. Others have felt that the *ludus* or "play" was merely that between two or more speakers, with just enough action to give the form of the interlude a dramatic status of its own. Whatever be the reason for the adoption of the name, the interludes are farcical and realistic, broadly humorful in spirit. They are brief in scope, turning usually on a single situation that requires only a limited number of actors and little external action.

Taken as a historical type, the interlude is itself an interlude between medieval and Elizabethan drama, between medieval pageant-wagon or street "station" and the Globe of London. The interludes flourished especially during the early and middle sixteenth century. They were given often and popularly received in Tudor banquet halls, in colleges and Inns.

The present interlude is a farcical presentation of the ancient triangle-situation. The three characters are the brazen and insolently unfaithful wife, the cowed, cuckolded, feeble and wife-oppressed husband, the openly profligate clergyman. The humor is not subtle. It turns upon the cumulative humiliations and indignities visited upon the undeceived deceived-husband until the latter responds with violence, only to repent of his retaliation at the "curtain." The butt of wit and abuse, Johan Johan is notable for the ironic contrast between his interior monologues and his "public" pronouncements, the former, menacing and threatening; the latter,

elicited often by his wife's "What sayest?"—conciliatory
and abjectly compromising. He leads the secret life of
Walter Mitty. Tyb herself is in the much-worn tradition
of the termagant wife which stretches from Noah *Uxor*
even to the Mrs. Zero of *The Adding Machine*. Indeed,
no figure until Mr. Zero was quite so oppressed by
domestic imperialism since Johan Johan. Both husbands
explode in defiance of their situations. But neither has
the courage or moral stamina to maintain an attitude
momentarily assumed under intolerable stress.

In general spirit, *Johan Johan* is the antithesis to the
spirit of *Everyman*. The treatment of priesthood and
the sacraments is one of light-hearted profaneness. Tyb
and Sir John together represent the world as Folly.
They are appetite and coarse humor indulged with
almost sadistic indifference to the plight of the cuckolded husband. That it was regarded as hilariously
funny is an index to the manners and humors of the
time as well as a tribute to the talent of its supposed
author.

The Four PP.

The Four PP. is less dramatic and more of a
"debate" than *Johan, the Husband*. It is in all prob-
ability a slightly earlier composition. William Middleton, a printer of law and medical books began printing
in 1541; he died in 1547. The present interlude, printed
by him, appeared about 1544, the title-page attributing
it to John Heywood. It has already been noted that
Heywood was implicated in a plot against Cranmer and
that, for his participation in it, Heywood very nearly
met a traitor's death at Tyburn, a penalty which he
escaped only by reading a recantation at Paul's Cross in
July of 1544.

Historians assume that Middleton decided to print
The Four PP. while Heywood was still the talk of the
town, especially that part of it known as the Inns of
Court, the haunt of students and practitioners of the

law. Middleton was perhaps doing more than taking advantage of a hot market. He may have thought that the work would be helpful to Heywood's reputation. *The Four PP.* presents a very unflattering picture of at least two chief figures of the older medieval order—a pardoner and a palmer. They are two types especially odious to the movers of the new Reformation order, to whose party Cranmer belonged. Of the two, the pardoner was the more objectionable, and his character is particularly debased by Heywood. Hence the publication might be read with sympathy by the Reformation party and its author considered not beyond redemption. As for the actual date of its original composition, there is but conjecture to fall back upon. A. W. Reed, a foremost authority, would assign the writing of the interlude to 1520-2.

The figures presented in the interlude lie midway between the medieval and the modern world: the older world of shrines, indulgences, and relics, and the newer one of medicines and drugs for health as well as the world of commerce, represented by the pedler.

In a literary perspective, the pardoner and the palmer belong to the receding world of Chaucer's Canterbury pilgrims. His most vivid and vital characterizations were the Pardoner of Rouncivalle and Alice of Bath, whose three visits to Jerusalem (and almost everywhere else) established her claim to a palm. Chaucer has no pedler, although his Friar with his packet of trinkets and toys for housewives partly supplies that loss. His only reference to an apothecary is in connection with his Doctor of Physic, the former having a "split-fee" relation to the latter. Heywood's Palmer will sustain no comparison with Alice. His Pardoner alone, especially his fraudulent relics, preserves the spirit of Chaucer's Pardoner in diluted form.

The Elizabethan drama of Shakespeare, following upon the Tudor interlude, does contain a brilliant picture of an apothecary, the haggard figure in *Romeo and Juliet*, and his grotesquely furnished shop. As for the pedler, Shakespeare's Autolycus of *The Winter's Tale* surpasses anything by Heywood. Still, perhaps Shakespeare profited by a look at the wares in the packet of Heywood's Pedler, so similar are the contents despite a few vivid additions by Shakespeare. We especially miss from the packet of Heywood's Pedler the fantastic ballads available to Autolycus' customers. Nor has Heywood's Pedler anything of the tricksterish agility of Shakespeare's "snapper-up of unconsidered trifles." In fact, Shakespeare's Autolycus almost combines the roles of pardoner and pedler. So skillfully does he present his wares that eager customers seek them "as if my trinkets had been hallowed and brought a benediction to the buyer." Thus did the older religion of the supernatural pass into the modern religion of the consumer.

As for the spiritual progeny of the Pothecary, the genius of comedy from Molière to Shaw has rejoiced over their absurdities. However, it was hardly until our own day, the period of *Babbitt*, that the descendants of the Pedler have been thought worthy of a central position in a work of literary art.

It is in Heywood's stage-world that almost for the last time we can see the four figures grouped together. The Pardoner and the Palmer are already on the long road into shameful exile, repudiated and denounced by the crusading spirit of the new Reformers.

The main components of Heywood's interlude are the following: 1) the desire of a Pedler to enjoy a holiday in the company of the other three, 2) the mutual antipathy of the members of the latter group, 3) the Pedler's suggestion that they form themselves into a society (in an effort to establish social harmony) with one as the leader, 4) the Pedler's improvisation of a tale-telling contest—who can tell the biggest lie—to determine who shall be chief man, 5) the victory of the Palmer, whose story turns out to be a satiric thrust at the character of woman, whose sex is not represented in the cast of the play.

We see the Pedler, as the play opens, desirous of a space of happy enjoyment from selling his wares. He is particularly pleased with the company he has encountered, and to spice work with play along with such "good fellows" is his ambition:

> For, by the faith of my body,
> I like full well this company
> . . .
> Who may not play one day in a week
> May think his thrift is far to seek.

He is eager and ready for any sport. After a song, he expresses himself as happy and pleased:

> This liketh me well, so may I thrive!

But at this juncture, the Pardoner reveals the latent divergence of temperament of the others, turning upon their rival pretensions and vanities. The Pardoner sounds the note of disharmony, protesting that social amenity is prohibited by such diversity of temper and disposition:

> But who can set in daliance
> Men set in such a variance

Whereupon the mutual disesteem of Pardoner, Pothecary, and Palmer is expressed. Each regards himself as the superior of the other two.

The Pedler, willing and resourceful, decides to form them into a sort of Salvation, Inc. For it is the particular boast of each that he contributes more than the others to the Salvation which lies beyond this life. The Pedler adopts a device whereby their sharply competitive temperaments may be subordinated to the rule of a leader. Since their vanity prevents a rational manner of choosing a leader, the Pedler adopts a device in harmony— ironically—with the professional habits of all three. They are already united by one bond: they are all equally given to lying. A contest or "debate" will be held. The Pedler will be the impartial judge, giving pre-eminence and leadership to the one who tells a tale most unlikely to be true—as it is put somewhat cautiously. The others agree.

The "debate" follows. Despite the elaborate fabrications of the Pardoner and the Pothecary, the Palmer wins. He adopts a bold and simple strategy. He merely comments that among the innumerable women met in his world-travels, he has yet to find one lacking in patience. His resultant winning of the contest is resented, however, by the losers. Thereupon, the Palmer benevolently releases them both from their promise of subordination to the winner of the contest. The interlude then shifts key, ending in an exhortation to all to live righteously and with charity.

As the drama was the major literary form of the sixteenth century, the novel is that of our time. If the reader were to cast about in the modern world for the reincarnation of the spirit of John Heywood, he might do worse than fix upon Sinclair Lewis. In style, both are loose-jointed, journalistic and breezy to the point of garrulousness. Both are constantly ambitious, if not always sure, of wit. But in spite of a certain aggressive naiveté of approach and ingenuousness of manner, both fully communicate through their limitations their unabating zest and joyous enthusiasm for satiric laughter at human folly and falseness. Sir John the priest and the Pardoner lived again in Elmer Gantry, the Pedler in George Babbitt and his pals, the Pothecary in Dr. Almus Pickerbaugh and his accomplices of *Arrowsmith*, and—for sake of symmetry—the Palmer in the itinerant, roving Dodsworths. It is enough to suggest that if Heywood's was one of those small voices not to be heard for all time, it was still strong enough to carry beyond the reach of a day.

FOOTNOTE TO *Introduction*

Current study of the history of the composition of *The Castle of Perseverance* points to the following possibility: that there have been several revisions or "editings" of the extant Macro version which is our only authority. These revisions are: 1) the entire vexillator portion of the play was added to the hypothetical original; 2) the scene of the Daughters of God at the end, together with several lines preceding it, was also an addition, but an addition slightly later than the vexillatory emendation; in the ending of the supposed original, the Blessed Virgin alone interceded for Mankind before God. The same study also assigns date and locale of origin. The composition of the play is placed in the north East Midlands, all portions presumably having originated in or near the city of Lincoln. The "original" version is assigned to the middle of the last decade of the fourteenth century. The vexillator revision is given to the year 1400, and the Daughters of God episode to the years 1402-05. —Jacob Bennett, "'Linguistic Study of the *Castle of Perseverance*." See *Dissertation Abstracts* (Ann Arbor, Michigan, 1960), XXI, 872.

Abraham and Isaac

THE STORY AS TOLD IN GENESIS

And it came to pass . . . that God did tempt Abraham, and said unto him, "Abraham," and he said, "Behold, here I am."

And He said, "Take now thy son, thine only son Isaac, whom thou lovest, and get thee into the land of Moriah; and offer him there for a burnt offering upon one of the mountains which I will tell thee of."

And Abraham rose up early in the morning and saddled his ass and took two of his young men with him, and Isaac his son, and cleft wood for the burnt offering, and rose up and went unto the place of which God had told him. Then on the third day Abraham lifted up his eyes and saw the place afar off. And Abraham said unto his young men, "Abide ye here with the ass; and I and the lad will go yonder and worship, and come again to you."

And Abraham took the wood of the burnt offering and laid it upon Isaac, his son; and he took the fire in his hand and a knife; and they went both of them together.

And Isaac spoke unto Abraham, his father, and said, "My father," and he said, "Here am I, my son." And he said, "Behold the fire and the wood, but where is the lamb for a burnt offering?" And Abraham said, "My son, God will provide himself a lamb for a burnt offering." So they went both of them together.

And they came to the place which God had told him of, and Abraham built an altar there and laid the wood in order, and bound Isaac, his son, and laid him on the altar upon the wood. And Abraham stretched forth his hand and took the knife to slay his son.

And the angel of the Lord called unto him out of heaven and said, "Abraham, Abraham," and he said, "Here am I."

And he said, "Lay not thine hand upon the lad, neither do thou any thing unto him, for now I know that thou fearest God, seeing thou hast not withheld thy son, thine only son from me."

And Abraham lifted up his eyes and looked, and behold a ram caught in a thicket by his horns; and Abraham went and took the ram and offered him up for a burnt offering in the stead of his son. And Abraham called the name of that place Jehovah-jireh; as it is said to this day, "In the mount of the Lord it shall be seen."

The Brome Version of the Play

The scenery requirements are minimal. A curtain, which separates in the center, cuts off part of the backstage, and there is an upper stage or balcony. The opening scene takes place in front of Abraham's tent in Beersheba. Father Abraham and his son Isaac enter from the left as if on their way home from the pastures. Abraham is a venerable and majestic patriarchal figure with long white hair and a flowing white beard. His countenance is aged but serene, his deep-set eyes suggesting a deeply meditative nature and a gaze directed to otherworldly things. He wears a loose white robe which reaches to his feet. In his left hand is a long staff which he uses as a cane although it is clear that his rugged frame does not require its support. Isaac is a handsome curly-haired lad of about nine years, dressed in a simple peasant frock which is tied around his waist by a cord and reaches to a point just above his bare knees. His is the frank, open face of innocent and all-trusting childhood. Both Abraham and Isaac wear open sandals on their bare feet, each sandal made of a full sole of leather roughly shaped to the foot and bound around the ankle by leather thongs. They walk

together to the front center of the stage where Abraham
places his right arm around Isaac's shoulder. Both kneel
in what appears to be a customary homecoming ritual.
Isaac folds his hands and lowers his head in prayer.
Abraham, his arm still circling his son's shoulder, raises
his eyes and his staff toward heaven.

ABRAHAM: (*in a firm, clear, but deeply reverent voice*)
Father of heaven, omnipotent,
   With all my heart to thee I call;
Thou has given me both land and rent,
And my livelihood thou hast me sent;
   I thank thee highly, evermore, for all.

First on the earth thou madest Adam,
   And Eve also, to be his wife;
All other creatures of these two came;
And now thou hast granted to me, Abraham,
   Here in this land to lead my life.

In my age thou hast granted me this,
   That this young child with me shall live; (wone)
I love nothing else so much, indeed, (i-wis)
Except thine own self, dear Father of bliss,
   As Isaac here, my own sweet son.

I have divers children mo'
   Which I love not half so well;
This fair sweet child, he cheers me so
In every place where that I go
   That no distress here may I feel. (fell)

And therefore, Father of heaven, I thee pray
   For his health and also for his grace;
Now, Lord, keep him both night and day,
That never distress nor no fear (fray)
   Come to my child in no place.
   He lowers his staff, looks tenderly at Isaac, and rises.
Now come on, Isaac, my own sweet child;
   Go we home and take our rest.

ISAAC: (*standing up and looking at his father with childish adoration*)

Abraham, my own father so mild,

    To follow thee I am full ready (prest)

        Both early and late.

ABRAHAM: (*again putting his arm around the lad's shoulder*)

    Come on, sweet child, I love thee best

        Of all the children that ever I begat.

Abraham and Isaac turn and go to the back of the stage. Abraham parts the curtains of the tent and follows Isaac inside.

The scene shifts to the upper stage where God and an angel appear. The bearded countenance of God is that of a more exalted Abraham. On his head is an ornate triple-tiered crown (symbol of the Trinity). He wears white pontifical robes, the stole with its patterned gold border caught in front with a gold sunburst. The angel is robed in white with large wings attached to the shoulders and a gold halo over his long hair which is parted in the center, combed down and toward the back, and curled at the end.

GOD: (*his hand raised in a pontifical gesture*)

Mine angel, fast hie thee thy way,

    And onto middle-earth anon thou go;

Abraham's heart now will I essay,

    Whether that he be steadfast or no.

Say I commanded him for to take

    Isaac, his young son that he loves so well,

And with his blood sacrifice he make,

    If any of my friendship he will feel. (fell)

Show him the way unto the hill

    Where that his sacrifice shall be.

I shall essay now his good will

    Whether he loveth better his child or me

All men shall take example by him

    My commandments how they shall keep.

God lowers his hand and goes off to left. The angel bows in acquiescence and goes off to the right to descend to the lower stage. Abraham (without his staff) comes forward from the tent and kneels down to pray.

ABRAHAM: *(hands raised upward in prayer)*
Now, Father of heaven, that formed all thing,
    My prayers I make to thee again,
For this day my tender offering
    Here must I give to thee, certain.
Ah, Lord God, Almighty King,
    What manner best will make thee most glad? (fain)
If I had thereof very knowing,
    It should be done with all my might, (main)
        Full soon anon.
    To do thy pleasure on a hill,
    Verily, it is my will,
        Dear Father, God in Trinity.
The angel enters from the right and stands beside the kneeling Abraham.

THE ANGEL: *(holding his hand over Abraham's head)*
Abraham, Abraham, wilt thou rest!
    Our Lord commandeth thee for to take
Isaac, thy young son that thou lovest best,
    And with his blood sacrifice that thou make.

Into the land of Vision thou go,
    And offer thy child unto thy Lord;
I shall thee lead and show all so.
    Unto God's behest, Abraham, accord,

And follow me upon this green.
ABRAHAM: *(deeply troubled, raising his eyes toward the angel)*
    Welcome to me be my Lord's messenger, (sond)
    And his hest I will not withstand; (withstond)
    Yet Isaac, my young son on earth, (in lond)
A full dear child to me hath been.

I had liefer, if God had been pleased,
    For to have forborne all the goods that I have

Than Isaac my son should have been harmed, (desseced)
   So God in heaven my soul may save!
I loved never thing so much on earth, (erde)
   And now I must the child go kill.
Ah! Lord God, my conscience is strongly stirred,
And yet, my dear Lord, I am sore afraid (aferd)
   To grudge anything against your will.

I love my child as my life,
   But yet I love my God much more,
For thou my heart would make any strife,
Yet will I not spare for child nor wife,
   But do after my Lord's lore.

Though I love my son never so well,
   Yet smite off his head soon I shall.
Ah! Father of heaven, to thee I kneel (knell)
A hard death my son shall feel (fell)
   For to honor thee, Lord, withal.

   THE ANGEL: (*raising his hand in blessing*)
Abraham, Abraham! This is well said,
   And all these commandments look that thou keep;
But in thy heart be nothing dismayed.
   ABRAHAM:
Nay, nay, forsooth, I hold me well pleased
   To please my God to the best that I have.

For though my heart be heavily set
   To see the blood of my own dear son,
Yet for all this I will not desist, (let)
(*The angel goes off. Abraham rises.*)
But Isaac, my son, I will go fetch, (fet)
   And come as fast as ever we can.

(*He returns to the tent and opens the curtain as he speaks.*)
Now, Isaac, my own son dear,
   Where art thou, child? Speak to me.
   ISAAC: (*discovered kneeling in prayer*)

My father, sweet father, I am here,
  And make my prayers to the Trinity.

ABRAHAM:
Rise up, my child, and fast come hither,
  My gentle bairn that art so wise,
For we two, child, must go together
  And unto my Lord make sacrifice.

  ISAAC: (*rising and coming out of the tent*)
I am full ready, my father, lo!
  Even at your hands I stand right here,
And whatsoever ye bid me do,
  It shall be done with glad cheer,
    Full well and fine.
  ABRAHAM: (*picking up a faggot from beside the tent*)
  Ah, Isaac, my own son so dear,
    God's blessing I give thee, and mine.

Hold this faggot upon thy back,
  And here myself fire shall bring.
  ISAAC: (*taking the faggot*)
Father, all this here will I pack;
  I am full fain to do your bidding.
  ABRAHAM: (*aside, as he picks up his sword and a box of coals*)
  Ah, Lord of heaven, my hands I wring;
    This child's words all to-wound my heart.

Now Isaac, son, go we our way
(*pointing to the right of the stage where an altar has been placed*)
  Unto yon mount, with all our main.
  ISAAC: (*following his father as they slowly proceed*)
Go we, my dear father, as fast as I may;
  To follow you I am full fain
    Although I be slender.
  ABRAHAM: (*aside*)
  Ah, Lord, my heart breaketh in twain,
    This child's words, they be so tender.

(*They arrive at Mount Vision.*)
Ah, Isaac, son, anon lay it down;
  No longer upon thy back it hold,
For I must make ready bound (boun)
  To honor my Lord God as I should.

  ISAAC: (*pointing to the altar*)
Lo, my dear father, where it is
  To cheer you always I draw me near;
But, father, I marvel sore of this,
  Why that ye make this heavy cheer.

And also, father, evermore dread I:
  Where is your quick beast that ye should kill?
Both fire and wood we have ready,
  But quick beast have we none on this hill.

A quick beast, I know well, must be dead
  Your sacrifice for to make.
  ABRAHAM: (*gazing at Isaac with dolorous intensity*)
Dread thee not, my child, I thee instruct; (rede)
Our Lord will send me unto this place (stead)
  Some manner of beast for to take,
    Through his sweet messenger. (sand)
  ISAAC: (*trembling—as Abraham places the coals beside
the altar*)
  Yea, father, but my heart beginneth to quake
    To see that sharp sword in your hand.

Why bear ye your sword drawn so?
  Of your countenance I have much wonder.
  ABRAHAM: (*aside*)
Ah, Father of heaven, so I am woe!
  This child here breaks my heart asunder.

  ISAAC:
Tell me, my dear father, ere that ye cease,
  Bear ye your sword drawn for me?
  ABRAHAM: (*his voice tremulous*)
Ah, Isaac, sweet son, peace! peace!
  For indeed thou breakst my heart in three.

ISAAC: (*wondering at his father's strange mood*)
Now truly, somewhat, father, ye think,
　That ye mourn thus more and more.
ABRAHAM: (*raising his eyes to heaven*)
Ah! Lord of heaven, thy grace let sink,
　For my heart was never half so sore.

ISAAC:
I pray you, father, ye let me that know,　(wit)
　Whether shall I have any harm or no.
ABRAHAM:
Indeed, sweet son, I may not tell thee yet;
　My heart is so full of woe.

ISAAC:　(*in most earnest entreaty*)
Dear father, I pray you, hide it not from me,
But some of your thought that ye tell me.
ABRAHAM: (*groaning heavily*)
Ah, Isaac, Isaac, I must kill thee!
ISAAC: (*falling to his knees*)
Kill me, father? Alas! What have I done?
If I have trespassed against you aught,
　With a rod ye may make me full mild;
And with your sharp sword kill me nought,
　For indeed, father, I am but a child.

ABRAHAM: (*putting his hand on Isaac's shoulder*)
I am full sorry, son, thy blood for to spill.
　But truly, my child, I may not choose.　(chese)
ISAAC: (*miserably*)
Now I would to God my mother were here on this hill!
　She would kneel for me on both her knees
　　To save my life.
And since that my mother is not here,
I pray you, father, change your cheer,
　　And kill me not with your knife.

ABRAHAM:
Forsooth, son, unless I thee kill,
　I should grieve God right sore, I dread;

It is his commandment and also his will
   That I should do this same deed.

He commanded me, son, for certain,
   To make my sacrifice with thy blood.
    ISAAC: *(in a tone of extreme wonderment)*
And is it God's will that I should be slain?

   ABRAHAM:
   Yea, truly, Isaac, my son so good,
     And therefore my hands I wring.

   ISAAC: *(bowing his head)*
Now, father, against my Lord's will
I will never grudge, loud or still;
   He might have sent me a better destiny
If it had been his pleasure.

   ABRAHAM: *(resting the sword against the altar)*
Forsooth, son, but if I did this deed,
   Grievously displeased our Lord will be.
   ISAAC:
Nay, nay, father, God forbid
   That ever ye should grieve him for me.

Ye have other children, one or two,
   The which ye should love well naturally. (by kind)
I pray you, father, make ye no woe,
For, be I once dead and from you go,
   I shall be soon out of your mind.

Therefore do our Lord's bidding,
   And when I am dead, then pray for me.
But, good father, tell ye my mother nothing;
Say that I am in another country dwelling.
   ABRAHAM: *(sighing deeply)*
   Ah! Isaac, Isaac, blessed must thou be!
My heart beginneth strongly to rise
   To see the blood of thy blessed body.
   ISAAC: *(comfortingly)*
Father, since it may be no other wise,
   Let it pass over as well as I.

But, father, ere I go unto my death,
   I pray you bless me with your hand.
   ABRAHAM: (*placing his hand on Isaac's head*)
Now, Isaac, with all my breath
   My blessing I give thee upon this land
      And God's also thereto, indeed, (i-wis)
   Isaac, Isaac, son, up thou stand,
      Thy fair sweet mouth that I may kiss.

   ISAAC: (*rising and receiving his father's kiss*)
Now farewell, my own father so fine,
   And greet well my mother in earth. (erde)
But I pray you, father, to hide my eyes (eyne)
   That I see not the stroke of your sharp sword (swerd)
      That my flesh shall defile.
   ABRAHAM: (*weeping*)
Son, thy words make me to weep full sore;
Now, my dear son Isaac, speak no more.
   ISAAC: (*tenderly*)
Ah! My own dear father, wherefore?
      We shall speak together here but a while.

And since that I must needs be dead,
   Yet, my dear father, to you I pray,
Smite but few strokes at my head,
   And make an end as soon as ye may,
      And tarry not too long.
   ABRAHAM: (*groaning heavily*)
   Thy meek words, child, make me afraid; (affray)
      So "Welaway!" may be my song,

Except only God's will.
   Ah! Isaac, my own sweet child,
Yet kiss me again upon this hill!
   In all this world is none so mild.

   ISAAC: (*after kissing his father*)
Now truly, father, all this tarrying
   It doth my heart but harm;

I pray you, father, make an ending.
 ABRAHAM: (*with gentle resolution*)
 Come up, sweet son, unto my arm.

I must bind thy hands two,
 Although thou be never so mild.
 ISAAC: (*horrified*)
Ah! Mercy, father! Why should ye do so?
 ABRAHAM: (*gently*)
 That thou shouldst not hinder, my child.

 ISAAC: (*with simple directness*)
Nay, indeed, father, I will not stop you.
 Do on for me your will;
And on the purpose that ye have set you
 For God's love keep it forth still.

I am full sorry this day to die,
 But yet I wish not my God to grieve;
Do as you please for me hardily,
 My fair sweet father, I give you leave.

But, father, I pray you evermore,
 Tell ye my mother no bit; (dell)
If she knew it, she would weep full sore,
 For indeed, father, she loveth me full well;
  God's blessing may she have!

Now farewell, my mother so sweet!
We two be like no more to meet.
 ABRAHAM: (*in a choked voice*)
Ah, Isaac, Isaac! Son, thou makest me to weep, (greet)
 And with thy words thou distemper'st me.

 ISAAC: (*kneeling and bowing his head*)
Indeed, sweet father, I am sorry to grieve you,
 I cry you mercy of that I have done,
And of all trespass that ever I did move you;
 Now, dear father, forgive me that I have done.
  God of heaven be with me!

ABRAHAM:

Ah, dear child, leave off thy moans;
In all thy life thou grieved me never once.
Now blessed be thou, body and bones,
    That ever thou wert bred and born!
Thou hast been to me child full good.
    But indeed, child, though I mourn never so fast,
    Yet must I needs here at the last
In this place shed all thy blood.

Therefore, my dear son, here shalt thou lie;
(lifting him up gently and placing him on the altar)
    Unto my work I must apply myself. (me stead)
Indeed I had as lief myself to die—
    If God will be pleased with my deed—
    And my own body for to offer.
ISAAC:

Ah! Mercy, father, mourn ye no more!
Your weeping maketh my heart sore
    As my own death that I shall suffer.

Your kerchief, father, about my eyes ye wind!
    ABRAHAM:

So I shall, my sweetest child in earth. (erde)
    ISAAC:

Now yet, good father, have this in mind,
    And smite me not often with your sharp sword,
        (swerd)
    But hastily that it be sped.

Here Abraham lays a cloth on Isaac's face, thus saying:
    ABRAHAM:

Now farewell, my child, so full of grace.
    ISAAC:

Ah! Father, father, turn downward my face,
    For of your sharp sword I am ever adread.

ABRAHAM: *(gently turning Isaac's body over)*
To do this deed I am full sorry,
    But, Lord, thy hest I will not withstand.

ISAAC:
Ah! Father of heaven, to thee I cry,
    Lord, receive me into thy hand!

ABRAHAM: (*picking up his sword*)
Lo! Now is the time come certain
    That my sword in his neck shall bite.
Ah! Lord, my heart riseth against this, (there-again)
    I may not find it in my heart to smite—
       My heart will not now thereto.
    Yet fain I would work my Lord's will;
    But this young innocent lieth so still,
    I may not find it in my heart him to kill.
       Oh! Father of heaven! What shall I do?

ISAAC:
Ah! Mercy, father, why tarry ye so
    And let me lie thus long on this heath?
Now I would to God the stroke were do!
Father, I pray you heartily, short me of my woe
    And let me not look thus after my death.

ABRAHAM: (*slowly raising his sword*)
Now, heart, why wouldest not thou break in three?
    Yet shall thou not make me to my God unmild.
I will no longer delay for thee,
For that my God aggrieved would be;
    Now take the stroke, my own dear child.

*As Abraham is about to strike, the angel appears
suddenly and takes the sword from Abraham's hand.*
THE ANGEL:
I am an angel, thou mayst see blithe,
    That from heaven to thee is sent.
Our Lord thank thee a hundred times (sithe)
    For the keeping of his commandment.

He knoweth thy will and also thy heart,
    That thou dreadest him above all thing;
And some of thy heaviness for to depart
    A fair ram yonder I gan bring.

(During this speech, a ram might be lowered from the upper stage onto a bramble bush at the rear of stage right, or the angel might draw a curtain at the back of the stage disclosing a ram caught in the briars.)

He standeth tied, lo, among the briars.
 Now, Abraham, amend thy mood,
For Isaac, thy young son that here is,
 This day shall not shed his blood.

Go, make sacrifice with yon ram.
Now, farewell, blessed Abraham,
 For unto heaven I go now home;
The way is full straight. (gain)
  Take up thy son so free.

 The angel departs.
 ABRAHAM: *(raising his hands to heaven)*
Ah! Lord, I thank thee of thy great grace!
 Now am I eased in divers wise.
 Arise up, Isaac, my dear son, arise!
  Arise up, sweet child, and come to me.

 ISAAC: *(unaware of the heavenly visitation)*
Ah! Mercy, father, why smight ye nought?
 Ah! Smite on, father, once with your knife.
 ABRAHAM: *(uncovering Isaac's face)*
Peace, my sweet son, and take no thought,
 For our Lord of heaven hath grant thy life
  By his angel now,
That thou shalt not die this day, son, truly.
 ISAAC: *(slowly sitting up in bewilderment)*
Ah! Father, full glad then were I.
 Indeed, father, I say, indeed, (i-wis)
  If this tale were true.
 ABRAHAM: *(embracing his son)*
  An hundred times, my son fair of hue,
For joy thy mouth now will I kiss.

ISAAC:

Ah! My dear father, Abraham,
  Will not God be wroth that we do thus?
  ABRAHAM:
No, no! Hardly, my sweet son,
For yon same ram he hath us sent
  Hither down to us.

Yon beast shall die here in thy stead,
  In the worship of our Lord alone.
Go, fetch him hither, my child, indeed.
  ISAAC: *(jumping down from the altar)*
Father, I will go seize him by the head,
  And bring yon beast with me anon.
  *Isaac runs to the bush, grasps the ram's head and
holds it.*
Ah! Sheep, sheep, blessed mote thou be,
  That ever thou were sent down hither!
Thou shalt this day die for me
In the worship of the holy Trinity.
  Now come fast and go we together
    To my father in haste. (hie)
Though thou be never so gentle and good,
Yet had I liefer thou sheddest thy blood,
    Indeed, sheep, than I.

  He leads the ram to his father.
Lo, father, I have brought here full smart
  This gentle sheep, and him to you I give;
But, Lord God, I thank thee with all my heart,
  For I am glad that I shall live
    And kiss once my dear mother.
  ABRAHAM: *(taking the ram)*
  Now be right merry, my sweet child,
  For this quick beast that is so mild
    Here I shall present before all other.

  ISAAC: *(bending down and placing the coals under
the faggot on the altar)*

And I will fast begin to blow;
    This fire shall burn a full good speed.
But, father, will I stoop down low,
Ye will not kill me with your sword, I trow?
    ABRAHAM: (*smiling*)
    No, hardly, sweet son, have no dread;
        My mourning is past.
    ISAAC: (*shuddering*)
    Yea! But I would that sword were in a fire, (gled)
        For, indeed, father, it makes me full ill aghast.

Here Abraham makes his offering, kneeling and saying thus:
    ABRAHAM:
Now, Lord God of heaven in Trinity,
    Almighty God omnipotent,
My offering I make in the worship of thee,
    And with this quick beast I thee present.
    Lord, receive thou mine intent,
        As thou art God and ground of our grace.

God appears on the upper stage.
    GOD:
Abraham, Abraham, well mote thou speed,
    And Isaac, thy young son thee by!
Truly, Abraham, for this deed
I shall multiply both your seed
    As thick as stars be in the sky,
        Both more and less;
    And thick as gravel in the sea,
    So thick multiplied your seed shall be;
        This grant I you for your goodness.

Of you shall come fruit great quantity, (won)
    And ever be in bliss without end.
For ye dread me as God alone
And keep my commandments every one,
    My blessing I give, wheresoever ye wend.

    ABRAHAM: (*bowing his head, then turning to Isaac*)
Lo! Isaac, my son, how think ye

By this work that we have wrought?
Full glad and blithe we may be,
    Against the will of God that we grudged nought
        Upon this fair heath.
ISAAC:
Ah! Father, I thank our Lord every way (dell)
That my wit served me so well
    For to dread God more than my death.

ABRAHAM: *(putting his arm around Isaac's shoulder)*
Why! Dearworthy son, wert thou adread?
    Hardily, child, tell me thy lore.
    ISAAC: *(clinging closely to his father)*
Yea! By my faith, father, now I realize (have I red)
    I was never so afraid before
        As I have been at yon hill.
    But, by my faith, father, I swear
    I will nevermore come there
        But it be against my will.

ABRAHAM: *(turning Isaac in the direction of home)*
Yea! Come on with me, my own sweet son,
And homeward fast now let us goon.
    ISAAC: *(looking up with sudden happiness)*
    By my faith, father, thereto I grant;
I had never so good will to go home
        And to speak with my dear mother.
    ABRAHAM: *(releasing Isaac and raising his arms upward)*
    Ah! Lord of heaven, I thank thee,
    For now may I lead home with me
    Isaac, my young son so free—
        The gentlest child above all other,
    This may I well avow. (avoee)
Now go forth, my blessed son.
    ISAAC: *(walking beside his father toward the tent)*
I grant, father, and let us gon,
    For, by my troth, were I at home,
    I would never go out under that haven. (forme)

I pray God give us grace evermo,
And all those that we beholden to.

*Abraham and Isaac enter the tent. A Doctor enters
from the left. He is an austere scholar, dressed in cleric's
robes.*

DOCTOR: (*addressing the audience*)

Lo, sovereigns and sirs, now have we showed
   This solemn story to great and small.
It is good learning to learned and ignorant, (lewd)
   And the wisest of us all,
      Without any searching. (berrying)
   For this story showeth
   How we should keep, to our power,
      God's commandments without grudging.

Trow ye, sirs if God sent an angel,
   And commanded you your child to slain,
By your troth is there any of you
   That either would grudge or strive against it?
      (thereagain)
How think ye now, sirs, thereby?
   I trow there be three or four or mo.
And these women that weep so sorrowfully
   When that their children die them fro,
      As nature will and kind—
   It is but folly, I may well avow,
   To grudge against God or to grieve you,
   For ye shall never see him mischiefed, well I know,
      By hand nor water. Have this in mind,

And grudge not against our Lord God
   In wealth or woe, whether that he you send,
Though ye be never so hard bestead;
   For when he will, he may it amend.
His commandments truly if ye keep with good heart,
   As this story hath now showed you before, (beforn)
And faithfully serve him while ye be safe, (quart)
   That ye may please God both even and morn.

Now Jesus, that wore the crown of thorn,
    Bring us all to heaven's bliss.
He raises his hand in blessing and so concludes the
play.

Noah's Flood

And God saw that the wickedness of man was great in the earth and that every imagination of the thoughts of his heart was only evil continually. And it repented the Lord that he had made man on the earth and it grieved him at his heart.

And the Lord said, "I will destroy man whom I have created from the face of the earth; both man and beast and the creeping thing and the fowls of the air; for it repenteth me that I have made them.

But Noah found grace in the eyes of the Lord. . . . And God said unto Noah, "The end of all flesh is come before me; for the earth is filled with violence through them; and, behold, I will destroy them with the earth.

"Make thee an ark of gopher wood; rooms shalt thou make in the ark, and shalt pitch it within and without with pitch. And this is the fashion which thou shalt make it of: the length of the ark shall be three hundred cubits, the breadth of it fifty cubits, and the height of it thirty cubits. A window shalt thou make to the ark, and in a cubit shalt thou finish it above; and the door of the ark shalt thou set in the side thereof; with lower, second, and third stories shalt thou make it.

"And behold, I, even I do bring a flood of waters upon the earth, to destroy all flesh, wherein is the breath of life, from under heaven; and every thing that is in the earth shall die. But with thee will I establish my covenant; and thou shalt come into the ark, thou, and thy sons, and thy wife, and thy sons' wives with thee. And of every living thing of all flesh, two of every sort shalt thou bring into the ark, to keep them alive with thee; they shall be male and female.". . .

And the Lord said unto Noah, "Come thou and all thy house into the ark; for thee have I seen righteous before me in this generation. Of every clean beast thou shalt take to thee by sevens, the male and the female: and of beasts that are not clean by two, the male and his female. . . .

"For yet seven days, and I will cause it to rain upon the earth forty days and forty nights; and every living substance that I have made will I destroy from off the face of the earth."

And Noah did according unto all that the Lord commanded him. . . . And Noah went in, and his sons, and his wife, and his sons' wives with him into the ark, because of the waters of the flood. Of clean beasts, and of beasts that are not clean, and of fowls, and of every thing that creepeth upon the earth, there went in two and two unto Noah into the ark, the male and the female, as God had commanded Noah.

And it came to pass after seven days that the waters of the flood were upon the earth. And the rain was upon the earth forty days and forty nights.

In the selfsame day entered Noah, and Shem, and Ham, and Japeth, the sons of Noah, and Noah's wife, and the three wives of his sons with them, into the ark. . . .

And the flood was forty days upon the earth; and the waters increased and bare up the ark, and it was lift up above the earth. . . . And every living substance was destroyed which was upon the face of the ground, both man, and cattle, and the creeping things, and the fowl of the heaven; and they were destroyed from the earth; and Noah only remained alive, and they that were with him in the ark.

And the waters prevailed upon the earth an hundred and fifty days. And God remembered Noah, and every living thing, and all the cattle that was with him in the ark: and God made a wind to pass over the earth, and the waters were assuaged. . . .

And the ark rested in the seventh month, on the

seventeenth day of the month, upon the mountains of Ararat. And the waters decreased continually until the tenth month: in the tenth month, on the first day of the month, were the tops of the mountains seen.

And it came to pass at the end of forty days that Noah opened the window of the ark which he had made. And he sent forth a raven, which went forth to and fro until the waters were dried up from off the earth. Also he sent forth a dove from him, to see if the waters were abated from off the face of the ground; but the dove found no rest for the sole of her foot, and she returned unto him into the ark, for the waters were on the face of the whole earth: then he put forth his hand, and took her, and pulled her in unto him into the ark.

And he stayed yet other seven days; and again he sent forth the dove out of the ark. And the dove came in to him in the evening; and, lo, in her mouth was an olive leaf plucked off, so Noah knew that the waters were abated from off the earth.

And he stayed yet other seven days, and again he sent forth the dove; which returned not again unto him any more. And it came to pass in the six hundredth and first year, in the first month, the first day of the month, the waters were dried up from off the earth; and Noah removed the covering of the ark and looked, and, behold, the face of the ground was dry. . . .

And God spake unto Noah, saying, "Go forth of the ark, thou, and thy wife, and thy sons, and thy sons' wives with thee. Bring forth with thee every living thing that is with thee, of all flesh, both of fowl and of cattle and of every creeping thing that creepeth upon the earth that they may breed abundantly in the earth, and be fruitful and multiply upon the earth."

And Noah went forth, and his sons and his wife and his sons' wives with him. Every beast, every creeping thing, and every fowl, and whatsoever creepeth upon the earth, after their kinds, went forth out of the ark.

And Noah builded an altar unto the Lord, and took of every clean beast and of every clean fowl and offered burnt offerings on the altar.

And the Lord smelled a sweet savour, and the Lord said in his heart, I will not again curse the ground any more for man's sake; for the imagination of man's heart is evil from his youth; neither will I again smite any more every thing living, as I have done. . . .

And God spake unto Noah, and to his sons with him, saying, "And I, behold, I establish my covenant with you and with your seed after you; and with every living creature that is with you, of the fowl, of the cattle, and of every beast of the earth with you; from all that go out of the ark, to every beast of the earth. And I will establish my covenant with you; neither shall all flesh be cut off any more by the waters of a flood; neither shall there any more be a flood to destroy the earth."

And God said, "This is the token of the covenant which I make between me and you and every living creature that is with you, for perpetual generations: I do set my bow in the cloud, and it shall be for a token of a covenant between me and the earth. And it shall come to pass, when I bring a cloud over the earth that the bow shall be seen in the cloud: And I will remember my covenant which is between me and you and every living creature of all flesh; and the waters shall no more become a flood to destroy all flesh.

The Play

(The Third Pageant: *Noah's Flood*)

presented by

The Water Carriers and the Drawers of Water from the River Dee

The pageant-wagon (or stage-on-wheels) for this play, the third play of the Chester Cycle, is an actual ark, a kind of shallow scow with bows at both ends and a small square superstructure in the middle, containing a casement window near the top, from the side of which rises a flagpole-like mast. The hull of the ark is elaborately decorated with paintings of the animals mentioned in the text. When the ark, drawn by horses, arrives at the place of performance, a gangplank is let down from the deck to the street, and a space around the ark is cleared so that there is room for action between the ark and the audience.

At the opening of the play, Noah and his wife, his three sons and their wives are standing in this open space. Noah, patriarchal with long white hair and flowing beard, wears a loose white robe, corded at the waist. His wife, his three sons and their wives are probably garbed in coarse sackcloth costumes, suggestive of primitive clothing. An alternative possibility is that their garments are made of animal hides. All of them wear simple sandals over bare feet.

The action begins with the spectacular appearance of God on the roof of a neighboring building, robed in pontifical vestments and wearing a gilded mask to enhance the effect of majesty. The original stage direction reads: "And first in some high place, or in clouds if it may be [simulated clouds placed on a roof?], God speaketh unto Noah standing without the Ark with all his family."

GOD: (*as if much troubled in spirit*)
I, God, that all the world have wrought,
Heaven and earth, and all of nought,
I see my people, in deed and thought,
   Are set foully in sin.
My ghost shall not linger in man,
That though fleshly liking is my foe, (fone)
But till six score years be gone,
   To look if they will desist. (blin)

Man that I made I will destroy,
Beast, worm, and fowl to fly;

For on earth they do me annoy, (nye)
  The folk that are thereon.
It harms me so heartfully,
The malice now that can multiply,
That sore it grieveth me inwardly
  That ever I made man.

Therefore, Noah, my servant free,
That righteous man art, as I see,
A ship soon thou shalt make thee
  Of trees dry and light.
Little chambers therein thou make;
And binding-pitch also thou take;
Within and out thou not slack (slake)
  To anoint it through all thy might.

Three hundred cubits it shall be long,
And fifty of breadth, to make it strong;
Of height fifty. The measure thou take, (fonge)
  Thus measure it about.
One window work through thy wit,
One cubit of length and breadth make it.
Upon the side a door shall sit
  For to come in and out.

Eating places thou make also;
Three-roofed chambers, one or two;
For with water I think to slay (slowe)
  Man that I can make.
Destroyed all the world shall be
Save thou; thy wife, thy sons three,
And all their wives also with thee
  Shall saved be, for thy sake.

  NOAH: (*on his knees with hands raised*)
Ah, Lord, I thank thee loud and still
That to me art in such will
And spares me and my house to spill,
  As now I soothly find.
Thy bidding, Lord, I shall fulfill,
And never more thee grieve nor offend, (grill)

That such grace hast sent me still
  Among all mankind.

(*turning and calling to his family*)
Have done, you men and women all!
Help, for ought that may befall,
To work this ship, chamber and hall,
  As God hath bidden us do.
  SHEM: (*showing an axe in his hand*)
Father, I am all ready prepared. (bowne)
An axe I have, by my crown,
As sharp as any in all this town,
  For to go thereto.

  HAM: (*eagerly raising his hatchet*)
I have a hatchet wonder-keen
To bite well, as may be seen;
A better ground, as I ween,
  Is not in all this town.
  JAPETH: (*displaying his hammer*)
And I can well make a pin,
And with this hammer knock it in;
Go and work without more din,
  And I am ready prepared. (bowne)

  NOAH'S WIFE:
And we shall bring timber to,
For we may nothing else do;
Women be weak to undergo
  Any great travail.
  SHEM'S WIFE: (*pointing to a chopping block*)
Here is a good hack-stock;
On this you may hew and knock;
Shall none be idle in this flock,
  Nor now may no man fail.

  HAM'S WIFE:
And I will go to gather pitch,
The ship for to caulk and pitch;

Anointed it must be every stick, (stitch)
   Board, tree, and pin.
JAPETH'S WIFE:
And I will gather chips here
To make a fire for you all, (in fere)
And for to get your dinner,
   Against you come in.
   Then they make gestures and movements as if laboring with divers tools.

NOAH: (*demonstrating the parts of the ship as he speaks*)
Now, in the name of God I will begin
To make the ship that we shall in,
That we be ready for to swim
   At the coming of the flood.
These boards I join here together
To keep us safe from the weather,
That we may row both hither and thither
   And safe be from this flood.

Of this tree will I make the mast,
Tied with cables that will last,
With a sail-yard for each blast,
   And each thing in their kind.
With topcastle and bowsprit,
With cords and ropes I have all meet
To sail forth at the next flood. (weete)
   This ship is at an end.
   (*Then Noah with all his family again make signs of laboring with divers tools.*)

Wife, in this vessel we shall be kept.
(*motioning her to ascend the gangplank*)
My children and thou, I would, in leapt.
   NOAH'S WIFE: (*truculently*)
In faith, Noah, I had as lief thou slept.
   For all thy frantic urgency (fare)
I will not do after thy advice. (red)
   NOAH: (*reasonably*)

Good wife, do now as I thee bid.
  NOAH'S WIFE: (*angrily*)
By Christ, not ere I see more need,
  Though thou stand all the day and stare.

  NOAH: (*wearily, to the audience*)
Lord, that women be crabbed aye,
And never are meek, that dare I say.
This is well seen by me today,
  In witness of you each one.
(*turning to his wife in mild entreaty*)
Good wife, let be all this bickering (bere)
That thou makes in this place here;
For all they (*indicating the audience*) ween thou art
    master—
  (*glumly*) And so thou art, by Saint John!

  GOD: (*speaking from the "clouds"*)
Noah, take thou thy household (meanye)
And in the ship hie that thou be;
For none so righteous man to me
  Is now on earth living.
Of clean beasts with thee thou take
Seven and seven, ere thou slacken; (slake)
He and she, mate to mate, (make)
  Quickly in that thou bring.

Of beasts unclean two and two,
Male and female, without more; (moe)
Of clean fowls seven also,
  The he and she together;
Of fowls unclean two and no more,
As I of beasts said before;
That shall be saved through my lore,
  Against I send the weather.

Of all meats that must be eaten
Into the ship look there be gotten,
For that no way may be forgotten;
  And do all this immediately, (bydeene)
To sustain man and beast therein

Aye till the water cease and end. (blyn)
This world is filled full of sin
  And that is now well seen.

Seven days be yet coming:
You shall have space them in to bring;
After that is my liking
  Mankind for to annoy. (noyle)
Forty days and forty nights
Rain shall fall for their unrights;
And that I have made through my mights
  Now think I to destroy.

NOAH:

Lord, at your bidding I am ready; (bain)
Since no other grace will gain,
It will I fulfill fain,
  For gracious I thee find.
A hundred winters and twenty
This ship making tarried have I,
If through amendment any mercy
  Would fall unto mankind.

(*calling to his family*)
Have done, you men and women all!
Hie you lest this water fall,
That each beast were in his stall,
  And into the ship brought.
Of clean beasts seven shall be,
Of unclean two; this God bade me.
This flood is nigh, well may we see;
  Therefore tarry you nought.

  *Then Noah shall go into the Ark with all his family,
except his wife, and the ark shall be boarded round
about, and on the boards all the beasts and fowls here-
after described must be painted that these words may
agree with the pictures.*

  SHEM: (*pointing to the pictures from the deck of the
ark*)
Sir, here are lions, leopards in,

Horses, mares, oxen, and swine;
Goats, calves, sheep, and kine
　Here sitten thou may see.
　HAM:
Camels, asses men may find,
Buck, doe, hart, and hind;
And beasts of all manner kind
　Here be, as thinketh me.

　JAPETH:
Take here cats and dogs too,
Otter, fox, polecat also;
Hares hopping gaily can go,
　Have cabbage here for to eat.
　NOAH'S WIFE: (*demonstrating from outside the Ark*)
And here are bears, wolves set,
Apes, owls, marmoset,
Weasels, squirrels, and ferret;
　Here they eat their meat.

　SHEM'S WIFE:
Yet more beasts are in this house:
Here cats maken it full lively;　(crouse)
Here a rat, here a mouse,
　They stand nigh together.
　HAM'S WIFE:
And here are fowls, less and more:
Herons, cranes, and bittern,　(byttour)
Swans, peacocks; and them before
　Meat for this weather.

　JAPETH'S WIFE:
Here are cocks, kits, crows,
Rooks, ravens, many roes,
Bucks, curlews. Whoever knows
　Each one in his kind?
And here are doves, ducks, drakes,
Redshanks running through the lakes;
And each fowl that music makes
　In this ship men may find.

Noah, annoyed that his wife has not come aboard, descends the gangplank and finds her chatting with a number of women in the audience, some of whom are members of the cast who have been mingling with the audience during the preceding action.

NOAH: (*somewhat pathetic in his anxiety and distress*)
Wife, come in! Why stands thou there?
Thou art ever perverse, that dare I swear.
Come in, on God's behalf! Time it were,
    For fear lest that we drown.
NOAH'S WIFE: (*scornfully*)
Yea, sir, set up your sail
And row forth with evil luck! (heale)
For, without any fail,
    I will not out of this town.

Unless I have my gossips every one,
One foot farther I will not gone;
They shall not drown, by Saint John,
    And I may save their life.
They loved me full well, by Christ;
Unless thou wilt have them in thy boat, (chist)
Else row forth, Noah, whither thou list,
    And get thee a new wife.

NOAH: (*returning to the ark*)
Shem, son, lo! thy mother is angry: (wraw)
Forsooth, such another I do not know.
SHEM:
Father, I shall fetch her in, I trow,
    Without any fail.
(*going down to his mother*)
Mother, my father after thee send,
And bids thee into yonder ship wend.
Look up and see the wind,
    For we be ready to sail.

NOAH'S WIFE:
Son, go again to him and say:
I will not come therein today.

(Noah and the other sons join Shem.)

NOAH:

Come in, wife, in twenty devils' way,
  Or else stand there without.

HAM:

Shall we all fetch her in?

NOAH:

Yea, sons, in Christ's blessing and mine:
I would you died you betime,
  For of this flood I am in doubt.

GOSSIP: *(to Noah's wife)*

The flood comes in, full fleeting fast,
  On every side it spreadeth full far;
For fear of drowning, I am aghast;
  Good gossip, let us draw near.

And let us drink ere we depart,
  For oft-times we have done so;
For at a draught thou drink'st a quart,
  And so will I do, ere I go.

*The gossips pass around a jug, presumably supplied
by Noah's wife. Noah, in despair, returns to the ark.*

JAPETH:

Mother, we pray you altogether—
For we are here your own children— (childer)
Come into the ship for fear of the weather,
  For His love that you bought!

NOAH'S WIFE:

That will I not, for all your call,
Unless I have my gossips all.

SHEM: *(with determination)*

In faith, Mother, yet you shall,
  Whether you will or nought.

The three sons drag their mother on to the ark.

NOAH:

Welcome, wife, into this boat.

NOAH'S WIFE: *(giving him "a lively blow")*

And have thou that for thy speech! (mote)

NOAH: *(ruefully)*

Ah! Hah! Marry, this is hot! (hote)

It is good to be still.

Ah, children, methinks my boat removes; (remeves)

Our tarrying here hugely me grieves.

Over the land the water spreads.

God do as he will!

All leave the deck and enter the door of the ship. Noah reappears at the casement window at the top of the central superstructure.

NOAH:

Ah! Great God that art so good!

Who works not thy will is mad. (wood)

Now all this world is on a flood,

As I see well in sight.

This window will I shut anon,

And into my chamber will I gone,

Till this water, so great one,

Be slacked through thy might.

Then Noah shall shut the window of the ark, and for a little space within board he shall be silent. Another manuscript suggests that during this interval all within sing the psalm "Save me, O God." Then he opens the window and looks around.

NOAH:

Now forty days are fully gone.

Send a raven I will anon,

If anywhere earth, tree, or stone

Be dry in any place;

And if this fowl come not again,

It is a sign, sooth to say, (sayne)

That dry it is on hill or plain,

And God hath done some grace.

(Then he shall send out the raven; and taking a dove in his hand let him say:)

Ah! Lord, wherever this raven be,

Somewhere is dry, well I see.
But yet a dove, by my loyalty,
　　After I will send.
Thou wilt turn again to me,
For of all fowls that may fly,
　　Thou art most meek and obedient. (hend)

*Then he shall send out the dove; and there shalt be
in the ship another dove bearing an olive branch in its
mouth, which shall be let down from the mast by a
string to Noah's hand; and afterwards let Noah say:*
Ah, Lord, blessed be thou aye,
That me hast comfort thus today;
By this sight I may well say
　　This flood begins to cease.
My sweet dove to me brought has
A branch of olive from some place;
This betokeneth God has done us some grace,
　　And is a sign of peace.

Ah, Lord, honored most thou be!
All earth dries now, I see,
But yet, till thou command me,
　　Hence I will not hie.
All this water is away;
Therefore as soon as I may
Sacrifice I shall do in faith (faye)
　　To thee devoutly.

GOD: (*speaking from "the clouds."*)
Noah, take thy wife anon,
And of thy children every one;
Out of the ship thou shalt gone
　　And they all with thee.
Beasts and all that can flie
Out anon they shall hie,
On earth to grow and multiply.
　　I will that it be so.

NOAH:
Lord, I thank thee through thy might;

Thy bidding shall be done in haste. (height)
And as fast as I may get ready (dighte)
   I will do thee honor,
And to thee offer sacrifice;
Therefore comes in all wise,
For of these beasts that be his, (hise)
   Offer I will this store.

(*Then going out of the ark with all his family, he
shall take his animals and birds and shall offer them
and make sacrifice.*)
Lord God in majesty,
That such grace hast granted me,
Where all was lost, safe to be.
   Therefore now I am ready, (bowne)
My wife, my children, my family
With sacrifice to honor thee
With beasts, fowls, as thou may see,
   I offer here right soon.

GOD:
Noah, to me thou art full able,
And thy sacrifice acceptable.
For I have found thee true and stable,
   On thee now must I be mindful: (myn)
Destroy Earth will I no more
For man's sin that grieves me sore;
For of youth man full yore
   Has been inclined to sin.

You shall now grow and multiply,
And earth again you edify;
Each beast and fowl that may fly
   Shall be afraid of you.
And fish in sea that may float (flytte)
Shall sustain you, I you promise; (behite)
To eat of them do not desist, (you ne lett)
   That clean be, you may know.

Thereas you have eaten before
Grass and roots, since you were born, (bore)

Of clean beasts now, less and more,
  I give you leave to eat;
Save blood and flesh both together (in feare)
Of long-dead carrion that is here,
Eat not of that in no manner;
  For that aye you shall avoid. (let)

Manslaughter also you shall flee;
For that is not pleasant to me.
That sheds blood, he or she,
  Ought-where amongst mankind,
That blood foully shed shall be,
And vengeance have, that men shall see;
Therefore beware now, all ye,
  You fall not in that sin.

A covenant now with thee I make,
And all thy seed for thy sake,
Of such vengeance for to slake,
  For now I have my will.
Here I bequeath thee a promise, (heaste)
That man, woman, fowl nor beast,
With water, while the world shall last,
  I will no more spill.

My bow between you and me
In the firmament shall be,
By very token that you may see
  That such vengeance shall cease,
That man nor woman shall never more
Be wasted by water as is before;
But for sin that grieveth me sore,
  Therefore this vengeance was.

Where clouds in the welkin be, (bene)
That same bow shall be seen
In tokening that my wrath and anger (tene)
  Shall never thus wreaked be.
The string is turned toward you,
And toward me is bent the bow,

That such weather shall never show;
  And this promise I thee.

My blessing now I give thee here,
To thee, Noah, my servant dear,
For vengeance shall no more appear.
And now, farewell, my darling dear.

The Second Shepherds' Play

And Joseph . . . went up from Galilee, out of the city of Nazareth into Judea, unto the city of David which is called Bethlehem . . . to be taxed with Mary, his espoused wife, being great with child.

And so it was that, while they were there, the days were accomplished that she should be delivered. And she brought forth her first born son and wrapped him in swaddling clothes and laid him in a manger, because there was no room for them in the inn.

And there were in the same country shepherds abiding in the field, keeping watch over their flock by night. And, lo, the angel of the Lord came upon them, and the glory of the Lord shone round about them: and they were sore afraid. And the angel said unto them, "Fear not: for, behold, I bring you good tidings of great joy, which shall be to all people. For unto you is born this day in the city of David a Saviour, which is Christ the Lord. And this shall be a sign unto you: Ye shall find the babe wrapped in swaddling clothes, lying in a manger."

And suddenly there was with the angel a multitude of the heavenly host praising God and saying, "Glory to God in the highest, and on earth peace, good will toward men."

And it came to pass, as the angels were gone away from them into heaven, the shepherds said to one another, "Let us now go even unto Bethlehem and see this thing which is come to pass which the Lord hath made known unto us." And they came with haste and found Mary and Joseph, and the babe lying in a manger.

And when they had seen it, they made known abroad

the saying which was told them concerning this child.
And all they that heard it wondered at those things
which were told them by the shepherds. . . . And the
shepherds returned, glorifying and praising God for all
the things that they had heard and seen, as it was told
unto them.

The Play

(Being the Second Play on This Subject
by "The Wakefield Master")

*The stage represents the open fields where the shep-
herds tend their sheep. At the back, on the right, is the
stable in Bethlehem where Joseph and Mary find refuge. At the left is the peasant cottage of Mak and his
wife Gill. Both of these structures are curtained off
when the play opens.*

*The First Shepherd enters, nearly frozen with the
cold. He wears rough peasant garb with burlap bound
about his feet and carries a shepherd's crook.*

FIRST SHEPHERD: (*shivering and teeth chattering*)
Lord, what these weathers are cold!
   And I am ill dressed. (happed)
I am nearly numb, (dold)
   So long have I napped;
My legs they fold,
   My fingers are chapped;
It is not as I would, (wold)
   For I am all lapped
     In sorrow.
    In storms and tempest,
    Now in the east, now in the west,
    Woe is him has never rest
     Mid-day nor morrow!

But we poor shepherds
   That walk on the moor,

In faith, we are nearly (nere-handys)
   Out of the door
No wonder, as it stands,
   If we be poor,
For the tilth of our lands
   Lies fallow as the floor,
       As ye know. (ken)
     We are so crippled, (hamyd)
     For-taxed and crushed, (ramyd)
     We are made hand-tamed (tamyd)
       With these gentlery men.

Thus they rob us our rest,
   Our Lady them curse! (wary)
These men that are bound to a lord, (lord-fest)
   They cause the plough tarry.
That, men say, is for the best;
   We find it contrary.
Thus are husbands oppressed
   In point to miscarry
      On life.
     Thus hold they us under,
     Thus they bring us in blunder!
     It were a great wonder
      And ever should we thrive. (thryfe)

There shall come a swain
   As proud as a peacock, (po)
He must borrow my wagon, (wane)
   My plough also;
Then I am full fain
   To grant ere he go.
Thus live we in pain,
   Anger and woe,
      By night and day.
     He must have, if he wanted, (langyd)
     If I should forego it.
     I were better be hanged
      Than once say him nay.

For may he get a paint sleeve,
    Or a brooch, nowadays,
Woe is him that him grieve
    Or once gainsays!
Dare no man him reprove, (reprefe)
    What mastery he mays;
And yet may no man believe
    One word that he says,
        No letter.
    He can may purveyance
    With boast and bragging, (bragance)
    And all is through maintenance
        Of men that are greater.

It does me good, as I walk
    Thus by mine own,
Of this world to talk
    In manner of moan.
To my sheep will I stalk
    And hearken anon;
There abide on a ridge, (balk)
    Or sit on a stone,
        Full soon. (soyne)
    For I believe, pardie,
    True men if they be,
    We get more company
        Ere it be noon. (noyne)

*The Second Shepherd enters. He is so wrapped up
in his own misery that he does not see the First Shepherd.*

SECOND SHEPHERD:
Bless us and Dominus!
    What may this bemean?
Why fares this world thus?
    Oft have we not seen!
Lord, these weathers are spitous,
    And the winds full keen,
And the frosts so hideous

They water my eyes—(een)
> No lie.
> Now in dry, now in wet,
> Now in snow, now in sleet,
> When my shoes freeze to my feet,
>> It is not all easy.

But, as far as I ken,
> Or yet as I go,
We poor wed-men
> Dree mickle woe:
We have sorrow then and then,
> It falls oft so.
Poor Copple, our hen,
> Both to and fro
>> She cackles;
>> But begin she to croak,
>> To groan or to cluck,
>> Woe is him our cock,
>>> For he is in the shackles.

These men that are wed
> Have not all their will;
When they are full hard situated, (sted)
> They sigh full still.
God wot they are led
> Full hard and full ill;
In bower nor in bed
> They say nought thereto. (theretill)
>> This tide,
>> My part have I fun,
>> I know my lesson!
>> Woe is him that is bound, (bun)
>>> For he must abide.

But now late in our lives—
> A marvel to me,
That I think my heart breaks (ryfys)
> Such wonders to see,
What that destiny drives

It should so be!—
Some men will have two wives,
  And some men three
     In store.
     Some are miserable that have any.
     But so far can I:
     Woe is him that has many,
      For he feels sore.

(*speaking to the audience*)
But, young men, of wooing,
  For God that you bought,
Be well ware of wedding,
  And think in your thought:
"Had I known" is a thing
  That serveth of nought.
Much still mourning
  Has wedding home brought,
     And griefs,
    With many a sharp shower;
    For thou may catch in an hour
    That shall be full sour
     As long as thou lives.

For, as ever read I Epistle,
  I have one to my company, (fere)
As sharp as a thistle,
  As rough as a briar; (brere)
She is browed like a bristle,
  With a sour-looking face; (chere)
Had she once wet her whistle,
  She could sing full clear
     Her paternoster.
    She is as great as a whale;
    She has a gallon of gall;
    By him that died for us all,
     I would I had run to I had lost her!

FIRST SHEPHERD: (*interrupting*)
God! Look over the row! (raw)

Full deafly ye stand.
SECOND SHEPHERD:
Yea, the devil in thy belly, (maw)
  So long tarrying! (tariand)
Saw'st thou ought of Daw?
  FIRST SHEPHERD:
  Yea, on a lea-land
Heard I him blow. (blaw)
  He comes here at hand,
     No far.
    Stand still.
  SECOND SHEPHERD: Why?
  FIRST SHEPHERD:
    For he comes, hope I.
  SECOND SHEPHERD:
    He will make us both a lie,
    But if we beware. (be war)

The Third Shepherd, a boy, enters.
  THIRD SHEPHERD: (*talking to himself*)
Christ's cross me speed,
  And Saint Nicholas!
Thereof had I need;
  It is worse than it was.
Whoso could take heed
  And let the world pass,
It is ever in dread (drede)
  And brittle as glass,
    And slides. (slithes)
    This world fared never so,
    With marvels more and more— (mo)
    Now in weal, now in woe,
    And all thing writhes.

Was never since Noah's flood
  Such floods seen,
Winds and rains so rude,
  And storms so keen!
Some stammered, some stood
  In doubt, as I imagine. (weyn)

Now God turn all to good!
   I say as I mean,
     For ponder:
    These floods so they drown,
    Both in fields and in town,
    And bear all down;
     And that is a wonder.

We that walk on the nights
   Our cattle to keep,
We see sudden sights
   When other men sleep.
(*suddenly becoming aware of the other two shepherds*)
Yet methinks my heart lightens; (lyghtys)
   I see shrews peep.
Ye are two tall men! (wyghtys)
   I will give my sheep
     A turn.
    But full ill have I meant;
    As I walk on this field, (bent)
    I may lightly repent,
     My toes if I spurn.

(*The two shepherds approach.*)
Ah, sir, God you save!
   And master mine!
A drink fain would I have
   And somewhat to dine.
   FIRST SHEPHERD: (*scornfully*)
Christ's curse, my knave,
   Thou art a worthless hind! (hyne)
   SECOND SHEPHERD:
What, the boy wants to rave!
   Abide until after (syne)
     We have made it.
    Ill thrift on thy pate!
    Though the shrew came late,
    Yet is he in state
     To dine—if he had it.

THIRD SHEPHERD:
Such servants as I,
  That sweats and works, (swynkys)
Eats our bread full dry;
  And that me displeases. (forthynkys)
We are oft wet and weary
  When master-men sleep; (wynkys)
Yet come full lately
  Both dinners and drinks.
      But thoroughly (nately)
      Both our dame and our sire,
      When we have run in the mire,
      They can nip at our hire,
        And pay us full lately.

But hear my truth, master:
  For the fare that you supply, (make)
I shall do thereafter—
  Work as I take.
I shall do a little, sir,
  And among every sport; (lake)
For yet lay my supper
  Never on my stomach
      In fields.
      Whereto should I argue? (threpe)
      With my staff can I leap;
      And men say, "Bargain cheap
        Badly yields."

FIRST SHEPHERD:
Thou wert an ill lad
  To ride on wooing
With a man that had
  But little of spending.
SECOND SHEPHERD:
Peace, boy, I bade.
  No more jangling,
Or I shall make thee full afraid,

By the Heaven's King!
    With thy pranks— (gawdys)
        Where are our sheep, boy? We scorn.
THIRD SHEPHERD:
    Sir, this same day at morn
    I them left in the corn
        When they rang Lauds.[1] (lawdys)

They have pasture good,
    They can not go wrong.
FIRST SHEPHERD:
That is right. By the cross, (roode)
    These nights are long!
Yet I would, ere we went, (yode)
    One gave us a song.
SECOND SHEPHERD:
So I thought as I stood,
    To mirth us among.
    THIRD SHEPHERD: (*agreeably*)
        I grant.
    FIRST SHEPHERD:
        Let me sing the tenory.
    SECOND SHEPHERD:
        And me the trebles so high.
    THIRD SHEPHERD:
        Then the mean falls to me.
            Let see how ye chant.

*While they are singing, Mak, a villager who is known
by them, enters. He has attempted to disguise himself
by means of a cloak in which he has wrapped himself
so that his face is barely visible.*
    MAK: (*speaking with an odd southern accent*)
Now Lord, for thy names seven,
    That made both moon and stars (starns)
Well more than I can name, (neven)
    Thy will, Lord, of me is lacking. (tharnys)

---

[1] The first of the morning hours of the Church.

I am all uneven;
> That unsettles oft my brain (harnes)
>> Continuously. (So styll)

FIRST SHEPHERD:
> Who is it that cries so piteously? (poore)

MAK:
> Would God ye knew how I fare! (foore)
> Lo, a man that walks on the moor,
>> And has not all his will.

SECOND SHEPHERD: (*recognizing him*)
Mak, where hast thou gone?
> Tell us tiding.

THIRD SHEPHERD:
Is he come? Then everyone
> Take heed to his thing.
(*He snatches Mak's cloak from him.*)

MAK: (*strutting grandiosely*)
What! I be a yeoman,
> I tell you, of the king;
The self and same,
> Messenger from a great lording,
>> And such. (sich)
>> Fie on you! Go hence!
>> Out of my presence!
>> I must have reverence.
>>> Why, who be I? (ich)

FIRST SHEPHERD:
Why make ye it so strange? (qwaynt)
> Mak, ye do wrong.

SECOND SHEPHERD:
But, Mak, do you deceive? (? lyst ye saynt)
> I believe that you want to. (lang)

THIRD SHEPHERD:
I believe the shrew can deceive! (paynt)
> The devil might him hang!

MAK: (*with mock severity*)
I shall make complaint,
> And make you all to be flogged (thwang)

At a word;
And tell even how ye do. (doth)

FIRST SHEPHERD:

But, Mak, is that truth? (sothe)
Now take out that southern tooth,
And put in a turd! (torde)

SECOND SHEPHERD: (*striking him*)

Mak, the devil in your eye!
A stroke would I give you.

THIRD SHEPHERD: (*threatening with his fist*)

Mak, know ye not me?
By God, I could hurt you.

MAK: (*suddenly obsequious and as if surprised to recognize them*)

God look you all three!
Methought I had seen you.
Ye are a fair company.

FIRST SHEPHERD:

Can ye now act yourself? (mene you)

SECOND SHEPHERD:

Shrewd joke! (iape)
Thus late as thou goes,
What will men suppose?
And thou hast an ill repute (noys)
Of stealing of sheep.

MAK: (*self-righteously*)

And I am true as steel,
All men know! (waytt)
But a sickness I feel
That holds me full hot; (haytt)
My belly fares not well,
It is out of shape. (astate)

THIRD SHEPHERD:

Seldom lies the devil
Dead by the gate!

MAK: (*pitiably*)

Therefore,
Full sore am I and ill;

If I stand stone still,
I eat not a needle
   This month and more.

FIRST SHEPHERD:
How fares thy wife? By my hood,
   How fares she? (sho)

MAK:
Lies sprawling-by the cross— (roode)
   By the fire, lo!
And a house full of brood.
   She drinks well, too;
Ill speed other good
   That she will do
     But so!
     Eats as fast as she can,
     And each year that comes to man
     She brings forth a baby— (lakan)
      And, some years, two.

But were I now more gracious
   And richer by far,
I were eaten out of house
   And of home. (harbar)
Yet is she a foul slut (dowse)
   If ye come near; (nar)
There is none that trows
   Or knows a worse (war)
     Than do I. (ken I)
     Now will ye see what I proffer?
     To give all in my coffer
     Tomorrow morning to offer
      For her funeral. (Hyr hed-mas penny)

SECOND SHEPHERD: (*drowsily*)
I believe so weary (forwakyd)
   Is none in this shire.
I would sleep if I taked
   Less to my hire.

THIRD SHEPHERD: (*shivering*)
I am cold and naked,
   And would have a fire.
  FIRST SHEPHERD: (*shaking the Second Shepherd*)
I am weary, exhausted, (for-rakyd)
   And run in the mire.
     Wake thou!
  SECOND SHEPHERD: (*lying down wearily*)
   Nay, I will lie down by,
   For I must sleep, truly.
  THIRD SHEPHERD: (*dropping down beside him*)
   As good a man's son was I
    As any of you.

But, Mak, come hither! Between
  Shall thou lie down.
  MAK:
Then might I hinder you, indeed, (bedene)
  Of what ye would whisper. (rowne)
[Note: Four lines of the ms. are missing]
(*They all lie down together.*)
    No dread.
(*raising himself stealthily on his elbows*)
   From my top to my toe,
   Manus tuas commendo,
   Poncio Pilato,[2]
    Christ's cross me speed.

   *Then he rises up, the shepherds being asleep, and
says:*
Now were time for a man
  That lacks what he would
To stalk privily then
  Into a fold,
And nimbly to work then,
  And be not too bold,
For he might rue the bargain,
  If it were told,
    At the ending.

---

[2] A spell invoking the aid of Pontius Pilate.

Now were time for to do it; (reyll)
But he needs good counsel
That fain would fare well,
    And has but little spending.

(*drawing an imaginary magic circle around the sleeping shepherds*)
But about you a circle
    As round as a moon,
Till I have done what I will,
    Till that it be noon,
That ye lie stone still
    Till that I be done.
And I shall say theretill
    Of good words a few: (foyne)
        "On height
        Over your heads my hand I lift.
        Out go your eyes! Fordo your sight!"
        But yet I must make better shift
            And it be right.

(*observing the shepherds carefully and listening to their snoring*)
Lord, what! they sleep hard!
    That may ye all hear.
Was I never a shepherd,
    But now will I learn. (lere)
If the flock be scared,
    Yet shall I nip near.
How! draw hitherward! (*stealing toward the sheep*)
    Now mends our cheer
        From sorrow.
    A fat sheep I dare say!
    A good fleece dare I lay.
    Repay it when I may,
        But this will I borrow.

He moves stealthily off to the right and comes back with a sheep (presumably stuffed). Then he crosses the stage to his own cottage, the curtain of which is now

drawn to reveal the interior. At the back is a crude
fireplace and cupboard with iron pots and mugs scat-
tered about. At the left is a rude bed with a cradle be-
side it. Mak's Wife sits on one of two rough chairs at a
spinning wheel. Clothing, burlap bags, and miscellane-
ous rags and cloths are hung on pegs on the right-hand
wall except at its center which is occupied by the door,
outside of which Mak now stands and shouts:

How, Gill, art thou in?
  Get us some light!
    HIS WIFE: *(from inside the house)*
Who makes such din
  This time of the night?
I am set for to spin;
  I hope not I might
Raise a penny to win.
  I shrew them on height
    So fares
    A housewife that has been
    To be aroused thus between.
    Here may no work be seen
      For such small chores.

    MAK: *(with noisy urgency)*
Good wife, open the door! (hek)
  See'st thou not what I bring?
    WIFE:
I may let thee draw the latch. (snek)
  Ah, come in, my sweeting!
    MAK: *(exhibiting the sheep as she opens the door)*
Yea, thou art not concerned (rek)
  About my long standing.
    WIFE: *(her attention fixed on the stolen sheep)*
By the naked neck
  Art thou like for to hang! (hyng)
    MAK: *(swaggering)*
    Do way!
  I am worthy my meat,
  For in a strait I can get

More than they that work and sweat
   All the long day.

Thus it fell to my lot, Gill.
  I had such grace!
  WIFE: (*lugubriously*)
It were a foul blot
  To be hanged for the case.
  MAK: (*full of easy self-confidence*)
I have 'scaped, Jelott,
  Oft as hard a blow. (glase)
  WIFE:
But as long goes the pot
  To the water, men says,
    At last
  Comes it home broken.
  MAK:
    Well know I the token;
    But let it never be spoken,
      But come and help fast!

I would he were skinned; (flain)
  I could well eat.
This twelvemonth was I not so fain
  Of one sheep meat.
  WIFE: (*full of trepidation*)
Come they ere he be slain
  And hear the sheep bleat—
  MAK: (*trembling*)
Then might I be taken: (tane)
  That were a cold sweat!
    Go fasten (spar)
  The front door.
  WIFE: (*obeying*) Yes, Mak,
  For if they come at thy back—
  MAK:
    Then might I buy for all the pack
    The devil of the war!

WIFE: (*chuckling*)
A good trick have I spied—
  Since thou knowest none—
Here shall we him hide
  Till they be gone—
In my cradle abide—
  Let me alone,
And I shall lie beside
  In childbed and groan.
  MAK: (*delighted with the scheme*)
    Do it, (Thou red)
    And I shall say thou wast delivered (lyght)
    Of a knave-child this night.
  WIFE:
    Now well is me day bright
      That ever was I bred!

This is a good disguise
  And a far cast!
Yet a woman's advice
  Helps at the last!
I care never who spies.
  Again go thou fast.
  MAK:
But I come ere they rise,
  Else blows a cold blast!
    I will go sleep.
(*He returns to the shepherds and observes them still slumbering.*)
    Yet sleeps all this company;
    And I shall go stalk privily
    As it had never been I
      That carried their sheep.
(*He lies down where he was and pretends to be asleep.*)

  The First and Second Shepherds rouse and stir.
  FIRST SHEPHERD:
Resurrex a mortruis! [3]

---

[3] The garbled Latin of this and the succeeding exclamation is obviously to be taken as a form of profanity.

Have hold my hand!
Judas carnas dominus!
  I may not well stand:
My foot sleeps, by Jesus,
  And I falter from fasting. (fastand)
I thought that we laid us
  Full near England.
  SECOND SHEPHERD: (*jumping up and stretching*)
    Ah, ye!
    Lord, what I have slept well.
    As fresh as an eel,
    As light I me feel
      As leaf on a tree.

  THIRD SHEPHERD: (*annoyed at being awakened*)
Blessing be herein!
  So me quakes,
My heart is out of skin,
  What-so it makes.
Who makes all this din?
  So my brow blackens, (blakes)
To the door will I win.
  Hark, fellows, wake! (wakes)
    We were four:
    See ye aught of Mak now?
  FIRST SHEPHERD:
    We were up ere thou.
  SECOND SHEPHERD:
    Man, I give God avow
      Yet went he nowhere. (nawre)

  THIRD SHEPHERD:
Methought he was lapped
  In a wolf-skin.
  FIRST SHEPHERD:
So many are happed
  Now—namely, within.
  THIRD SHEPHERD:
When we had long napped,
  Methought with a trick (gin)

A fat sheep he trapped;
  But he made no din.
  SECOND SHEPHERD:
      Be still!
    Thy dream makes thee mad; (woode)
    It is but phantom, by the cross. (roode)
  FIRST SHEPHERD:
    Now God turn all to good
      If it be his will.

Finally seeing Mak, they rouse him.
  SECOND SHEPHERD:
Rise, Mak! For shame!
  Thou lyest right long.
  MAK: *(as if dazed by this sudden awakening)*
Now Christ's holy name
  Be us among!
What is this, for Saint Jame,
  I may not well move! (gang)
I trow I be the same.
  Ah, my neck has lain wrong—
(They help him to his feet.)
      Enough!
    Mickle thank! Since yester-even,
    Now, by Saint Stephen,
    I was flayed with a dream— (swevyn)
      My heart that slew. (of-sloghe)

I thought Gill began to croak
  And travail full sad,
Well-nigh at the first cock,
  Of a young lad
For to mend our flock.
  Then be I never glad;
I have tow on my distaff (rok)
  More than ever I had.
      Ah, my head!
    A house full of young stomachs! (tharnes)
    The devil knock out their brains! (harnes)

Woe is he who has many children, (barnes)
  And thereto little bread.

I must go home, by your leave,
  To Gill, as I thought.
I pray you look in my sleeve
  That I steal nought;
I am loath you to grieve
  Or from you take aught.
  THIRD SHEPHERD: (*as Mak departs*)
Go forth; ill might thou thrive!
  Now would I we sought,
      This morn,
    That we had all our store.
  FIRST SHEPHERD: (*starting off to the left*)
    But I will go before.
    Let us meet.
  SECOND SHEPHERD: Where? (Whore)
  THIRD SHEPHERD:
      At the crooked thorn.

*The shepherds leave the stage. Mak arrives at the
door of his cottage anl knocks. Gill, inside, sits at her
spinning wheel.*
  MAK: (*shouting angrily*)
Undo this door! Who is here?
  How long shall I stand?
  WIFE: (*continuing her work*)
Who makes such a racket? (bere)
  Now walk in the waning moon! [4] (wenyand)
  MAK: (*in pleading tones*)
Ah, Gill, what cheer?
  It is I, Mak, your husband.
  WIFE: (*rising wearily and opening the door*)
Then may we see here
  The devil in a noose, (bande)
      Sir Guile!
    Lo, he comes with a clamor (lote)

---

[4] An unlucky time.

As if he were held in the throat.
   I may not sit at my work (note)
    A hand-long while.

MAK: (*to the audience*)
Will ye hear what fare she makes
   To get her a pretext? (glose)
And does naught but plays (lakys)
   And claws her toes.
   WIFE: (*to the audience*)
Why, who wanders? Who wakes?
   Who comes? Who goes?
Who brews? Who bakes?
   Who makes me thus hose?
     And then, (than)
    It is sad to behold,
    Now in hot, now in cold,
    Full woeful is the household
     That lacks a woman.

But what end hast thou made
   With the shepherds, Mak?
   MAK:
The last word that they said
   When I turned my back,
They would look that they had
   Their sheep, all the pack.
I hope they will not be well paid
   When they their sheep lack,
     Pardie!
    But how-so the game goes,
    To me they will suppose,
    And make a foul noise,
     And cry out upon me.

But thou must do as thou promised. (hyght)
   WIFE: (*wrapping the sheep in swaddling clothes and placing it in the cradle which she then covers with a cloth*)
   I accord me theretill;

I shall swaddle him right
  In my cradle.
If it were a greater sleight,
  Yet could I help till.
I will lie down straight.
  Come cover me.
    MAK: (*tucking her in bed*)
               I will.
    WIFE:
      Behind!
    Come Coll and his mate, (maroo)
    They will nip us full close (naroo)
    MAK:
    But I may cry, "Out, harrow!" (haroo)
      The sheep if they find.

    WIFE:
Harken aye when they call;
  They will come anon.
Come and make ready all;
  And sing by thine own;
Sing lullaby thou shall,
  For I must groan
And cry out by the wall
  On Mary and John,
    For sore.
    Sing lullay on fast,
    When thou hearest at the last;
    And unless I play a false cast,
      Trust me no more!

*Mak sits down by the cradle. At the opposite end of
the stage, the shepherds return from their flock.*
    THIRD SHEPHERD:
Ah, Coll, good morn!
  Why sleepest thou not?
    FIRST SHEPHERD:
Alas that ever was I born!
  We have a foul blot.
A fat wether have we lost. (lorn)

THIRD SHEPHERD:
Marry, God forbid! (forbott)
SECOND SHEPHERD:
Who should do us that scorn?
That were a foul spot.
FIRST SHEPHERD:
Some shrew.
I have sought with my dogs
All Horbury thickets,[5] (shrogys)
And of fifteen hogs,
Found I but one ewe.

THIRD SHEPHERD:
Now believe me, if ye will,
By Saint Thomas of Kent,
Either Mak or Gill
Was at that assent.
FIRST SHEPHERD:
Peace, man, be still!
I saw when he went.
Thou slanderest him ill;
Thou ought to repent
Good speed.
SECOND SHEPHERD:
Now as ever might I thrive, (the)
If I should even here die,
I would say it were he
That did that same deed.

THIRD SHEPHERD:
Go we thither, I advise, (rede)
And run on our feet.
Shall I never eat bread
The truth till I know. (wytt)
FIRST SHEPHERD:
Nor drink in my head,
With him till I meet.
SECOND SHEPHERD:

---

[5] Four miles from Wakefield.

I will rest in no stead
   Till that I him greet,
     My brother.
    One thing I will swear: (hight)
    Till I see him in sight
    Shall I never sleep one night
     There I do another.

The shepherds cross the stage to Mak's cottage. As they approach, Mak's wife begins to groan noisily while Mak intones a hoarse lullaby.

THIRD SHEPHERD:
Will ye hear how they hack?
   Our sire likes to croon.
FIRST SHEPHERD:
Heard I never none bawl (crak)
   So clear out of tune.
Call on him.
   SECOND SHEPHERD: (*pounding on the door*)
      Mak!
Undo your door soon.
   MAK: (*as if annoyed at being disturbed*)
Who is that spake (spak)
   As it were noon
     On high? (loft)
    Who is that, I say?
   THIRD SHEPHERD: (*to the others*)
    Good fellows, would it were day.
   MAK: (*opening the door*)
    As far as ye may,
     Good, speak soft,

Over a sick woman's head,
   That is at mal-ease;
I had liefer be dead
   Ere she had any annoyance (dyseasse)
   WIFE: (*with weak pathos, from her bed*)
Go to another homestead!
   I may not well breathe; (quease)

Each foot that ye tread
  Goes through my nose, (nese)
    So hie!
  FIRST SHEPHERD:
    Tell us, Mak, if ye may,
    How fare ye, I say?
  MAK: (*with innocent surprise*)
    But are ye in this town today?
      Now how fare ye?

Ye have run in the mire,
  And are wet yet.
I shall make you a fire
  If ye will sit.
A nurse would I hire;
  Think ye on it.
Well quit is my hire;
  My dream—this is it,
(*pointing to the cradle*)
    A season.
    I have bairns, if ye knew,
    Well more than enough. (enewe)
    But we must drink as we brew,
      And that is but reason.

I would ye dined ere ye went. (yode)
  Methink that ye sweat.
  SECOND SHEPHERD:
Nay, neither mends our mood (mode)
  Drink nor meat. (mete)
  MAK:
Why, sirs, ails you aught but good?
  THIRD SHEPHERD:
    Yea, our sheep that we tend (gete)
    Are stolen as they pastured. (yode)
    Our loss is great. (grette)
  MAK: (*offering them a mug*)
    Sirs, drink!
  Had I been there, (thore)
  Some should have bought it full sore.

FIRST SHEPHERD:

> Marry, some men believe that you were, (wore)
>> And that us bothers. (forthinkys)

SECOND SHEPHERD:

Mak, some men believe (trowys)
> That it should be ye.

THIRD SHEPHERD:

Either ye or your spouse,
> So say we.

MAK: *(in righteous indignation)*

Now, if ye have suspicion (suspowse)
> To Gill or to me,

Come and rip up our house,
> And then may ye see
>> Who had her.
>> If I any sheep fetched, (fott)
>> Either cow or young bull, (stott)
>> And Gill, my wife, rose not
>>> Here since she laid her,

As I am true and loyal, (lele)
> To God here I pray

That this be the first meal
> That I shall eat today. *(pointing to the cradle)*

FIRST SHEPHERD:

Mak, as have I bliss, (ceyll)
> Advise thee I say:

He learned timely to steal
> That could not say nay.

The shepherds begin to search the cottage.

WIFE: *(groaning)*

>> I become faint! (swelt)
>> Out, thieves, from my house! (wonys)
>> Ye come here to rob us, for the nonce. (nonys)

MAK:

> Hear ye not how she groans? (gronys)
>> Your hearts should melt.

WIFE: (*raising herself on her elbow as the shepherds approach the cradle*)

Out, thieves, from my bairn!
  Nigh him not there! (thor)
  MAK: (*indignantly*)
Wist ye how she had labored, (farne)
  Your hearts would be sore.
Ye do wrong, I you warn,
  That thus come before
To a woman that has labored. (farne)
  But I say no more.
  WIFE: (*groaning*)
    Ah, my middle!
    I pray to God so mild,
    If ever I you beguiled,
    That I eat this child
      That lies in this cradle.

  MAK: (*in anguished tones*)
Peace, woman, for God's pain!
  And cry not so!
Thou spillest my brain,
  And makest me full woe.
  SECOND SHEPHERD: (*giving up the search*)
I trow our sheep be slain.
  What find ye two?
  THIRD SHEPHERD:
All work we in vain;
  As well may we go.
    But, blast it, (hatters)
  I can find no flesh,
  Hard nor soft, (nesh)
  Salt nor fresh,
    But two empty platters.

Live cattle but this,
  Tame nor wild,
None, as have I bliss,
  As loud as he smelled. (smylde)

WIFE:

No, so God me bless, (blys)
  And give me joy of my child!
  FIRST SHEPHERD: *(apologetically)*
We have marked amiss;
  I hold us beguiled.
  SECOND SHEPHERD: *(to Mak)*
      Sir, done.
    Sir—our Lady him save!
    Is your child a boy? (knave)
  MAK: *(proudly)*
    Any lord might him have
      This child to his son.

When he wakens, he snatches, (kyppys)
  That joy is to see.
  THIRD SHEPHERD:
In good time to his hips (hyppys)
  And in happiness! (cele)
But who was his godparents (gossyppys)
  So soon ready? (rede)
  MAK: *(as if grateful to the godparents)*
So fair fall their lips! (lyppys)
  FIRST SHEPHERD: *(aside)*
  Hark now, a lie! (le)
  MAK:
      So God them thank,
    Parkin, and Gibbon Waller, I say,
    And gentle John Horne, in good faith, (fay)
    He made all the commotion (garray)
      With his long legs.[6] (great shank)

  SECOND SHEPHERD:
Mak, friends will we be,
  For we are all one.
  MAK: *(truculently)*
We? Now I hold for me,
  For amends get I none.

---

[6] John Horne creates a commotion in the *First Shepherds' Play* in a quarrel with Gyb.

Farewell all three!
   All glad were ye gone.
(*The Shepherds leave.*)
   THIRD SHEPHERD: (*gloomily*)
Fair words may there be,
   But love is there none
      This year.
   FIRST SHEPHERD:
      Gave ye the child anything?
   SECOND SHEPHERD:
      I trow, not one farthing!
   THIRD SHEPHERD: (*starting back*)
      Fast again will I fling;
         Abide ye me there.

   *He returns to the cottage and walks in without
knocking.*
Mak, take it to no grief
   If I come to thy bairn.
   MAK:
Nay, thou dost me great wrong, (reprefe)
   And foul hast thou fared. (farn)
   THIRD SHEPHERD: (*approaching the cradle*)
The child will it not grieve, (grefe)
   That little day-star. (starn)
Mak, with your leave, (leyfe)
   Let me give your bairn
      But sixpence.
   MAK: (*attempting to stay between the cradle and the
Shepherd*)
      Nay! Do way! He sleeps.
   THIRD SHEPHERD: (*edging closer*)
      Methinks he peeps.
   MAK: (*in panic*)
      When he wakens, he weeps.
         I pray you go hence!

   *The other shepherds, tired of waiting, come wander-
ing in.*

THIRD SHEPHERD: (*pressing toward the cradle*)
Give me leave him to kiss,
 And lift up the cloth. (*clout*)
(*seeing the head of the sheep*)
What the devil is this?
 He has a long snout!
(*The other shepherds come close to look at the baby.*)
 FIRST SHEPHERD: (*bemused*)
He is marked amiss.
 We wait ill about.
 SECOND SHEPHERD: (*scornful of Mak and his Wife*)
Ill-spun woof, indeed, (i-wys)
 Ever comes foul out.
(*with sudden recognition*)
      Aye, so!
  He is like to our sheep!
 THIRD SHEPHERD: (*pressing forward*)
  How, Gib, may I peep?
 FIRST SHEPHERD: (*lifting the sheep from the cradle*)
  I trow nature will creep
   Where it may not walk. (go)

 SECOND SHEPHERD: (*angrily*)
This was a quaint trick (gawde)
 And a far cast!
It was a high fraud!
 THIRD SHEPHERD: (*moving toward the bed*)
 Yea, sirs, it was. (wast)
Let us burn this bawd
 And bind her fast.
A false scold (skawde)
 Hangs at the last!
     So shalt thou.
  Will ye see how they swaddle
  His four feet in the middle?
  Saw I never in a cradle
   A horned lad ere now!

 MAK: (*in an aggrieved tone of wronged innocence*)
Peace bid I! What!
 Let be your scoffing! (fare)

I am he that him begat,
  And yon woman him bare.

FIRST SHEPHERD: *(in high amusement)*
What devil shall he be called? (hatt)
  "Mak?" Lo, God, Mak's heir!

SECOND SHEPHERD: *(in surly rejoinder)*
Let be all that.
  Now God give him trouble, (care)
    I say. (sagh)

WIFE: *(blubbering)*
  A pretty child is he
  As sits on a woman's knee;
  A darling, pardie,
    To make a man laugh. (laghe)

THIRD SHEPHERD: *(examining the sheep)*
I know him by the ear-mark;
  That is good token!

MAK: *(whining)*
I tell you, sirs, hark!
  His nose was broken;
Afterwards told me a clerk
  That he was bewitched. (forspoken)

FIRST SHEPHERD:
This is a false work;
  I would fain be avenged. (wrokyn)
    Get weapon!

WIFE: *(earnestly)*
  He was taken with an elf,
  I saw it myself;
  When the clock struck twelve,
    Was he misshapen.

SECOND SHEPHERD: *(disgusted)*
Ye two are well gifted, (feft)
  Alike in a homestead.

FIRST SHEPHERD: *(angrily)*
Since they maintain their theft,
  Let do them to death. (dede)

MAK: (*on his knees, trembling*)
If I trespass again, (eft)
  Strike off my head!
With you will I be left.
  THIRD SHEPHERD: (*snatching a cover from the bed*)
  Sirs, take my advice: (rede)
     For this trespass
   We will neither curse nor quarrel, (flyte)
   Fight nor chide, (chyte)
   But have done as quickly, **(tyte)**
     And cast him in canvass.

*They drag Mak outside where they toss him in the
blanket. Finally dropping him and leaving him groaning, they return to the fields. He reenters his hut as the
cottage curtain closes.*

FIRST SHEPHERD: (*rubbing his hands*)
Lord, what! I am sore
  In point for to burst!
In faith, I may no more;
  Therefore will I rest.
  SECOND SHEPHERD: (*opening and closing his hand*)
As a sheep of seven score
  He weighed in my fist.
For to sleep anywhere (ay-whore)
  Methink that I wish. (lyst)
  THIRD SHEPHERD: (*sitting down on the ground*)
    Now I pray you
  Lie down on this green.
  FIRST SHEPHERD: (*shaking his head*)
  On these thieves yet I ponder. (mene)
  THIRD SHEPHERD: (*wearily*)
   Whereto should ye trouble? (tene)
    Do as I say you.

*They all lie down as if to sleep. Suddenly, an Angel,
white robed with golden angel-wings and a gold halo,
appears in the "heaven" or top story of the stage and
sings "Gloria in excelsis." Then he holds up his right
hand in command to the shepherds.*

ANGEL:

Rise, shepherds gentle, (hend)
  For now is he born
That shall take from the fiend
  That Adam had doomed; (lorn)
That devil to destroy (sheynd)
  This night is he born;
God is made your friend
  Now at this morn.
        He commands (behestys)
        At Bethlehem go see,
        There lies that free
        In a crib full poorly
          Between two beasts. (bestys)

The Angel disappears.
FIRST SHEPHERD: *(rubbing his eyes)*

This was a rare voice (stevyn)
  That ever yet I heard.
It is a marvell to tell, (neven)
  Thus to be scared.
  SECOND SHEPHERD: *(wonderingly)*
Of God's son of heaven
  He spake upward.
All the wood on a lightning (levyn)
  Methought that he made (gard)
      Appear.
    THIRD SHEPHERD:
      He spake of a bairn
      In Bethlehem, I you warn.
    FIRST SHEPHERD:
        That betokens yon star; (starne)
        Let us seek him there.

  SECOND SHEPHERD:
Say, what was his song?
  Heard ye not how he sang it, (crakyd it)
Three breves to a long?
    THIRD SHEPHERD:
    Yea, marry, he trilled it; (hakt it)

Was no crochet wrong,
  Nor no thing that lacked it.
  FIRST SHEPHERD:
For to sing us among,
  Right as he performed it, (knakt it)
      I can.
  SECOND SHEPHERD:
      Let see how ye croon.
      Can ye bark at the moon?
  THIRD SHEPHERD:
      Hold your tongues! Have done!
  FIRST SHEPHERD:
      Hark after, then.
(sings "Gloria in excelsis.")

  SECOND SHEPHERD:
To Bethlehem he bade
  That we should go; (gang)
I am full feared (fard)
  That we tarry too long.
  THIRD SHEPHERD:
Be merry and not sad;
  Of mirth is our song;
Everlasting glad
  To reward may we win (fang)
      Without trouble. (noyse)
  FIRST SHEPHERD:
      Hie we thither therefore, (for-thy)
      If we be wet and weary,
      To that child and that lady!
          We have it not to lose.

  SECOND SHEPHERD:
We find by the prophecy—
  Let be your din!—
Of David and Isaiah (Isay)
  And more than I remember, (myn)
They prophesied by clergy
  That in a virgin
Should he alight and lie

To quench our sin
    And slake it,
    Our kind from woe.
For Isaiah said so:
    Ecce virgo
        Concipiet[7] a child that is naked.

THIRD SHEPHERD:
Full glad may we be,
    And abide that day
That lovely to see,
    That all mights may.
Lord, well were me,
    For once and for aye,
Might I kneel on my knee
    Some word for to say
        To that child.
        But the angel said,
        In a crib was he laid;
        He was poorly arrayed,
            Both meek and mild.

FIRST SHEPHERD:
Patriarchs that has been
    And prophets before, (beforne)
They desired to have seen
    This child that is born.
They are gone full clean;
    That have they lost. (lorne)
We shall see him, I believe, (weyn)
    Ere it be morn,
        As a sign. (to token)
        When I see him and feel,
        Then know I full well
        It is true as steel
            That prophets have spoken:

To so poor as we are
    That he would appear,

---

[7] "Behold, a virgin will conceive"

First find and declare
  By his messenger.

SECOND SHEPHERD:

Go we now, let us fare;
  The place is us near.

THIRD SHEPHERD:

I am ready and eager; (yare)
  Go we in together (fere)
    To that bright.
    Lord, if thy will be—
    We are ignorant all three—
    Thou grant us some kind of joy (somkyns gle)
      To comfort thy wight.

They go to the stable. The curtain is drawn, revealing Mary in white robes, wearing a halo and holding the child on her lap. The First Shepherd enters and kneels before the babe.

FIRST SHEPHERD:

Hail, comely and clean!
  Hail, young child!
Hail, Maker, as I mean,
  Of a maiden so mild!
Thou hast cursed, I believe, (weyne)
  The devil so wild;
The false guiler of evil, (teyn)
  Now goes he beguiled.
    Lo, he merries!
    Lo, he laughs, my sweeting!
    A well-faring meeting!
    I have held my promise. (hetyng)
      Have a bob of cherries.

SECOND SHEPHERD: *(entering and kneeling)*

Hail, sovereign Saviour,
  For thou hast us sought!
Hail, noble child and flower,
  That all thing hast wrought!
Hail, full of favor,
  That made all of nought!

Hail! I kneel and I cower.
  A bird have I brought
      To my bairn.
    Hail, little tiny baby! (mop)
    Of our creed thou art head, (crop)
    I would drink of thy cup, (cop)
        Little day-star! (starn)

THIRD SHEPHERD: *(entering and kneeling)*
Hail, darling dear,
  Full of Godhead! (godhede)
I pray thee be near
  When that I have need.
Hail, Sweet is thy cheer!
  My heart would bleed
To see thee sit here
  In so poor clothing, (wede)
      With no pennies.
    Hail! Put forth thy fist! (dall)
    I bring thee but a ball:
    Have and play thee withal,
        And go to the tennis.

MARY:
The Father of heaven,
  God omnipotent,
That set all in order, (on seven)
  His Son has he sent.
My name did he name
  And alighted ere he went.
I conceived him full even
    Through might as he meant,
        And now is he born.
      He keep you from woe!
      I shall pray him so.
      Tell forth as ye go,
        And treasure this morn.

FIRST SHEPHERD:
Farewell, lady,

So fair to behold,
With thy child on thy knee!

SECOND SHEPHERD:
But he lies full cold.
Lord, well is me!
   Now we go, thou behold.

THIRD SHEPHERD:
Forsooth, already
   It seems to be told
      Full oft.

FIRST SHEPHERD:
   What grace we have found! (fun)

SECOND SHEPHERD:
   Come forth; now are we saved! (won)

THIRD SHEPHERD:
   To sing are we bound: (bun)
      Let us begin mightily! (Let take on loft)

They go out singing.

The Castle of Perseverance

(ABRIDGED)

THE BANNS

The following stanzas constituted the announcement or advertisement of the play. They were delivered in a public place a week before the performance by two vexillators (or flagbearers) dressed as heralds, and accompanied by trumpeters to attract attention. After a flourish of trumpets:

FIRST VEXILLATOR:

Glorious God, in all degrees Lord most of might,[1]
    That heaven and earth made of nought, both sea and
        land,
The angels in heaven him to serve bright,
    And mankind in middle-earth he made with his hand,
And our lovely Lady, that lantern is of light,
    Save our liege lord, the king, the leader of this land,
And all the royalty of this realm, and teach them the
        right,
    And all the good commoners of this town that before
        us stand
      In this place!
    We muster you with honor, (menshepe)
    And ask you for generous friendship.
    Christ save you all from hardship,
      That will know our case!

SECOND VEXILLATOR:

The cause of our coming, you to declare,

---

[1] This modernization of the language of the text attempts to preserve as much as possible of the original rhythms, alliterations, and rhymes, and permits itself occasional awkwardness and a very few minor liberties of translation to do so.

Every man in himself forsooth he it may find.
When mankind into this world born is full bare—
    And bare shall buried be at the last end—
God him giveth two angels full alert and full ready,
        (yare)
    The good angel and the bad, to him for to lend.
The good teacheth him goodness; the bad, sin and sor-
        row; (sare)
    When the one hath the victory, the other goeth be-
        hind, (be-hende)
        By reason. (skyll)
        The good angel coveteth evermore man's salvation,
        And the bad beats him ever to his damnation.
        And God hath given man free arbitration
            Whether he will himself save or his soul peril.

FIRST VEXILLATOR:
Spilt is man sadly when he to sin assent!
    The bad angel then bringeth him three enemies so
        stout:
The World, the Fiend, the foul Flesh so lovely and cour-
        teous; (jent)
    They laden him full lustily with sins all about.
Filled with Pride and Covetousness, to the World is he
        went,
    To maintain his manhood; all men to him bow. (lout)
After, Ire and Envy the Fiend hath to him lent,
    Backbiting and Enditing, with all men for to trouble,
        Full even.
        But the foul Flesh, homeliest of all,
        Sloth, Lust, and Lechery began to him call,
        Gluttony, and other sins, both great and small.
            This man's soul is soiled with sins more than
            seven.
(*Lines 40 to 130 omitted*)

SECOND VEXILLATOR:
Grace if God will grant us of his great might,
    These parts in costume we purpose us to play
This day seventh before you in sight,

At [name of town is inserted] on the Green, in royal
    array.
(*Lines 135 to 143 omitted*)

FIRST VEXILLATOR:

Deus, our lifelong we love you, thus taking our leave.
    Ye manly men of [name of town], thus Christ save you
        all!
May he maintain your mirth and keep you from grief,
    (greve)
    That formed was of Mary mild in an ox stall.
Now, mercy be all [name of town], and well may ye
    thrive! (cheve)
    And all our faithful friends, thus fair may ye fall!
Yea, and welcome be ye when ye come, our worth for
    to prove, (preve)
    And worthy to be worshipped in bower and in hall
        And in every place.
        Farewell, fair friends,
        That lovely will listen and tarry! (lendis)
        Christ keep you from fiends!
    (*To the trumpeters*)
        Trump up, and let us pace!

The Play

The presentation of this play calls for a quite elaborate theatre, crudely described by a diagram affixed at the end of the manuscript and ingeniously reconstructed by Richard Southern in his The Medieval Theatre in the Round. *Apparently, a temporary theatre was created for each place of performance by digging a circular ditch, which constituted the boundaries of the theatre, and piling the dirt around the inside edge of the ditch to make an artificial hill on which spectators might sit or stand. In the center of this circle was a representation of a castle on stilts, a raised platform supported by four legs, beneath which a simple bed or cot was visible. At*

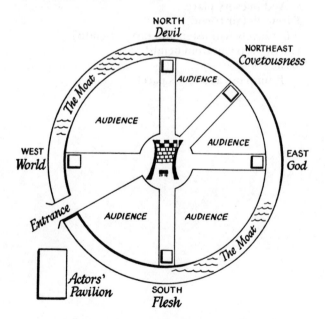

intervals around the edge of the circle (as indicated in the accompanying diagram) were five curtained scaffolds provided with stairs or ramps for the actors. The audience sat or stood in roughly triangular formations, leaving clear aisles leading from the scaffolds to a circular area around the castle which served as a central acting place. The outside ditch was filled with water when possible, in which case the audience entered a break in the hill by crossing a bridge over the moat. Southern argues that some of the entrances and exits must have been by this same bridge and therefore suggests that a tent or pavilion was erected across the ditch to serve as a dressing room. The stage directions in the following text are in general agreement with the conclusions of Southern's painstaking analysis of the complicated staging of this play.

The beginning of the play is announced by the blowing of trumpets in front of the West Scaffold, the Scaffold of the World. At the end of the trumpet call, the curtain of the scaffold slowly opens, revealing the oversized and sumptuously dressed figure of World, gold crowned and ermine robed. He is seated on a gilded throne, receiving the homage of his attendants Lust and Folly, his treasurer Covetousness, his messenger Backbiter, and an extremely malignant and evil-looking Boy.

WORLD: *(rising, strutting, and throwing out his arms)*
Worthy people in all this world wide,
By wild wood dwelling and every way-went,
Precious in price, pricked in pride,
Through this proper playing place, in peace be ye bent!
Prepare you, bold bachelors, under my banner to abide,
Where bright helmets be battered and backs are broken. (schent)
Ye, sirs seemly, all same sitteth on side,
For both by sea and by land my messengers I have sent:
All the World my name is minded; (ment)

All about my proclamation is blown; (blowe)
In every coast I am known; (knowe)
I do men clothe in rich gown (rowe)
Till they be doomed to death's blow. (dent)

*World concludes his announcement (Lines 170 to
195) and takes his seat regally on his throne. The trumpeters, meanwhile, have taken places in front of the
North Scaffold where a trumpet blast announces the
opening of the curtain which reveals a complete medieval Devil with a fearsome masked face, seated on a
bench and accompanied by his attendants Pride, Envy,
and Wrath.*

DEVIL:

Now I sit, Satan, in my sad sin,
    As devil doughty, in dregs as a dragon! (drake)
I champ and I chase, I chock on my chin,
    I am boisterous and bold, as Belial the black. (blake)
What folk that I rip, they gape and grin.
    Indeed, from Carlyle into Kent my chatter they take!
Both the back and the buttock bursteth all in burning;
        (brenne)
    With works of vengeance, I work them much wrack;
        (wrake)
        In woe is all my delight. (wenne)
        In care I am cloyed
        And foul I am annoyed
        But mankind be destroyed
            By ditches and by dens. (denne)

(pointing to his attendants)
Pride is my prince, in pearls bedecked; (y-pyth)
    Wrath, this wretch, with me shall go;
Envy into war with me shall walk brave; (wyth)
(Lines 212 to 226 omitted)

Gather you together, you boys on this green!
On this broad bugle a blast when I blow,
    All this world shall be mad, indeed as I ween,
        And to my bidding bind.
        Swiftly on side,

On bench will I bide
To plague, this tide,
    All wholly, Mankind.

*The trumpeters, now in front of the opposite South
Scaffold of the Flesh, signal the opening of the third
curtain which reveals the mountainous figure of Flesh,
seated on a wine cask and accompanied by his male attendants, the corpulent Gluttony, the recumbent Sloth,
and the sinuous scarlet woman Lechery.*

FLESH: (*leering grossly at the audience*)
I abide, as a broad bursting gut, high on these towers!
            (towris)
    Everybody is the better that to my bidding is bent.
I am Mankind's fair Flesh, flourished in flowers; (flowris)
    My life is to lusts and pleasure lent;
With hangings of taffeta I cover my towers; (towris)
    In mirth and in melody my mind is mixed; (i-ment)
Though I be clay and clod, clapped under grasses,
            (clowris)
    Yet would I that my will in the world went
        Full true, I you promise. (be-hyth)
        I love well mine ease,
        In lusts me to please
        Though sin my soul seize,
            I give not a mite. (myth)

(*pointing to his attendants*)
In Gluttony gracious now am I grow;
    Therefore, he sitteth seemly here by my side.
In Lechery and liking sunk am I low;
    And Sloth, my sweet son, is bound to abide.
(*Lines 252 to 265 omitted*)
    Behold the World, the Devil, and Me!
With all our mights, we kings three,
    Night and day busy we be
        For to destroy Mankind
            If that we may!
        Therefore on hill
        Sit you all still

And see with good will
 Our rich array!

*The trumpeters have retired. From under the castle
at the center, in striking contrast to these three pompous figures with their retinues, the pathetic little character of Mankind slowly and tentatively emerges into
the light. He wears only a plain white mantle, falling
from his head, which represents the chrisom in which
the consecrated oil was wrapped when he was baptized
and which was customarily thrown over the child at the
baptism ceremony. Slightly behind him at right and left
respectively walk his Good Angel (wearing a white
belted robe and large wings) and his Bad Angel (in red).
During Mankind's speech, the trio slowly circle the castle.*

MANKIND:

After our first father's kind, (kende)
 This night I was of my mother born.
From my mother I walk, I went.
 Full faint and feeble I walk you beforn.
I am naked of limb and loin, (lende)
 As mankind is shaped and shorn.
I know not whither to go nor to linger, (lende)
 To help myself midday nor morn.
  For shame I stand and am stupefied. (chende)
 I was born this night in bloody color, (ble)
 And naked I am, as ye may see.
 Ah! Lord God in Trinity,
  How Mankind is wretched! (unthende)

Whereto I was to this world brought
 I know not; but to woe and weeping
I am born, and have right nought
 To help myself in any doing.
I stand and study, all full of thought
 But bare and poor is my clothing;
A poor chrisom my head hath caught

That I took at my christening:
  Certes, I have no more.
    From earth I came, I know right well, (wele)
    And as earth I stand this while; (sele)
    Of mankind it is great pity (dele)
      Lord God, I cry thy mercy! (ore)

Two angels be assigned to me.
  The one teacheth to good;
On my right side ye may him see;
  He came from Christ that died on cross. (rode)
Another is ordained here to be,
  That is my foe by fen and flood;
He is about, in every degree,
  To draw me to those devils mad (wode)
    That in hell be thick.
    Such two hath every man alive
    To rule him and his wits five:
    When man doth evil, the one will shrive;
      The other draweth to wickedness. (wycke)

But since these angels have to me befallen (falle)
  Lord Jesus! to you I ask a boon, (bone)
That I may follow, by street and stall,
  The angel that came from heaven's throne.
Now, Lord Jesus in heaven's hall,
  Hear, when I make my moan!
Merciful Christ, to you I call!
  As a grisly ghost I grumble and groan,
    I suppose, right full of thought.
    Ah! Lord Jesus! Whither may I go? (goo)
    A chrisom I have, and no more (moo)
    Alas! men may be wondrous woeful (woo)
      When they be first forth brought!

  GOOD ANGEL:
Yea, forsooth, and this is well seen:
  Of woeful woe man may sing,
For each creature helpeth himself immediately, (be-
      dene)

Save only man, at his coming.
Nevertheless, turn thee from harm (tene)
   And serve Jesus, heaven's king,
And thou shalt, by groves green,
    Fare well in everything.
       That Lord thy life hath lent. (lante)
     Have him always in thy mind,
     That died on cross for mankind,
     And serve him to thy life's end,
       And certainly thou shalt not want!

BAD ANGEL:

Peace, angel! Thy words are not wise!
   Thou counsellest not aright!
He shall draw himself to the World's service
   To dwell with kaiser, king, and knight,
     That in land be him not like.
    Come on with me, still as stone!
    Thou and I to the World shall go (goon)
    And then thou shalt see anon
     How soon thou shalt be rich.

(*Lines 348 to 376 omitted*)

   MANKIND: (*in bewilderment*)

Whom to follow, I have no way of knowing! (wetyn I
     ne may!)
   I stand in study and begin to rave.
I would be rich in great array,
   And fain I would my soul save!
     As wind in water I wave.
(*to the Bad Angel*)
     Thou wouldst to the World I me took;
     And he would that I it forsook.
     Now, so God me help, and the holy book,
      I know not which I may have!

BAD ANGEL:

Come on, man! Whereof hast thou care?
   Go we to the World, I advise thee, quickly; (blyve)
For there thou shalt be able to right well fare;

In case you hope to thrive
>No lord shall be like thee. (thee lyche)
>Take the World to thine intent,
>And let thy love be thereon lent;
>With gold and silver rich rent
>>Anon thou shalt be rich.

MANKIND: *(with enthusiasm)*
Now, since thou hast promised me so,
>I will go with thee and assay;
I will not stop for friend nor foe,
>But with the World I will go play,
>>Certain, a little while. (throwe)
>>In this World is all my trust,
>>To live in liking and in lust.
>>When he and I have once kissed, (cust)
>>>We shall not part, I trow.

GOOD ANGEL: *(in pleading tones)*
Ah! Nay, man! For Christ's blood (blod)
>Come again by street and stile!
The World is wicked, and full mad, (wod)
>And thou shalt live but a while.
>>What covetest thou to win?
>>Man, think on thine ending day
>>When thou shalt be closed under clay!
>>And if thou think of that array,
>>>Certain, thou shalt not sin.
Homo, memento finis! et in eternum non peccabis.
(Man, consider the end! and in eternity you will not
>>>fail.)

BAD ANGEL: *(impatiently)*
Yea, on thy soul thou shalt think in good time.
>Come forth, man, and take no heed!
Come on, and thou shalt hold him in.
>Thy flesh thou shalt foster and feed
>>With lovely life's food.
>>With the World thou mayest be bold
>>Till thou be sixty winters old.

When thy nose waxes cold,
  Then mayest thou draw to good.

MANKIND:

I vow to God, and so I may
  Make merry a full great time! (throwe)
I may live many a day;
  I am but young, as I trow,
    For to do as I should.
    Might I ride by swamp and rill (syke)
    And be rich and lordlike,
    Certain, then should I be frisky (fryke)
      And a merry man on earth.

(Lines 431 to 529 omitted:
  The Bad Angel leads Mankind away from the Good
Angel. The Good Angel grieves at having been forsaken
and retires either to an obscure place under the castle
or to the pavilion outside the theatre. Suddenly, music
is heard from the direction of the Scaffold of the World
where World is strutting again. He brags that he is lord
of "king, knight, and kaiser" and is not concerned about
God. He then orders his attendants Lust, or Liking, and
Folly to go forth and advertise the advantages of serving
the World. They descend to the inner circle and address
the audience. The Bad Angel, leading Mankind around
the circle, meets them and greets them enthusiastically.)

BAD ANGEL:

How, Lust! Liking and Folly!
  Give me your close attention! (entent)
I have brought, by downs dry,
  To the World a great present!
I have beguiled him full quaintly;
  For, since he was born, I have tempted him. (hym
      blent)
He shall be servant good and true; (try)
  Among you his will is lent;
    To the World he will him take;
    For, since he could know, I understand,

I have enticed him in every land.
His Good Angel, by street and strand,
    I have caused him to forsake.
(*Lines 543 to 561 omitted*)

FOLLY:
With rich rents I shall him bind
    With the World till he be buried; (pytte)
And then shall I, long ere his end,
    Make that caitiff to be knit
        On the World when he is beset sore.
        Come on, Man! Thou shalt not rue,
        For thou wilt be to us true.
        Thou shalt be clad in clothes new
            And be rich evermore.

MANKIND: (*delighted*)
Marry, fellow, grammercy!
    I would be rich and of great renown.
For good I have no interest truly
    So that I be lord of tower and town,
        By bushes and banks brown.
        Since that thou wilt make me
        Both rich of gold and fee,
        Go forth! for I will follow thee
            By dale and every town.

A flourish of trumpets. Then Lust, Folly, the Bad Angel, and Mankind go to the Scaffold of the World.
    LUST: (*addressing World*)
How, lord! Look out! For we have brought
    A servant of noble fame!
Of worldly good is all his thought;
    Of lust and folly he hath no shame.
        He would be great of name;
        He would be at great honor
        For to rule town and tower;
        He would have for his paramour
            Some lovely worthy dame.

WORLD: (*greeting Mankind*)
Welcome, sir, seemly in sight!
   Thou art welcome to worthy clothes, (wede)
For thou wilt be my servant day and night;
   With my service I shall thee foster and feed;
Thy back shall be adorned with gold coins bright;
   Thou shalt have buildings by banks broad; (brede)
To thy body shall kneel kaiser and knight
      And ladies lovely in face, (lere)
     Where that thou walk, by sty or by street.
     But God's service thou must forsake
     And wholly to the World thee take
     And then a man I shall thee make
      That none shall be thy peer.

MANKIND: (*holding out his hand*)
Yes, World, and thereto here my hand
   To forsake God and his service.
For rewards thou give me house and land
   That I reign richly at my desire. (enprise)
So that I fare well by street and strand.
   While I dwell here in worldly wise,
I reek never of heaven's punishment (wonde)
   Nor of Jesus, that gentle justice.
      Of my soul I have no care. (rewthe)
     What should I reckon of doomsday,
     So that I be rich, and of great array?
     I shall make merry while I may
      And thereto here my troth. (trewthe)

WORLD: (*heartily*)
Now, certain, sir, thou sayest well!
   I hold thee true from top to the toe.
But thou were rich, it were greaty pity, (del)
   And all men that will fare so.
Come up, my servant true as steel! (stel)
(*Mankind mounts the Scaffold of the World.*)
   Thou shalt be rich whereso thou go;
Men shall serve thee at meals (mel)
   With minstrelsy and trumpet blow,

With meats and drinks abundant; (trye)
Lust and Liking shall be thy ease;
Lovely ladies thee shall please;
Whoso do thee any harm, (disesse)
    He shall be hanged high!

(*to Lust and Folly as they mount the scaffold*)
Liking, look alive! (be-lyve)
Have him clothed quickly (swythe)
In robes abundant (ryve)
    With rich array.
Folly, thou fool, (fonde)
By street and strand (strond)
Serve him at hand (honde)
    Both night and day.

(*Lines 635 to 651 omitted:*
   *Lust and Folly take Mankind aside to dress him,
probably behind a curtain at the rear of the scaffold.
No stage direction indicates what happens to the Bad
Angel. Presumably, he continues to accompany Man-
kind.*)

   *Backbiter enters the place, probably from the pavilion
outside. He is an evil-looking, cantankerous old man.*
  BACKBITER: (*to the audience*)
All things I cry against the peace (pes)
    To knight and knave. This is my nature. (kende)
Yea! worthy dukes on their thrones (edes)
    In bitter sorrow I bind
Crying and care, chiding and strife (ches)
    And sad sorrow to them I send.
Yea! loud lyings latched in deceit (les)
    Of tales untrue is all my mind. (mende)
        Man's bane about I bear.
    I will that ye observe, all those that are here;
    For I am known far and near;
    I am the World's messenger;
        My name is Backbiter.
(*Lines 664 to 689 omitted*)

Therefore, I am mad messenger
  To leap over lands fallow, (leye)
Through all the world, far and near,
  Unsaid sayings for to say.
In this place I hunt here
  For to spy a secret trick, (pley)
For when Mankind is clothed clear
  Then shall I teach him the way
      To the deadly sins seven.
    Here I shall abide with my peace
    The wrong to do him for to choose, (chese)
    For I think that he shall lose (lese)
      The blessing of high heaven.

*On the Scaffold of the World, which Backbiter now
approaches, Lust and Folly bring forth Mankind. He
now appears like a jaunty young dandy, smartly and ex-
pensively dressed from the feather in his cap to his
highly polished boots. During the remainder of the play
he will age gradually until, at the conclusion, he will be
a feeble and tottering old man. (The presentation
speeches of Lust and Folly, lines 703 to 728, are omitted.)*

WORLD:

Now, Folly, fair thee befall!
  And Lust, blessed be thou aye!
Ye have brought Mankind to my hall
  Certainly in a noble array!
With World's wealth within these walls (wall)
  I shall endow him of what I may.
Welcome, Mankind, to thee I call!
  Cleanlier clothed than any clay
      By down, dale, and ditch.
    Mankind, I counsel that thou rest
    With me, the World, as it is best.
    Look thou hold my hands fast (feste)
      And ever thou shalt be rich.

MANKIND: (*complacently*)

How should I but I thy behests hold? (helde)
  Thou workest with me wholly my will;

Thou endowest me with fen and field, (felde)
   And high halls by holts and hill;
In worldly weal my mind I rule; (welde)
   In joy I strut with jewels genteel; (jentyll)
On blissful banks my bower is built; (bylde)
   In vainglory I stand still;
      I am bold as a knight.
     Whoso against the World will speak
     Mankind shall on him be revenged; (wreke)
     In strong prison I shall him confine, (steke)
      Be it wrong or right!

WORLD:

Ah, Mankind, well thee betide,
   That thy love in me is set!
In my bowers thou shalt abide,
   And yet fare much the better. (bette)
I endow thee in all my buildings wide,
   In the grave till thou be put. (deth)
I make thee lord of much pride,
   Sir, at thine own mouth's command. (mette)
      I find in thee no treason.
     In all this world, by sea and sand,
     Parks, places, lawns, and land,
     Here I give thee with my hand,
      Sir, an open season.

Go to my treasurer, Sir Covetousness!
   Look thou tell him as I say!
Bid him make thee master in his house,
   With pennies and pounds for to play.
Look thou give not a louse
   Of the day that thou shalt die. (deye)
(addressing Backbiter who stands waiting below)
Messenger, do now thy service; (use)
   Backbiter, teach him the way!
      Thou art sweeter than mead.
     Mankind, take with thee Backbiting!
     Leave him for no sort of thing!

Flibbertigibbet with his flattering
Stands Mankind in good stead.

BACKBITER:

Backbiting and Detraction
Shall go with thee from town to town.
Have done, Mankind, and come down!
(*Mankind descends from the scaffold.*)
 I am thine own page.
I shall bear thee witness with my might, (myth)
When my lord, the World, it commands. (behyth)
(*pointing to the Northeast Scaffold of Covetousness*)
Lo, where Sir Covetousness sits
 And waits for us on his stage.

(*Lines 789 to 817 omitted:*
 Backbiter leads Mankind to the Scaffold of Covetousness where Covetousness, clad in gold and wearing a crown and bracelets of jingling coins, sits enthroned amidst his moneybags. During the journey the Good Angel laments and the Bad Angel rejoices.)

BACKBITER:

Sir Covetousness, God thee save,
 Thy pence and thy pounds all!
I, Backbiter, thine own knave,
 Have brought Mankind unto thine hall.
The World bade thou shouldst him have,
 And endow him, whatsoever befall.
In green grass till he be in grave,
 Put him in thy precious care, (pall)
 Covetousness! It were all a pity. (rewthe)
 While he walketh in worldly weal, (wolde)
 I, Backbiter, am with him close: (holde)
 Lust and Folly, those barons bold,
 To them he hath plighted his troth. (trewthe)

COVETOUSNESS: (*raising his sceptre to which jingling coins are attached*)

Oh, Mankind! Blessed must thou be!
 I have loved thee dearly many a day,

And so I know well that thou dost me.
  Come up and see my rich array!
(Mankind mounts the scaffold.)
It were a great point of pity
  Unless Covetousness were to thy liking. (pay)
*(rising from his throne and gesturing toward it with
        his sceptre)*
Sit up right here in this seat; (se)
  I shall teach thee of World's story (lay)
        That fadeth as a flood.
      With goods enough I shall thee store,
      And yet our game is but lost (lore)
      Unless thou covetest much more
        Than ever shall do thee good.

Thou must give thee to simony,
  Extortion, and false measure; (asyse)
Help no man but thou have a why;
  Pay not thy servants their service;
Thy neighbors see thou destroy;
  Tithe not in any wise;
Hear no beggar, though he cry—
  And then shalt thou full soon rise.
      And when thou deal in merchandise,
      See that thou be subtle in sleights;
      And also swear all by deceits;
      Buy and sell by false weights;
        For that is normal covetousness. (coveytyse)

(Lines 856 to 895 omitted:
  *Mankind joyfully accepts the offer and the way of
life proposed, and takes his place on the throne. Covetousness waves his sceptre in the direction of the North
Scaffold of the Devil.)*

  COVETOUSNESS: *(calling joyously)*
Pride, Wrath, and Envy,
  Come forth, the Devil's children three!
(turning to address the South Scaffold of the Flesh)
Lechery, Sloth, and Gluttony,

   To man's flesh ye are fiends free!
Drive down over dales dry!
   Be now blithe as any bee!
Over hill and farm ye you hie
   To come to Mankind and to me
        From your doughty dens!
      As dukes doughty, ye you dress!
      When ye six be come, I guess,
      Then be we seven, and no less,
        Of the deadly sins.

(*Lines 909 to 1013 omitted:*
   On the Scaffold of the Devil, Pride, Wrath, and Envy
bid farewell to Belial who exhorts them to do everything
in their power to lead Mankind to hell. On the Scaffold
of the Flesh, Lechery and Sloth take their leave of
Flesh who urges them to exert themselves to keep Man-
kind away from the bliss of heaven. They descend from
their respective scaffolds, dressed in lordly array. Pride,
tall and overbearing, leads his procession with his nose
in the air, followed by red-faced Wrath, who cavorts
furiously behind him, and Envy, who has hooks for
hands which he reaches out toward members of the
audience. From the opposite direction come sinuous
Lechery, a lascivious female who leers at the audience,
and Sloth, a short, sluggish tub of a man barely able to
move. They all line up in front of the Scaffold of
Covetousness.)

   PRIDE: (*acting as spokesman, being the first of the*
deadly sins)
What is thy will, Sir Covetousness?
   Why hast thou after us sent?
When thou criedest, we began to tremble (agryse)
   And come to thee now by assent.
        Our love is on thee fixed. (lent)
      I, Pride, Wrath, and Envy,
      Gluttony, Sloth, and Lechery,
      We are come all six for thy cry,
        To be at thy commandment.

COVETOUSNESS: *(opening his arms)*
Welcome be ye, brethren all,
 And my sister, sweet Lechery!
Know ye why I began to call?
 For ye must me help, and that in haste. (hy)
Mankind is now come to my hall
 With me to dwell, by downs dry;
Therefore ye must, whatso befall,
 Endow him with your folly;
     And else ye do him wrong,
      For when Mankind is naturally covetous,
      He is proved wrathful and envious,
      Gluttonous, slothful, and lecherous.
         They are other times about. (amonge)
(Lines 1035 to 1047 omitted)

PRIDE:
In entertainment and jokes I grow glad!
 Mankind, take good heed, (hed)
And do as Covetousness thee bade!
 Take me in thine heart, precious Pride;
See thou be not lorded over; (over-lad)
 Let no bachelor thee mistreat; (mysbede)
Make thyself to be doughty and feared; (drad)
 Beat boys till they bleed;
     Cast them in dire distresses; (kettis)
     Friends, father, and mother harm; (dere)
     Respect them in no manner.
     And hold no kind of man thy peer,
      And use these new fashions. (iettis)

Look thou make many a boast, (bost)
 With long pointed, curling toes on thy shoes;
Jag thy clothes in every way (cost)
 Or else men should consider thee but a goose.
It is thus, Man, well thou knowest. (wost)
 Therefore do as no man does;
And every man value as a turd; (thost)
 And of thyself make great honor; (ros)
     Now see thyself on every side.

Every man thou shalt shun and shove; (shelfe)
And hold no man better than thyself;
Till death's dent thy body bury, (delfe)
    Put wholly thine heart in Pride.
(Lines 1074 to 1090 omitted)

WRATH: *(ranting and raving)*
Be also angry as if thou wert mad. (wode)
    Make thee be feared by lonely dales! (dales derne)
Whoso thee angers, by fen or flood,
    See thou be avenged completely! (yerne)
Be ready to spill man's blood!
    See that thou frighten them, by far off fields! (feldis
        ferne)
Always, Man, be full of wrath! (mod)
    My loathsome laws see thou learn,
        I counsel, by anything.
        Quickly take vengeance, Man, I advise; (rede)
        And then shall no man overshadow you, (thee
            overlede)
        But of thee they shall have dread,
            And bow to thy bidding.

MANKIND: *(bowing low in acknowledgment)*
Wrath, for thy counsel gentle (hende)
    Have thou God's blessing and mine!
What caitiff of all my kind (kende)
    Will not bow, he shall suffer; (a-byn)
With my vengeance I shall him hurt, (schende)
    And avenge myself, by God's eyes. (yne)
(Lines 1110 to 1120 omitted)

ENVY: *(presenting himself as Wrath retires)*
Envy with Wrath must drive
    To haunt Mankind also.
When any of thy neighbors will thrive,
    See that thou have Envy thereto.

(Lines 1125 to 1150 omitted:
    Mankind accepts Envy as his "chief counsel.")

GLUTTONY: *(waddling up as Envy retires)*
In gay gluttony a sport thou begin!
　Order thee meat and drinks good.
See that no treasure escapes from thee, (thee part
　　　　a-twynne)
　But gorge thyself and feed with all kinds of food.
With fasting shall man never heaven win:
　These great fasters, I hold them mad. (wode)
Though thou eat and drink, it is no sin.
　Fast no day, I advise, by the cross. (rode)

(Lines 1159 to 1180 omitted:
　Mankind greets Gluttony.)

LECHERY: *(sidling up toward Mankind)*
Yea, when thy flesh is fairly fed,
　Then shall I, lovely Lechery,
Be bobbed with thee in bed;
　Hereof serve meat and drinks rich. (trye)
In love thy life shall be led;
　Be a lecher till thou die!

(Lines 1187 to 1210 omitted:
　Mankind remarks that few men will forsake Lechery.)

SLOTH: *(slowly approaching Mankind)*
Yea! when ye be in bed brought both,
　Wrapped well in worthy robes, (wede)
Then I, Sloth, will be wroth
　Unless two derelicts I may breed.
When the mass-bell sounds, (goth)
　Lie still, man, and take no heed.

(Lines 1217 to 1240 omitted:
　Mankind approves of Sloth's speech.)

MANKIND: *(addressing the audience)*
"Mankind" I am called by nature, (kynde)
　With cursedness in condition joined, (knet)
In sorry sweetness my time I spend,
　With seven sins sad beset.

Much mirth I move in mind,
  With melody at my mouth's might. (met)
My proud power shall I not limit (pende)
  Till I be put in pain's pit,
    To hell snatched from hence.
   In dale of dole till we are down,
   We shall be clad in a gay gown.
   I see no man but they use some
     Of these seven deadly sins.

(Lines 1254 to 1354 omitted:

  *The Good Angel reappears in the inner circle and
grieves bitterly. Shrift and Penance, dressed alike in
priestly garments except that Penance carries a scourge,
appear and inquire of the Good Angel the reason for
his grief. The Good Angel replies that he is lamenting
because of the imminent destruction of Mankind, and
begs Shrift to help. Shrift promises to do what he can.
The three then go to the Scaffold of Covetousness
where they observe Mankind enthroned and surrounded
by the seven deadly sins.)*

  SHRIFT: *(to Mankind)*
What, Mankind! How goeth this?
  What dost thou with these devils seven?
Alas, alas! Man, all amiss!
  Rejoice in the might of God in heaven,
    I advise, so have I rest.
    These loathsome rogues away thou send (lyfte)
    And come down and speak with Shrift.
    And draw thee quickly to some thrift!
      Truly, it is the best.

  MANKIND: *(scornfully)*
Ah, Shrift, thou art well known (benote)
  Here to Sloth, that sitteth herein.
He saith thou might have come to man's dwelling (cote)
  On Palm Sunday, in good time.
    Thou art come too soon!
    Therefore, Shrift, by thy fay,

Go forth till on Good Friday!
Attend to thee then well I may;
I have now else to do. (doon)

(Lines 1358 to 1548 omitted:
Shrift urges Mankind to confess, and Penance coun-
sels repentance. Mankind is finally persuaded to ac-
cept their advice. He descends from the scaffold, con-
fesses to Shrift, and is granted absolution. He then asks
to be directed to a place where he will be safe from the
attacks of the seven deadly sins.)

SHRIFT:

To such a place I shall thee direct, (kenne)
There thou mayest dwell without strife (dystaunce)
And always keep thee from sin—
Into the Castle of Perseverence.
If thou wilt to heaven win
And keep thee from worldly strife, (dystaunce)
Go to yon Castle and keep thee therein,
For it is stronger than any in France. (Fraunce)
To yon Castle I thee send.
That Castle is a precious place,
Full of virtue and of grace:
Whoso liveth there his life's space,
No sin shall him harm. (schende)

(Lines 1562 to 1695 omitted:
Shrift leads Mankind toward the Castle. The Bad
Angel reminds him that he is only forty years old and
too young to reform. The Good Angel encourages him
to continue his journey to the Castle where he is given
good advice by the seven moral virtues: Meekness, Pa-
tience, Charity, Abstinence, Chastity, Industry, and
Generosity. These stately ladies, clad in long flowing
robes of different colors, have presumably descended
from inside the Castle to greet him upon his arrival.
Mankind is touched by their teachings and agrees to
adhere to them.)

MEEKNESS: *(leading him to the stairway to the Castle)*
Mercy may mend all thy moan.

   Come in here at thine own will!
(Mankind enters the Castle and appears on its battlements while the Virtues sing, "Cum sancto sanctus eris, etc."—"With sanctity thou art blessed.")
We shall thee defend from thy foes (fon)

   If thou keep thee in this Castle still.
Stand herein as still as stone, (ston)

   Then shall no deadly sin thee destroy: (spylle)
Whether that sins come or go, (gon)

   Thou shalt with us thy bower build: (bylle)

      With virtues we shall thee advance. (vaunce)

   This Castle is of so quaint a device (gynne)

   That whosoever holds him therein,

   He shall never fall in deadly sin:

      It is the Castle of Perseverance.
Qui perseverauerit usque in finem, hic saluus erit.
(Matthew XXIV, 13: "But he that endureth to the end, the same shall be saved.")

(Lines 1710 to 1718 omitted:

   The Virtues sing Eterne rex altissime—*"Eternal Highest King." No stage direction is given, but it may be assumed that they stand guard around the Castle.)*

   The Bad Angel suddenly appears in the central acting place and rages at the sight of Mankind safe in the Castle.

BAD ANGEL:

Nay! By Belial's bright bones,

   There shall he no while dwell!
He shall be won from these dwellings, (wonys)

   With the World, the Flesh, and the Devil of hell!

      They shall my will work. (awreke)

   The sins seven, the kings three,

   To Mankind have enmity;

   Sharply they shall help me,

      This Castle for to break.

(calling to Backbiter)
How! Flibbertigibbet Backbiter!
  Swift our message see thou make!
Sharp about look thou bear it (bere)
  Say, Mankind his sins hath forsake.
With yon wenches he will himself protect; (were)
  All to holiness he hath him take.
In my heart it doth me hurt; (dere)
    The boast that those mothers make
        My gall begins to grind.
      Flibbertigibbet, run about quickly! (a rasche)
      Bid the World, the Fiend, and the Flesh
      That they come to fight fiercely (fresche)
        To win against Mankind.

BACKBITER:

I go! I go on ground glad!
  Swifter than ship with rudder!
I make men bemazed and mad,
  And every man to kill other
      With a sorry mien. (chere)
    I am glad, by Saint James of Galys,
    Of shrewdness to tell tales
    Both in England and in Wales,
        And, faith, I have many a companion. (fere)

*The Bad Angel and Backbiter go together to the
Scaffold of the Devil where Belial sits enthroned in
solitary grandeur. His attendants, Pride, Envy, and
Wrath, stand in a knot in a far corner of the scaffold
with their backs to the audience.*
Hail, set in thy throne! (selle)
Hail, dungy devil in thy dell!
Hail, low in hell!
I come to thee, tales to tell.

BELIAL:

Backbiter, boy, always by holt and heath,
Say now, I say, what tidings? Tell me the truth!

BACKBITER:

Painful tales I may thee say,
   To thee no good, I guess!
Mankind is gone now away
   Into the Castle of Goodness!
There he will both live and die (deye)
   In dale of dross till death him dress.
Hath thee forsaken, forsooth I say,
   And all thy works, more and less!
         To yon Castle he gan to creep.
   Yon mother, Meekness, truth to say, (sayn)
      And all yon maidens on yon plain,
         For to fight they be full fain,
            Mankind for to keep.

Pride, Envy, and Wrath, hearing this, suddenly turn about in excitement.

PRIDE:

Sir King, what are your thoughts? (what wytte)
We be ready throats to cut. (kytte)

BELIAL: *(to Backbiter and the Bad Angel)*

Say, vagabonds, have ye hard grace!
   And evil death may ye die!
Why let ye Mankind from you pass
      Into yon Castle, from us away?
         With pain I shall you flay!
      Harlots! at once
      From this spot! (wonys)
         By Belial's bones,
            Ye shall smart! (abeye)

He snatches a long whip and beats them until they fall on the ground. When their punishment is concluded, Backbiter slowly pulls himself to his feet and runs to the Scaffold of the Flesh.

BACKBITER:

Hail, King I call!
Hail, Prince, proudly arrayed in magnificence! (palle)
Hail, gentle in hall!
Hail, Sir King, fair thee befall!

FLESH:
King Backbiting,
Full ready in robes to reign, (rynge)
Full glad tiding,
By Belial's bones, I believe thou bring.

BACKBITER:
Yea, for God! out I cry
　On thy two sons and thy daughter young! (ying)
Gluttony, Sloth, and Lechery
　Hath put me in great mourning.
They let Mankind go up high
　Into yon castle at his liking,
Therein for to live and die
　With those ladies to make ending,
　　　The flowers fair and fresh.
　　He is in the Castle of Perseverance,
　　And put his body to penance.
　　Of hard hap is now thy chance,
　　　Sir King, Mankind's Flesh.

(Lines 1813 to 1853 omitted:
　Flesh turns to Gluttony, Sloth, and Lechery, berates
them for their negligence, and beats them. Backbiter
watches with delight and then runs to the Scaffold of
the World whom he informs of the escape of Man-
kind and advises that Covetousness be punished. A
horn is blown to summon Covetousness who descends
from his Scaffold and angrily confronts World.)

COVETOUSNESS:
Sir Bulging Bold, (bowde)
Tell me why blow ye so loud?
　WORLD:
Loud, doomed one! The devil thee burn!
　I pray God give thee a foul hap!
Say, why lettest thou Mankind
　Into yon Castle for to escape?
　　　I believe thou beginst to rave
　　Now, for Mankind is went,

All our game is lost: (schent)
Therefore, a sore driving blow, (dent)
    Harlot, thou shalt have!

World and Backbiter fall on Covetousness and beat him.

COVETOUSNESS:

Mercy! Mercy! I will no more!
    Thou hast me rapped with rueful blows! (rowtis)
I scowl! I sob! I sigh sore!
    Mine head is clattered all to bits! (clowtis)

(Lines 1869 to 2186 omitted:
    The World, Flesh, and the Devil announce their intentions to storm the Castle and seize Mankind. Meekness reminds her sisters that it is their duty to defend Mankind. Then Belial leads Pride, Wrath, and Envy to the Castle where they engage in a debate with Meekness, Patience, and Charity. This talk without action enrages Belial.)

BELIAL:

What, for Belial's bones!
    Whereabouts chide ye?
Have done, ye boys, all at once!
    Lash down these mothers, all three!
Work wrack to this dwelling! (wonys)
    Your doughty deeds now let see!
        Dash them to tatters! (daggys)
    Have do, boys blue and black! (blake)
    Work these wenches woe and destruction! (wrake)
    Clarions cry up at top pitch (krake)
        And blow your broad bagpipes! (baggys)

(Lines 2200 to 2427 omitted:
    They assault the Castle with slings, lances, shot, and bows. A stage direction appended to the plan of the Castle reads: "He that schal pleye Belyal, loke that he haue gunnepowder brennyn [burning] *in pyps in his hands and in his eris and in his ers, whanne he goth to bat* [tel].*" The Virtues defend the Castle by hurling*

*roses, symbolic of Christ's passion, and drive off the
attackers, who retreat to their respective Scaffolds.
Then Flesh leads Gluttony, Sloth, and Lechery in an
attack upon the Castle. After a preliminary debate between Gluttony and Abstinence, Lechery and Chastity,
Sloth and Industry, they also attack the Castle and are
defeated. The World then attempts to conquer Mankind by appealing to Covetousness to use his skill to
lure Mankind away from the Virtues. Covetousness
approaches the Castle and addresses Mankind in a tone
of gentle reasonableness.)*

COVETOUSNESS:

How, Mankind! I am annoyed (a-tenyde)
   For thou art there so in that hold.
Come and speak with thy best friend,
   Sir Covetousness! Thou knowest me of old.
What the devil! Shalt thou there longer linger (lende)
   With great penance in that Castle cold?
Into the world, if thou wilt, wend
   Among men to bear thee bold,
      I advise, by Saint Guile.
    How, Mankind! I thee say,
    Come to Covetousness, I thee pray.
    We two shall together play,
      If thou wilt, awhile.

*(Lines 2440 to 2479 omitted:
   The virtues attempt to turn Covetousness aside; he
replies that he is not talking to them but to Mankind
and again appeals to him to leave the Castle.)*

MANKIND: *(now an old man)*
Covetousness, whither should I wend?
   What way wouldst that I should hold?
To what place wouldst thou me send?
   I begin to wax hoary and cold;
My back begins to bow and bend:
   I crawl and creep and wax all cold.
Age maketh man full wretched, (unthende)

Body and bones, and all unwieldy. (unwolde)
  My bones are feeble and sore;
    I am arrayed in a loose gown; (sloppe)
  As a young man I may not hop;
  My nose is cold and begins to drop;
    My hair waxeth all hoar.

COVETOUSNESS:
Peter! thou hast the more need
  To have some goods in thine age—
Marks, pounds, lands and lead, (lede—meaning metal
      or a leaden seal)
  Houses and homes, castle and cage!
Therefore do as I thee teach! (rede)
  To Covetousness cast thy kinship! (parage)
Come, and I shall thy request present; (bede)
  The worthy World shall give thee wage,
    Certainly, not a little. (lyth)
    Come on, old man! It is no reproof (reprefe)
    That Covetousness be to thee dear. (lefe)
(*Lines 2504 to 2515 omitted*)

MANKIND: (*unmoved by the argument*)
  I will not do these ladies despite
  To forsake them for so little. (lyt)
  To dwell here is my delight;
    Here are my best friends.

COVETOUSNESS:
Yea! up and down thou take the way
  Through this world to walk and wend,
And thou shalt find, sooth to say,
  Thy purse shall be thy best friend.
Thou shalt sit all day and pray;
  No man shall come to thee nor send.
But if thou have a penny to pay,
  Men shall to thee then listen and lend,
    And cool all thy care.
    Therefore to me thou cling and hold, (helde)
    And be covetous whilst thou may thee control.
      (welde)

If thou be poor and needy and eld,
    Thou shalt often evil fare.

MANKIND:

Covetousness, thou sayest a good reason. (skyl)
    So great goods me will advance,
All thy bidding do I will.
    I forsake the Castle of Perseverance;
In Covetousness I will me hide (hyle)
    For to get some sustenance.

(Lines 2538 to 2687 omitted:
    Mankind descends from the Castle. The Virtues
plead with him to remain, but the Bad Angel persuades
him that the female cackle of the Virtues is not to be
heeded. Mankind walks off with Covetousness while
the Good Angel laments and the World exults.)

WORLD:

Ah, ah! This game goeth as I would. (wolde)
    Mankind will never the World forsake!
Till he be dead and under mold
    Wholly to me he will him take.
To Covetousness he hath him yielded; (yolde)
    With my weal he will awake.
For a thousand pounds I would not (nolde)
    But Covetousness were Man's mate, (make)
        Certain, on every wise.
      All these games he shall bewail,
      For I, the World, am of this entail;
      In his most need I shall him fail,
        And all for Covetousness. (Coveytyse)
During this speech Covetousness has escorted Man-
kind to a bower under the Castle which is furnished
with a bed and a chest or "cupboard" nearby.

COVETOUSNESS:

Now, Mankind, beware of this:
    Thou art a party well in age;
I would not thou fared amiss;
    Go we now nigh my castle cage.

In this bower I shall thee bless; (blys)
 Worldly weal shall be thy wage;
Much more than is thine, indeed, (y-wys)
  Take thou in this trust payment, (terage)
   And see that thou do wrong.
   Covetousness, it is no sore,
   He will thee endow full of store,
   And always, always, say "more and more";
    And that shall be thy song.

MANKIND:

Ah, Covetousness, have thou good grace!
 Certain thou bearest a true tongue:
"More and more," in many a place,
 Certain, that song is often sung.
I know never man, by banks base,
 So say, in clay till he were buried: (clonge)
"Enough, enough" had never space;
  That full song was never sung,
   Nor I will not begin.
   Good Covetousness, I thee pray
   That I might with thee play!
   Give me goods enough ere that I die, (dey)
    To live in world's joy. (wynne)

COVETOUSNESS: (*opening the chest and pulling out a handful of gold coins*)

Have here, Mankind, a thousand marks! (marke)
 I, Covetousness, have thee this gotten. (gote)
Thou mayest purchase therewith both pond and park,
 And do therewith much business. (note)
Lend no man hereof, for no distress, (karke)
 Though he should hang by the throat,
Monk nor friar, priest nor clerk;
 Nor help therewith church nor cottage, (cote)
  Till death thy body delve.
  Though he should starve in a cave.
  Let no poor man thereof have;
  In green grass till thou be in grave,
   Keep somewhat for thyself. (selve)

MANKIND:

I vow to God, it is great husbandry:
  Of thee I take these nobles round.
I shall me hasten, and that in speed, (hye)
  To hide this gold under the ground.
There shalt it lie till that I die;
  It may be kept there safe and sound.
Though my neighbor should be hanged high,
  Thereof getteth he neither penny nor pound.
    Yet am I not well at ease;
   Now would I have castle walls,
   Strong steeds and stiff in stalls.
   With high woods and high halls,
    Covetousness, thou must me endow. (sese)

(*Lines 2752 to 2778 omitted:*

Covetousness leaves Mankind exulting over his fortune and declaring that if he can have wealth he will forego heaven. Whether he actually buries the gold or not is not clear. Suddenly, Death makes a dramatic entrance from outside the theatre. A sepulchral figure from his skull-mask to the bones represented on his tights, he appears to be a walking skeleton, wearing only the tattered suggestion of a monk's hood and gown. He carries a spear or dart in his right hand.)

DEATH:

Oh! Now it is time high
  To cast Mankind to death's blow! (dynt)
In all his works he is unsly;
  Much of his life he hath misspent.
To Mankind I come nigh.
  With rueful raps he shall be rent.
When I come, each man dreads therefore, (forthi)
  But yet is there no help hoped for, (i-went)
    High hill, holt, nor heath.
   Ye shall me dread, every one;
   When I come, ye shall groan!
   My name in land is left alone:
    I'm known as "Dreary Death."

(Lines 2792 to 2830 omitted)

To Mankind now will I reach;
   He hath whole his heart on Covetousness. (Covey-
        tyse)
A new lesson I will him teach,
   That he shall both shun and shudder! (gryse)
No one in land shall be his physician; (leche)
   I shall him prove of my enterprise;
With this point I shall him breach,
   And pester him in woeful wise;
      Nobody shall be his help. (bote)

*(He approaches Mankind, threatening him with his
dart.)*

      I shall thee shape a sorry shape: (schappe)
      Now I kill thee with my blow! (knappe)
      I reach to thee, Mankind, a rap
         To thine heart's root. (rote)

(He strikes Mankind, who falls to one knee.)

MANKIND:

Ah, Death, Death! Dismal is thy drift!
   Dead is my destiny!
Mine head is cloven all in a cleft! (clyfte)
   For cap of sorrow now I cry;
Mine eyelids may I not lift;
   My brains wax all empty;
I may not once my head up raise. (schyfte)
   With Death's dent now I die!
      Sir World, I am caught! (hent)
      World! World! Have me in mind!
      Good Sir World! Help now Mankind!
      But thou me help, Death shall me grind;
      He hath dealt to me a dent!

World, my wit waxeth wrong;
   I change, both hide and hue;
Mine eyelids wax all tearful; (outewronge)
   But thou me help sore it shall me rue!
Now hold that thou has promised me long!

For all fellowships old and new,
Release me from my pains strong!
  Some charm from harm thou me brew,
      That I may of thee praise! (yelpe)
     World, for old acquaintance,
     Help me from this sorry chance!
     Death hath lopped me with his lance!
      I die but thou me help!

WORLD:

Oh, Mankind, hath Death with thee spoke?
  Against him helps no gage!
I would thou wert in the earth locked, (be-loke)
  And another had thine heritage!
Our bond of love shall soon be broke;
  In cold clay shall be thy cage.
Now shall the World on thee be avenged. (wroke)
  For thou hast done so great outrage;
     Thy goods thou shalt forego.
     World's goods thou hast foregone,
     And with fools thou shalt be torn.
     Thus have I served here before, (be-forn)
      A hundred thousand more! (moo)

MANKIND:

Oh, World, World! ever worth woe!
  And thou, sinful Covetousness, (Coveytyse)
When that a man shall from you go,
  Ye work with him in a wondrous wise!
The wit of this world is sorrow and woe.
  Beware, good men, of this guise!
Thus hath he served many and more. (mo)
  In sorrow slaked all his assize;
     He beareth a blighting tongue.
     While I laid with him my lot,
     Ye saw how fair he me promised; (be-hett)
     And now he would I were a clot
      In cold clay for to cling.

(Lines 2896 to 2982 omitted:

World calls to the Boy who descends from World's Scaffold and approaches the bed where he is made heir to Mankind's treasure. Mankind objects that he is not of his kin. The Boy replies arrogantly that World has given it to him. Mankind asks his name. Boy replies, "My name is I-wot-never-who." Mankind crawls to the bed under the Castle and lies down to die.)

Certain, a verse that David spake　(spak)
　　In the Psalter, I find it true:
Tesaurizat, et ignorat cui congregabit ea.
(Psalm XXXIX, 6: *He heapeth up riches, and knoweth not who shall gather them.*)
Treasure, treasure, it hath not strength;　(tak)
　　It is other men's, old and new.
Oh, oh! My goods go all to wrack!
　　Sorely man Mankind rue!
　　　　God keep me from despair!
　　All my goods, without fail,
　　I have gathered with great travail;
　　The world hath ordained of his entail;
　　　　I know never who to be mine heir.

Now, good men, take example of me!
　　Do for yourself while ye have space!
For many men thus served be
　　Through the world in divers place.
I bulge and bleach in bloody color,　(ble)
　　And as a flower fadeth my face.
To hell I shall both fare and flee,
　　But God me grant of his grace.
　　　　I die certainly.
　　Now my life I have lost.　(lore)
　　My heart breaketh. I sigh sore.
　　A word may I speak no more.
　　　　I put me in God's mercy.

Heaving a great sigh, he dies. Mankind's Soul, a white-robed figure, crawls from beneath the bed. The Soul

steps out into the inner circle where he is met by the
Good Angel and the Bad Angel.

SOUL:

"Mercy!" This was my last tale
  That ever my body was about.
But Mercy help me in this vale,
  Of dooming drink sore I me fear. (coute)
(*The soul looks back toward the body on the bed.*)
Body, thou didst brew a bitter bale,
  To thy lusts when thou began to bow! (loute)
Thy pitiable soul shall be frigid. (a-kale)
  I buy thy deeds with rueful route;
      And all it is for guile.
    Ever thou hast been covetous,
    Falsely to get land and house;
    To me thou hast brewed a bitter juice;
      So welaway the while!

(*turning to the Good Angel*)
Now, sweet angel, what is thy counsel? (red)
  The right advice thou me teach!
Now my body is dressed for death, (ded)
  Help now me, and be my physician! (leche)
Save thou me from devil's dread!
  Thy worthy way thou me teach!
I hope that God will help and be my heed, (hed)
  For "Mercy" was my last speech:
      Thus made my body his end.
(*A page of the ms. is here lost.*)

BAD ANGEL:

    Witness of all that was about,
    Sir Covetousness he had him out;
    Therefore he shall, without doubt,
      With me to hell pit.

GOOD ANGEL:

Yea, alas, and welawoe!
  Against Covetousness can I not tell.
Reason while I from thee go,
  For, wretched soul, thou must to hell!

Covetousness, he was thy foe;
  He hath thee shaped a shameful shell.
Thus hath served many and more, (mo)
    Till they be drawn to death's dell,
      To bitter bale's bower.
      Thou must to pain, by right reason.
      With Covetousness, for he is the reason,
      Thou art trapped full of treason,
        But Mercy be thy succor.

(Lines 3048 to 3060 omitted:
    The Good Angel sorrowfully leaves the theatre.)

SOUL: *(gazing about frantically)*
Alas, Mercy! thou art too long!
  Of sad sorrow now may I sing!
Holy Writ it is full wrong,
  But Mercy passeth everything.
I am ordained to pains strong;
  In woe is dressed my dwelling;
In hell on hooks I shall hang; (honge)
  But Mercy from a well spring,
    This devil will have me away.
    Welaway! I was full mad (wod)
    That I forsook mine Angel Good,
    And with Covetousness stood
      Till that day that I should die. (dey)

BAD ANGEL:
Yea! Why wouldst thou be covetous,
  And draw thee again to sin?
I shall thee brew a bitter juice!
  In bulging bonds thou shalt burn; (brenne)
In high hell shall be thine house;
  In pitch and tar to groan and grin,
Thou shalt lie drowned as a mouse;
  There may no man therefrom thee win,
    For that same while. (wyll)
    That day the ladies thou forsook
    And to my counsel thou thee took,

Thou were better hanged upon a hook
  Up on gibbet hill.

(Lines 3087 to 3127 omitted:
  The Bad Angel hoists the Soul on his back and starts
in the direction of a gaping Hell-mouth beneath the
Scaffold of Belial.)

To devil's dell
I shall bear thee to hell.
I will not dwell.
(to the audience)
Have good day! I go to hell!

  From the Pavilion outside the theatre enter the Four
Daughters of God: Mercy, Truth, Righteousness, and
Peace. These are four comely and stately women clothed
in simple mantles: Mercy in white, Truth in green,
Righteousness in red, and Peace in black.
  MERCY:
A moan I heard of "mercy" made, (meve)
  And to me, Mercy, began cry and call;
Unless it have mercy, sore it shall me grieve,
  For else it shall to hell fall.
Righteousness, my sister chief,
  This ye heard: so did we all;
For we were made friends dear (leve)
  When the Jews proffered Christ vinegar and gall
    On the Good Friday.
    God granted that remission,
    Mercy and absolution
    Through virtue of his passion,
      To no man should be said "Nay."

Therefore, my sisters, Righteousness,
  Peace, and Truth, to you I tell,
When man crieth "mercy," and will not cease,
  Mercy shall be his washing well:
    Witness of holy kirk.
    For the least drop of blood
    That God bled on the cross, (rode)

It had been satisfaction good
  For all Mankind's work.

(Lines 3152 to 3217 omitted:
  Righteousness and Truth contend that Mankind
should pay the penalty for his misdeeds, but Peace agrees
with Mercy. At the conclusion of the debate, all four
agree to approach the throne of God.)

PEACE:

Righteousness and Truth, do by my counsel! (red)
  And Mercy, go we to yon high place!
(pointing to the Scaffold of God)
We shall inform the high Godhead
  And pray him to judge this case.
Ye shall tell him your intent
  Of Truth and Righteousness;
And we shall pray that his judgment
  May be passed by us, Mercy and Peace.
    All four, now go we hence
    Quickly to the Trinity;
    And there shall we soon see
    What that his judgment shall be
      Without any remedy. (deffens)

All four daughters approach the Scaffold of God and
stand at a respectful distance as the curtain of the scaf-
fold opens, revealing the majestic figure of Deity,
crowned with gold and wearing pontifical vestments.

TRUTH:

Hail, God of might!
We come, thy daughters in sight,
Truth, Mercy, and Right,
And Peace, peaceful in fight.

MERCY:

We come to prove (preve)
If Man, that was to thee full dear; (leve)
If he shall go (cheve)
To hell or heaven, by thy leave.

RIGHTEOUSNESS:
I, Righteousness,
Thy daughter, as I guess,
Let me, nevertheless,
At this trial put me in press.

PEACE:
Peaceable King,
I, Peace, thy daughter young, (yinge)
Hear my praying
When I pray thee, Lord, of a thing.

GOD: *(raising his hand in blessing)*
Welcome, in fellowship, (fere)
Brighter than blossoms on briar, (brere)
My daughters dear!
Come forth, and stand ye me near.

TRUTH:
Lord, as thou art King of kings, crowned with crown,
  As thou lovest me, Truth, thy daughter dear,
Let never me, Truth, to fall down,
  My faithful Father, without peer!
      Quia veritatem delexisti.
      (Because you have esteemed truth.)
For in all truth stands thy renown,
  Thy faith, thy hope, and thy power.
Let it be seen, Lord, now at thy judgment, (dome)
  That I may have my true prayer
      To do truth to Mankind.
    For if Mankind be doomed by right
    And not by mercy, most of might,
    Here my truth, Lord, I thee plight,
      In prison man shall be pinned.

Lord! How should Mankind be saved
  Since he died in deadly sin,
And all thy commandments he depraved,
  And of false Covetousness he would never desist?
      (blyne)
(Lines 3265 to 3307 omitted)

I pray thee, Lord, as I have space,
Let Mankind have due distress,
In hell for to be burnt. (brent)
In pain look he be still,
Lord, if it be thy will,
Or else I have no skill
By thy true judgment.

MERCY:

O pater maxime, et Deus tocius consolaciounis, qui
consolatur nos in omni tribulacione nostra!
(II Corinthians I, 4: O greatest Father, and the God of
all comfort, who comforteth us in all our tribuations)
O thou Father, of might most,
Merciful God in Trinity!
I am thy daughter, well thou knowest,
And Mercy from heaven thou broughtest free.
Show me thy grace in every coast!
In this case my comfort be!
Let me, Lord, never be lost
At thy judgment, whatever it be,
Of Mankind.
If man's sin had never come about, (in cas)
I, Mercy, should never on earth have had place;
Therefore, grant me, Lord, thy grace,
That Mankind may me find.

(*Lines 3328 to 3366 omitted*)

Lord, though that man hath done more wrong than
good,
If he die in very contrition,
Lord, the least drop of thy blood
For his sins maketh satisfaction.
As you died, Lord, on the cross, (rode)
Grant me my petition!
Let me, Mercy, be his food,
And grant him thy salvation,
Quia dixisti, "misericordiam amabo."
(Because thou hast said, "I will cherish mercy.")
Mercy shall I sing and say,

And *miserere* (have mercy) shall I pray
For Mankind ever and aye;
   Misericordias domini in eternum cantabo.
   (The mercy of God I will sing in eternity.)

RIGHTEOUSNESS:

Righteous King, Lord God Almighty, (almyth)
   I am thy daughter Righteousness.
Thou hast loved me ever, day and night,
   As well as other, as I guess:
      Justicias Dominus justicia dilexit.
      (The just God has prized justice.)
If thou Mankind from pain acquit, (e-quite)
   Thou dost against thine own process.
Let him in prison to be thrust (pyth)
   For his sin and wickedness!
      Of a boon I thee pray:
      Full often he hath thee, Lord, forsaken, (for-sake)
      And to the devil he hath him taken; (take)
      Let him lie in hell's lake,
         Doomed for ever and aye!
         Qui Deum, qui se genuit, dereliquit.
         (Because he forsook God, who bore himself.)
(*Lines 3394 to 3483 omitted*)

PEACE:

Peaceable King in Majesty!
   I, Peace, thy daughter, ask thee a boon
Of Man, how-so it be.
   Lord, grant me mine asking soon,
That I may evermore dwell with thee,
   As I have ever yet done,
And let me never from thee flee,
   Especially at thy judgment (dome)
      Of man, thy creature.
      Thou my sisters, Right and Truth,
      Of Mankind have no pity, (rewthe)
      Mercy and I full sore us move (mewythe)
         To catch him to our cure.
(*Lines 3497 to 3548 omitted*)

Lord, for thy pity and that peace
  Thou suffered in thy passion,
Bound and beaten, in very truth, (without les)
  From the foot to the crown,
Tanquam ouis ductis es.
(As a sheep you have been led.)
  When *gutte sanguis* (drops of blood) ran down
Yet the Jews would not cease
  But on thy head they thrust a crown,
      And on the cross thee nailed—
    As piteously as thou wert tortured, (pynyd)
    Have mercy on Mankind,
    So that he may find
      Our prayer may him avail.

THE FATHER: (*raising his right hand*)
Ego cogito cogitaciones pacis, non affliccionis.
(Jeremiah XXIX, 11: I think thoughts of peace, not of
evil.)
Fair befall thee, Peace, my daughter dear!
  On thee I think and on Mercy.
Since ye accorded be all in fellowship, (fere)
  My judgment I will give you by,
Not after deserving to do harshness, (reddere)
  To doom Mankind to tormentry,
But bring him to my bliss full clear,
  In heaven to dwell endlessly,
      At your prayers for this. (for-thi)
    To make my bliss perfect, (perfyth)
    I mingle with my most might (myth)
    All peace, some truth, and some right,
      And most of my mercy.

Misericordia Domini plena est terra. Amen!
(The earth is full of the lovingkindness of God.)
My daughters gentle, (hende)
Lovely and lithesome to linger, (lende)
Go to yon fiend
And from him take Mankind!
  Bring him to me!

And set him here by my knee,
In heaven to be,
In bliss with gaiety and glee.

TRUTH:
We shall fulfill
Thy behests, as right and proper, (skylle)
From yon ghost gruesome (grylle)
Mankind to bring to thee. (thee tylle)

The Daughters of God make obeisance to the Almighty and proceed to the Scaffold of the Devil where they address the Bad Angel.

PEACE:
Ah, thou foul wight!
Let go that soul quickly! (tyth)
In heaven's light
Mankind soon shall be placed. (pyth)

RIGHTEOUSNESS:
Go thou to hell,
Thou devil bold as a bell,
Therein to dwell
In brass and brimstone to boil. (welle)

They take the Soul away from the Bad Angel and lead him to the Scaffold of God where they present him.

MERCY:
Lo, here Mankind
Lighter than leaf is on limb! (lynde)
That hath been tortured, (pynyd)
Thy mercy, Lord, let him find.

THE FATHER: (*sitting in judgment*)
My mercy, Mankind, give I thee.
Come, sit at my right hand. (honde)
(*The Soul ascends the scaffold and obeys.*)
Full well have I loved thee,
Unkind though I thee found. (fonde)
As a spark of fire in the sea,
My mercy is sin quenching. (quenchande)
Thou hast cause to love me

Above all things in land,
    And keep my commandment.
    If thou me love and dread,
    Heaven shall be thy meed;
    My face thee shall feed.
      This is my Judgment.

Ego occidam, et vivificabo; percuciam et sanabo; et nemo est qui de manu mea possit eruere. (Deuteronomy XXXII, 39: I kill and I make alive; I wound and I heal; neither is there any that can deliver out of my hand.)

King, kaiser, knight, and champion,
    Pope, patriarch, priest, and prelate in peace,
Duke doughtiest in deed by dale and by down,
    Little and much, the more and the less,
All the states of the world is at my behest. (renoun)
    To me shall they give account at my worthy dais.
When Michael his horn bloweth at my dread command,
      (dom)
    The count of their conscience shall put them in press
      And yield a reckoning
    Of their space how they have spent;
    And of their true talent,
    At my great Judgment,
      An answer shall me bring.

Ecce! requiram gregem meum de manu pastorum.
(Behold! I require my flock at the hand of the shepherds.)
And I shall inquire of my flock and of their pasture,
    How they have lived and led their people subject.
      (soiet)
The good on the right side shall stand full sure;
    The bad on the left side there shall I set.
The seven deeds of mercy, whoso was used (had ure)
    To fulfill: the hungry for to give meat;
Or drink to the thirsty; the naked, vesture;
    The poor of the pilgrim home for to fetch; (fette)
      Thy neighbor that hath need;

Whoso doth mercy, according to his ability, (myth)
To the sick, or in prison put, (pyth)
He doth to me—I shall him requite: (quyth)
  Heaven's bliss shall be his meed.

*Et qui bona egerunt, ibunt in vitam eternam: qui vero
mala, in ignem eternum.*
(And whoso does good, they will go to eternal life; ver-
ily, who does evil, to eternal flames.)
And they that well do in this world here, wealthy shall
          awake;
  In heaven they shall be hailed in bounty and in bliss;
And they that evil do, they shall to hell's lake,
  In bitter bales to be burned; my judgment it is.
My virtues in heaven then shall they quake:
  There is no wight in the world that may escape this!
All men example hereat may take
  To maintain the good and mend what's amiss.
(*To the audience*)
        Thus endeth our play! (gamys)
      To save you from sinning,
      Ever at the beginning,
      Think on your last ending!
        Te, Deum, laudamus!

  The curtains close on all the scaffolds.

Everyman

Here beginneth a treatise how the High Father of Heaven sendeth death to summon every creature to come and give account of their lives in this world and is in manner of a moral play.

Since the play is about Everyman, the scene is actually anywhere. When performed on the steps of a cathedral, it had the advantage of a majestic background which reinforced the moral of the play. When performed on a stage, whether fixed or mobile, it might have been backed up by a tapestry depicting an outdoor scene. Off to one side is the opening of a sepulchre, as a constant reminder of the transitoriness of human life.

The play is announced by a Messenger, dressed as a herald in a dark-colored tunic with filigreed gold stripes, belted and covering more than half his upper legs which are clad in hose. He wears nimble-looking slippers on his feet. A medium-brimmed, loose velvet hat trimmed with feathers adds to his heraldic and official bearing. He carries a long golden trumpet on which he sounds a fanfare to command the attention of the audience. When comparative silence seems assured, he opens the play in grave and measured accents.

MESSENGER:
I pray you all give your audience,
And hear this matter with reverence,
By figure a moral play—
The *Summoning of Everyman* called it is,
That of our lives and ending shows
How transitory we be all day.
This matter is wondrous precious,

But the intent of it is more gracious,
And sweet to bear away.
The story saith,—Man, in the beginning,
Look well, and take good heed to the ending,
Be you never so gay!
Ye think sin in the beginning full sweet,
Which in the end causeth thy soul to weep,
When the body lieth in clay.
Here shall you see how FELLOWSHIP and JOLLITY,
Both STRENGTH, PLEASURE, and BEAUTY
Will fade from thee as flower in May.
For ye shall hear, how our Heaven King
Calleth EVERYMAN to a general reckoning:
Give audience, and hear what he doth say.

*God enters the stage or appears on a balcony of the
cathedral if there is one. Wearing a long white flowing
gown, he presents a venerable and majestic appearance,
his bearded face suggesting the patriarch Abraham. A
golden halo is suspended over his head.*

GOD:

I perceive here in my majesty
How that all creatures be to me unkind,
Living without dread in worldly prosperity:
Of ghostly sight[1] the people be so blind,
Drowned in sin, they know me not for their God;
In worldly riches is all their mind,
They fear not my righteousness, the sharp rod;
My law that I showed, when I for them died,
They forget clean, and shedding of my blood red;
I hanged between two, it cannot be denied;
To get them life I suffered to be dead;
I healed their feet; with thorns hurt was my head:
I could do no more than I did truly,
And now I see the people do clean forsake me.
They use the seven deadly sins damnable;
As pride, covetise, wrath, and lechery,
Now in the world be made commendable;

---

[1] Spiritual insight.

And thus they leave of angels the heavenly company;
Everyman liveth so after his own pleasure,
And yet of their life they be nothing sure:
I see the more that I them forbear
The worse they be from year to year;
All that liveth appaireth[2] fast,
Therefore I will in all the haste
Have a reckoning of Everyman's person;
For, and [3] I leave the people thus alone
In their life and wicked tempests,
Verily they will become much worse than beasts;
For now one would by envy another up eat;
Charity they all do clean forget.
I hoped well that Everyman
In my glory should make his mansion,
And thereto I had them all elect;[4]
But now I see, like traitors deject,[5]
They thank me not for the pleasure that I to them
     meant,
Nor yet for their being that I them have lent;
I proffered the people great multitude of mercy,
And few there be that asketh it heartily;
They be so cumbered with worldly riches,
That needs on them I must do justice,
On Everyman living without fear.
Where art thou, DEATH, thou mighty messenger?

Death appears dramatically at the entrance of the tomb. A sepulchral figure from his skull-mask to the skeletal bones represented on his tights, he appears to be a walking anatomy, wearing only the tattered suggestion of a monk's hood and gown. He carries a dart, instrument of death, sickle or an hour-glass in his right hand.

DEATH: *(in hollow tones)*
Almighty God, I am here at your will,

---

[2] Degenerates.
[3] If.
[4] Numbered among the Redeemed.
[5] Abject.

Your commandment to fulfil.

GOD: (*raising his hand with austere dignity*)

Go thou to Everyman
And show him in my name
A pilgrimage he must on him take,
Which he in no wise may escape,
And that he bring with him a sure reckoning
Without delay or any tarrying.

DEATH: (*advancing to the center of the stage*)

Lord, I will in the world go run over all
And cruelly outsearch both great and small.
Every man will I beset that liveth beastly
Out of God's laws and dreadeth not folly.
He that loveth riches I will strike with my dart,
His sight to blind, and from heaven to depart,
Except that alms be his good friend,
In hell for to dwell, world without end.

(*Everyman appears a short distance away, walking
casually toward the stage. He is a handsome gentleman
in his early thirties and in the pink of health. Very
much the dandy, he wears a loose velvet cap, falling
over one ear but not completely covering his lustrous
bobbed hair. A loose white shirt with long loose sleeves
is partly revealed beneath his magnificent satin-lined
and fur trimmed tunic, which reaches from his shoulders to a point halfway between hips and knees. His
dark tights terminate in pointed shoes which match the
tunic. He carries a large account book, the record of his
life. God withdraws as he enters.*)

Lo, yonder I see Everyman walking;
Full little he thinketh on my coming;
His mind is on fleshly lusts and his treasure,
And great pain it shall cause him to endure
Before the Lord Heaven King.
Everyman, stand still; Whither art thou going
Thus gaily? Hast thou thy Maker forgot?

*Everyman pauses as if momentarily annoyed by the
petition of a wayside beggar.*

EVERYMAN: (*in an arrogant and contemptuous tone*)

Why askst thou?
Wouldest thou wete? [6]

    DEATH: (*with grave solemnity*)
Yea, sir, I will show you:
In great haste I am sent to thee
From God out of his majesty.

    EVERYMAN: (*troubled and surprised*)
What, sent to me?

    DEATH:
Yea, certainly.
Though thou have forgot him here,
He thinketh on thee in the heavenly sphere,
As, ere we depart, thou shalt know.

    EVERYMAN: (*visibly shaken*)
What desireth God of me?

    DEATH:
That shall I show thee:
A reckoning he will needs have
Without any longer respite.

    EVERYMAN: (*defensively and a trifle beseechingly*)
To give a reckoning longer leisure I crave;
This blind matter troubleth my wit.

    DEATH: (*as Everyman looks uncertainly at his book*)
On thee thou must take a long journey.
Therefore thy book of count with thee thou bring;
For turn again thou cannot by no way,
And look thou be sure of thy reckoning:
For before God thou shalt answer, and show
Thy many bad deeds and good but a few;
How thou hast spent thy life, and in what wise,
Before the Chief Lord of paradise.
Have ado that we were in that way
For, wete thou well, thou shalt make none attournay. [7]

    EVERYMAN:
Full unready I am such reckoning to give.
I know thee not. What messenger art thou?

---

[6] Would you like to know?

[7] Make ready to journey with me, for, know you well, you will
have no attorney.

DEATH: (*opening his robe to reveal more of the skele-
ton*)
I am Death that no man dreadeth.[8]
For every man I arrest and no man spareth;
For it is God's commandment
That all to me should be obedient.

EVERYMAN: (*stunned by the impact of sudden reali-
zation, his manner now conciliatory and ingratiating*)
O Death, thou comest when I had thee least in mind;
In thy power it lieth me to save,
Yet of my good will I give thee, if ye will be kind;
Yea, a thousand pound shalt thou have,
And defer this matter till another day.

DEATH: (*in a stern and peremptory manner*)
I set not by gold, silver, nor riches,
Nor by pope, emperor, king, duke, nor princes.
For and I would receive gifts great,
All the world I might get;
But my custom is clean contrary.
I give thee no respite: come hence, and not tarry.

EVERYMAN: (*his tone now desperate and beseeching*)
Alas, shall I have no longer respite?
I may say Death giveth no warning:
To think on thee, it maketh my heart sick,
For all unready is my book of reckoning.
But twelve year, and I might have abiding,[9]
My counting book I would make so clear
That my reckoning I should not need to fear.
Wherefore, Death, I pray thee, for God's mercy,
Spare me till I be provided of remedy.

DEATH:
Thee availeth not to cry, weep, and pray,
But haste thee lightly that thou wert gone the journey,
And prove thy friends if thou can.
For, wete thou well, the tide abideth no man,[10]
And in the world each living creature

---

[8] Death, who dreads no man.

[9] If I might have a stay of but twelve years.

[10] Time, or tide, waits for no man.

For Adam's sin must die of nature.

EVERYMAN: (*urgently but with faltering hope*)
Death, if I should this pilgrimage take,
And my reckoning surely make,
Show me, for saint charity,
Should I not come again shortly?

DEATH: (*abruptly*)
No, Everyman; and thou be once there,
Thou mayst never more come here,
Trust me, verily.

EVERYMAN:
O gracious God in the high seat celestial,
Have mercy on me in this most need!
Shall I have no company from this vale terrestrial
Of mine acquaintance that way me to lead?

DEATH:
Yea, if any be so hardy
That would go with thee and bear thee company.
Hie[11] thee that thou wert gone to God's magnificence,
Thy reckoning to give before his presence.
What, weenest[12] thou thy life is given thee,
And thy worldly goods also?

EVERYMAN: (*in a state of bewilderment*)
I had wend so, verily.

DEATH:
Nay, nay; it was but lent thee;
For as soon as thou art go,[13]
Another a while shall have it, and then go therefro
Even as thou hast done.
Everyman, thou art mad; thou hast thy wits five,
And here on earth will not amend thy life,
For suddenly I do come.

EVERYMAN: (*wildly looking about in panic*)
O wretched caitiff,[14] whither shall I flee,
That I might scape this endless sorrow!

---

[11] Hurry.
[12] Thinkest. *Wend* (below) is the past tense.
[13] Gone.
[14] Despicable person.

(to Death, in abject entreaty)
Now, gentle Death, spare me till tomorrow
That I may amend me
With good advisement.
   DEATH: *(raising his dart)*
Nay, thereto I will not consent,
Nor no man will I respite;
But to the heart suddenly I shall smite
Without any advisement.
And now out of thy sight I will me hie;
See thou make thee ready shortly,
For thou mayst say this is the day
That no man living may scape away.
   Death turns abruptly and stalks off, disappearing inside the sepulchre.
   EVERYMAN: *(in anguished tones)*
Alas, I may well weep with sighs deep;
Now have I no manner of company
To help me in my journey and me to keep;
And also my writing is full unready.
How shall I do now for to excuse me?
I would to God I had never be gete! [15]
To my soul a full great profit it had be;
For now I fear pains huge and great.
The time passeth; Lord, help, that all wrought! [16]
For though I mourn, it availeth nought.
The day passeth, and is almost a-go;
I wot not well what for to do.
To whom were I best my complaint to make?
What, and I to Fellowship thereof spake,
And showed him of this sudden chance?
For in him is all mine affiance;[17]
We have in the world so many a day
Be on good friends in sport and play.
   (Fellowship is seen approaching Everyman. Perhaps a trifle younger, he is very much like Everyman in ap-

----

[15] Begotten.
[16] Lord who created all things, help!
[17] Trust.

*pearance except that his dress is more gaudy. He wears
a jaunty feather in his cap and carries a lute suspended
from his neck by a broad gold band.*)

I see him yonder, certainly;

I trust that he will bear me company;

Therefore to him will I speak to ease my sorrow.

(*calling out*)

Well met, good Fellowship, and good morrow!

　FELLOWSHIP: (*coming up to him and grasping his
hand*)

Everyman, good morrow by this day.

Sir, why lookest thou so piteously?

If any thing be amiss, I pray thee, me say,

That I may help to remedy.

　EVERYMAN: (*groaning*)

Yea, good Fellowship, yea,

I am in great jeopardy.

　FELLOWSHIP:

My true friend, show to me your mind;

I will not forsake thee, unto my life's end,

In the way of good company.

　EVERYMAN: (*brightening but betraying some dubious-
　　　　　ness*)

That was well spoken, and lovingly.

　FELLOWSHIP:

Sir, I must needs know your heaviness;

I have pity to see you in any distress;

If any have you wronged ye shall revenged be,

Though I on the ground be slain for thee,—

Though that I know before that I should die.

　EVERYMAN:

Verily, Fellowship, gramercy.[18]

　FELLOWSHIP: (*heartily*)

Tush! by thy thanks I set not a straw.

Show me your grief, and say no more.

　EVERYMAN:

If I my heart should to you break,

---

[18] Thank you.

And then you to turn your mind from me,
And would not me comfort, when you hear me speak,
Then should I ten times sorrier be.

FELLOWSHIP:
Sir, I say as I will do in deed.

EVERYMAN:
Then be you a good friend at need:
I have found you true here before.

FELLOWSHIP:
And so ye shall evermore;
For, in faith, and thou go to Hell,
I will not forsake thee by the way!

EVERYMAN:
Ye speak like a good friend; I believe you well;
I shall deserve it, and I may.[19]

FELLOWSHIP: (*with gusty off-handedness*)
I speak of no deserving, by this day.[20]
For he that will say and nothing do
Is not worthy with good company to go;
Therefore show me the grief of your mind,
As to your friend most loving and kind.

EVERYMAN:
I shall show you how it is;
Commanded I am to go a journey,
A long way, hard and dangerous,
And give strait count without delay
Before the high judge Adonai.
Wherefore I pray you, bear me company,
As ye have promised, in this journey.

FELLOWSHIP: (*stepping back as if having been struck*)
That is matter indeed! Promise is duty,
But, and I should take such a voyage on me,
I know it well, it would be to my pain:
Also it make me afeard, certain.
But let us take counsel here as well as we can,
For your words would fear[21] a strong man.

---

[19] I shall make it up to you, if I have an opportunity.
[20] A mild oath.
[21] Frighten.

EVERYMAN:

Why, ye said, if I had need,
Ye would me never forsake, quick nor dead,
Though it were to hell truly.

FELLOWSHIP: (*evasively*)

So I said, certainly,
But such pleasures be set aside, thee sooth to say;[22]
And also, if we took such a journey,
When should we come again?

EVERYMAN: (*slowly and solemnly*)

Nay, never again till the day of doom.

FELLOWSHIP: (*throwing up his hands*)

In faith, then will not I come there!
Who hath you these tidings brought?

EVERYMAN:

Indeed, Death was with me here.

FELLOWSHIP: (*turning as if to leave, his bland amiability transformed into impatient irritation*)

Now, by God that all hath bought,[23]
If Death were the messenger,
For no man that is living today
I will not go that loath journey—
Not for the father that begat me!

EVERYMAN: (*holding his arm to detain him*)

Ye promised otherwise, pardie.[24]

FELLOWSHIP:

I wot well I say so truly;
And yet if thou wilt eat, and drink, and make good
    cheer,
Or haunt to women, the lusty company,
I would not forsake you, while the day is clear,
Trust me, verily!

EVERYMAN:

Yea, thereto ye would be ready;
To go to mirth, solace, and play,
Your mind will sooner apply

---

[22] To tell you the truth.
[23] Redeemed.
[24] A mild version of "by God."

Than to bear me company in my long journey.

FELLOWSHIP: (*vehemently*)

Now, in good faith, I will not that way.
But and thou wilt murder, or any man kill,
In that I will help thee with a good will!

EVERYMAN: (*beseechingly*)

O that is a simple advice indeed.
Gentle fellow, help me in my necessity;
We have loved long, and now I need,
And now, gentle Fellowship, remember me.

FELLOWSHIP:

Whether ye have loved me or no,
By Saint John, I will not with thee go.

EVERYMAN: (*in anguished pleading*)

Yet I pray thee, take the labor, and do so much for me
To bring me forward,[25] for saint charity.
And comfort me till I come without the town.

FELLOWSHIP: (*pulling away*)

Nay, and thou would give me a new gown,
I will not a foot with thee go;
But and you had tarried I would not have left thee so.
And as now, God speed thee in thy journey,
Far from thee I will depart as fast as I may.

EVERYMAN: (*As Fellowship edges away, he puts a hand
    on his arm to restrain him.*)

Whither away, Fellowship? Will you forsake me?

FELLOWSHIP:

Yea, by my fay,[26] to God I betake[27] thee.

EVERYMAN:

Farewell, good Fellowship; for this my heart is sore;
Adieu for ever: I shall see thee no more.

FELLOWSHIP: (*as he walks hastily off*)

In faith, Everyman, farewell now at the end;
For you I will remember that parting is mourning.

EVERYMAN: (*looking after the departing figure*)

Alack! Shall we thus depart indeed?

---

[25] To start me on my journey.

[26] Faith.

[27] Commend.

Our Lady, help, without any more comfort,
Lo, Fellowship forsaketh me in my most need:
For help in this world whither shall I resort?
Fellowship herebefore with me would merry make;
And now little sorrow for me doth he take.
It is said, in prosperity men friends may find,
Which in adversity be full unkind.
Now whither for succor shall I flee
Since that Fellowship hath forsaken me?
To my kinsmen I will truly,
Praying them to help me in my necessity;
I believe that they will do so,
For kind will creep where it may not go.[28]
I will go say,[29] for yonder I see them.
Where be ye now, my friends and kinsmen?

During the last two lines, Cousin and Kindred approach. Representing Everyman's relatives, they may be visualized as well-dressed, established people, somewhat over middle age. Cousin, a man, wears clothing much like Everyman's though somewhat more subdued to indicate his status as a "solid citizen." Kindred, a woman, is garbed in a relatively sober loose-fitting medieval gown, made of costly material richly embroidered at the hem.

KINDRED: (*with a ceremonious curtsey*)
Here we be now at your commandment.
Cousin, I pray you show us your intent
In any wise, and not spare.

COUSIN: (*with masculine heartiness*)
Yea, Everyman, and to us declare
If ye be disposed to go any whither,
Fore wete[30] you well, we will live and die together.

KINDRED:
In wealth and woe we will with you hold,

---

[28] Natural instinct will creep where it can't walk. The intent of Everyman's use of the proverb is somewhat obscure. He seems to mean that if he cannot have his choice of companionship (Fellowship), he will have to settle for what is available (relatives).

[29] Try.

[30] Know.

For over his kin a man may be bold.

    EVERYMAN: *(with a deeply troubled expression)*
Gramercy, my friends and kinsmen kind.
Now shall I show you the grief of my mind:
I was commanded by a messenger
That is an high king's chief officer;
He bade me go a pilgrimage to my pain,
And I know well I shall never come again;
Also I must give a reckoning straight,
For I have a great enemy, that hath me in wait,
Which intendeth me for to hinder.

    KINDRED: *(still sympathetic but a trifle more remote)*
What account is that which ye must render?
That would I know.

    EVERYMAN: *(pointing to his book)*
Of all my works I must show
How I have lived and my days spent;
Also of ill deeds that I have used
In my time since life was me lent;
And of all virtues that I have refused.
Therefore I pray you go thither with me,
To help to make mine account, for saint charity.

    COUSIN: *(with a derisive guffaw at the absurdity of the
        suggestion)*
What, to go thither? Is that the matter? [31]
Nay, Everyman, I had liefer fast bread and water
All this five year and more.

    EVERYMAN:
Alas, that ever I was bore!
For now shall I never be merry
If that you forsake me.

    KINDRED: *(encouragingly)*
Ah, sir; what, ye be a merry man!
Take good heart to you, and make no moan.
But one thing I warn you, by Saint Anne,
As for me, ye shall go alone.

    EVERYMAN: *(directly and bluntly)*
My Cousin, will you not with me go?

---

[31] Proposal.

COUSIN: *(moving off slightly with a limping gait)*
No, by our Lady: I have the cramp in my toe.
Trust not to me, for, so God me speed,
I will deceive you in your most need.

KINDRED:
It availeth not us to tice.[32]
Ye shall have my maid with all my heart;
She loveth to go to feasts, there to be nice,[33]
And to dance, and abroad to start:
I will give her leave to help you in that journey
If that you and she may agree.

EVERYMAN: *(angrily)*
Now show me the very effect of your mind.
Will you go with me, or abide behind?

KINDRED: *(turning to go)*
Abide behind? Yea, that I will and [34] I may!
Therefore farewell until another day.
　　She exits abruptly with a touch of offended dignity.

EVERYMAN: *(bowing his head)*
How should I be merry or glad?
For fair promises to me make,
But when I have most need, they me forsake.
I am deceived; that maketh me sad.

COUSIN: *(in a brusque, businesslike tone)*
Cousin Everyman, farewell now,
For verily I will not go with you;
Also of mine own an unready reckoning
I have to account; therefore I make tarrying.
Now, God keep thee, for now I go.
　　He goes off quickly, forgetting his limp.

EVERYMAN: *(sighing mournfully)*
Ah, Jesus, is all come hereto?
Lo, fair words maketh fools feign;
They promise and nothing will do certain.
My kinsmen promised me faithfully
For to abide with me steadfastly,

---

[32] Entice.
[33] Foolish or wanton.
[34] If.

And now fast away do they flee:
Even so Fellowship promised me.
What friend were best me of to provide?
I lose my time here longer to abide.
Yet in my mind a thing there is;—
All my life I have loved riches;
If that my good now help me might,
He would make my heart full light.
I will speak to him in this distress.—
(*turning around and calling*)
Where art thou, my Goods and riches?

Rising from the left rear corner of the stage, where he has been concealed behind crates and bales of merchandise, the roly-poly figure of Goods peers over the barricade of earthly treasures. He wears a kind of turban covered with gold coins so loosely attached that they jingle when he moves his head.

GOODS: (*in a colorless, brazen voice*)
Who calleth me? Everyman? What haste thou hast.
I lie here in corners, trussed and piled so high,
And in chests I am locked so fast,
Also sacked in bags, thou mayst see with thine eye,
I cannot stir; in packs low I lie.
What would ye have, lightly me say.

EVERYMAN: (*in a commanding tone*)
Come hither, Goods, in all the haste thou may,
For of counsel I must desire thee.

With difficulty, Goods lifts his corpulent body to surmount the pile and struggles uncertainly over the bales and boxes toward Everyman. He is further hampered by his long, heavy, purple velvet gown and by the fact that his hands are rendered useless because each one clutches a bag of gold. He collapses immediately upon reaching Everyman's side.

GOODS: (*gasping and wheezing*)
Sir, and ye in the world have trouble or adversity,
That can I help you to remedy shortly.

EVERYMAN: (*as if explaining to a subordinate*)
It is another disease that grieveth me;

In this world it is not, I tell thee so.
I am sent for another way to go,
To give a straight account general
Before the highest Jupiter of all;
And all my life I have had joy and pleasure in thee.
Therefore I pray thee go with me,
For, peradventure, thou mayst before God Almighty
My reckoning help to clean and purify;
For it is said ever among
That money maketh all right that is wrong.

GOODS:

Nay, Everyman, I sing another song.
I follow no man in such voyages;
For and I went with thee
Thou shouldst fare much the worse for me;
For because on me thou did set thy mind,
Thy reckoning I have made blotted and blind,
That thine account thou cannot make truly;
And that hast thou for the love of me.

EVERYMAN:

That would grieve me full sore,
When I should come to that fearful answer.
(*peremptorily*)
Up, let us go thither together.

GOODS: (*making no effort to rise*)

Nay, not so, I am too brittle, I may not endure;
I will follow no man one foot, be ye sure.

EVERYMAN: (*puzzled and bemused*)

Alas, I have thee loved, and had great pleasure
All my life-days on good and treasure.

GOODS:

That is to thy damnation, without lesing,[35]
For my love is contrary to the love everlasting.
But if thou had me loved moderately during,
As to the poor give part of me,[36]
Then shouldst thou not in this dolor be,
Nor in this great sorrow and care.

---

[35] Lying.
[36] As to have given part of me to the poor.

EVERYMAN: (*heavily*)
Lo, now was I deceived ere I was ware,[37]
And all I may wyte[38] my spending of time.
GOODS:
What, weenest[39] thou that I am thine?
EVERYMAN:
I had wend so.
GOODS:
Nay, Everyman, I say no;
As for a while I was lent thee,
A season thou hast had me in prosperity;
My condition is man's soul to kill;
If I save one, a thousand I do spill;
Weenest thou that I will follow thee?
Nay, from this world, not verily.
EVERYMAN:
I had wend otherwise.
GOODS: (*coldly and relentlessly*)
Therefore to thy soul Good is a thief;
For when thou art dead, this is my guise
Another to deceive in the same wise
As I have done thee, and all to his soul's reprief.[40]
EVERYMAN: (*emerging from his stupor, and raging*)
O false Good, cursed thou be!
Thou traitor to God, that hast deceived me.
And caught me in thy snare.
GOODS: (*unmoved*)
Marry, thou brought thyself in care,
Whereof I am glad,
I must needs laugh; I cannot be sad.
EVERYMAN: (*in a sudden transition from railing to pleading as he kneels beside Goods and holds out his hands in entreaty*)
Ah, Good, thou hast had long my hearty love;
I gave thee that which should be the Lord's above.

---

[37] Before I was aware.
[38] Blame.
[39] Thinkest. *Wend* in the next line is the past tense, *thought*.
[40] Reproach.

But wilt thou not go with me in deed?
I pray thee truth to say.

GOODS: (*laboriously getting on his feet*)
No, so God me speed,
Therefore farewell, and have good day.

Without ceremony, he heaves his way back over the barricade and disappears.

EVERYMAN: (*looking distractedly about the stage, then moving forward to address the audience*)
O to whom shall I make my moan
For to go with me in that heavy journey?
First Fellowship said he would with me gone;
His words were very pleasant and gay,
But afterwards he left me alone.
Then spake I to my kinsmen all in despair,
And also they gave me words fair;
They lacked no fair speaking,
But all forsake me in the ending.
Then went I to my Goods that I loved best
In hope to have comfort, but there had I least;
For my Goods sharply did me tell
That he bringeth many into hell.
Then of myself I was ashamed,
And so I am worthy to be blamed;
Thus may I well myself hate.
Of whom shall I now counsel take?
I think that I shall never speed
Till that I go to my Good-Deeds,
But alas, she is so weak
That she can neither go nor speak;
Yet will I venture on her now.—

(*Wearily pulling himself together and as if benumbed by woe, he moves gropingly about the stage.*)
My Good-Deeds, where be you?

Unobserved by the audience until now, a slight figure wrapped in the white habit of a nun has been lying at the rear right corner of the stage. From beneath her hood, her head rising slightly and weakly from the ground, comes a weak, exhausted voice.

GOOD-DEEDS:

Here I lie cold on the ground;

Thy sins hath me sore bound,

That I cannot stir.

EVERYMAN: (*staggering to her side and kneeling*)

O, Good-Deeds, I stand in fear;

I must you pray of counsel,

For help now should come right well.

GOOD-DEEDS: (*in a gentle, benign voice*)

Everyman, I have understanding

That ye be summoned account to make

Before Messias, of Jerusalem King;

And you do by me,[41] that journey with you will I take.

EVERYMAN: (*with bowed head*)

Therefore I come to you my moan to make;

I pray you, that ye will go with me.

GOOD-DEEDS: (*struggling to sit up*)

I would full fain, but I cannot stand verily.

EVERYMAN:

Why, is there anything on you fall? [42]

GOOD-DEEDS: (*abandoning the attempt to sit up, and leaning weakly on one arm*)

Yea, sir, I may thank you of all;

If ye had perfectly cheered me,

Your book of account now full ready had be.

Look, the books of your works and deeds eke;[43]

Oh, see how they lie under the feet,

To your soul's heaviness.

Our Lord Jesus, help me!

EVERYMAN: (*picking up his book and opening it*)

For one letter here I cannot see.[44]

GOOD-DEEDS: (*in a quiet admonitory tone*)

There is a blind reckoning in time of distress!

EVERYMAN: (*frantically*)

Good-Deeds, I pray you, help me in this need,

---

[41] If you accept my advice.

[42] Has anything happened to you?

[43] Also.

[44] For I cannot make out a single letter.

Or else I am for ever damned indeed;
Therefore help me to make reckoning
Before the redeemer of all things,
That king is, and was, and ever shall.

GOOD-DEEDS:

Everyman, I am sorry of your fall,
And fain would I help you, and I were able.

EVERYMAN: (*with the deepest humility*)

Good-Deeds, your counsel I pray you give me.

GOOD-DEEDS:

That shall I do verily;
Though that on my feet I may not go.
I have a sister, that shall with you also,
Called Knowledge, which shall with you abide
To help you to make that dreadful reckoning.

As if mystically summoned, there enters a magnificent queenly figure, wearing a royal diadem and richly figured royal robes of state. She approaches and stands over Everyman, looking down at him.

KNOWLEDGE: (*in slow, measured accents*)

Everyman, I will go with thee, and be thy guide,
In thy most need to go by thy side.

EVERYMAN: (*rising and looking toward heaven*)

In good condition I am now in every thing,
And am wholly content with this good thing;
Thanked be God my Creator.

GOOD-DEEDS: (*in a stronger voice*)

And when she hath brought you there
Where thou shalt heal thee of thy smart,
Then go with your reckoning and your Good-Deeds
    together
For to make you joyful at heart
Before the blessed Trinity.

EVERYMAN:

My Good-Deeds, gramercy!
I am well content, certainly,
With your words sweet.

KNOWLEDGE:

Now go we together lovingly

To Confession, that cleansing river.

EVERYMAN: (*tremulously*)

For joy I weep; I would we were there;
But, I pray you, give me cognition
Where dwelleth that holy man Confession.

KNOWLEDGE:

In the house of salvation:
We shall find him in that place,
That shall us comfort by God's grace.

(*Knowledge takes Everyman by the arm and leads him to a representation of a hermit's cell, from which a coarsely clad monk emerges. The monk carries a scourge. A rosary hangs from the cord which pulls his rough gown together at the waist.*)

Lo, this is Confession; kneel down and ask mercy,
For he is in good conceit[45] with God Almighty.

EVERYMAN: (*kneeling*)

O glorious fountain that all uncleanness doth clarify,
Wash from me the spots of vices unclean,
That on me no sin may be seen;
I come with Knowledge for my redemption,
Repent with hearty and full contrition;
For I am commanded a pilgrimage to take,
And great accounts before God to make.
Now, I pray you, Shrift, mother of salvation,
Help my good deeds for my piteous exclamation.

CONFESSION: (*in a liturgically modulated voice*)

I know your sorrow well. Everyman;
Because with Knowledge ye come to me,
I will you comfort as well as I can,
And a precious jewel I will give thee,
Called penance, wise voider of adversity;
Therewith shall your body chastised be
With abstinence and perseverance in God's service:
(*holding out the scourge which Everyman takes*)
Here shall you receive that scourge of me
Which is penance strong that ye must endure

---

[45] Esteem.

To remember thy Savior was scourged for thee
With sharp scourges, and suffered it patiently;
So must thou, or thou escape that painful pilgrimage;
Knowledge, keep him in this voyage,
And by that time Good-Deeds will be with thee.
But in any wise, be sure of mercy,
For your time draweth fast, and ye will saved be,
Ask God mercy, and He will grant truly,
When with the scourge of penance man doth him bind,
The oil of forgiveness then shall he find.

EVERYMAN: (*gazing at the scourge which he raises aloft*)
Thanked be God for his gracious work!
For now I will my penance begin;
This hath rejoiced and lighted my heart,
Though the knots be painful and hard within.

KNOWLEDGE: (*taking the scourge and examining it*)
Everyman, look your penance that ye fulfil,
What pain that ever it to you be,
And Knowledge shall give you counsel at will
How your accounts ye shall make clearly.

EVERYMAN: (*slowly taking off his rich tunic*)
O eternal God, O heavenly figure,
O way of rightwiseness, O goodly vision,
Which descended down in a virgin pure
Because he would Everyman redeem,
Which Adam forfeited by his disobedience;
O blessed Godhead, elect and high-divine,
Forgive my grievous offence;
Here I cry thee mercy in this presence.
O ghostly treasure, O ransomer and redeemer
Of all the world, hope and conductor,
Mirror of joy, and founder of mercy,
Which illumineth heaven and earth thereby,
Hear my clamorous complaint, though it late be;
Receive my prayers; unworthy in this heavy life
Though I be, a sinner most abominable,
Yet let my name be written in Moses' table;
O Mary, pray to the Maker of all thing,

Me for to help at my ending,
And save me from the power of my enemy,
For Death assaileth me strongly;
And, Lady, that I may be means of thy prayer
Of your Son's glory to be partaker,
By the means of his passion I it crave,
I beseech you, help my soul to save.—
(*rising with his book in his left hand*)
Knowledge, give me the scourge of penance;
My flesh therewith shall give a quittance;
I will now begin, if God give me grace.

KNOWLEDGE: (*giving him the scourge*)
Everyman, God give you time and space;
Thus I bequeath you in the hands of our Savior,
Thus may you make your reckoning sure.

EVERYMAN: (*advancing to the front of the stage with Knowledge beside him as Confession retires into his cell*)
In the name of the Holy Trinity,
My body sore punished shall be:
(*With his right hand, he lashes his back furiously. During the scourging, Good-Deeds rises gradually to her feet.*)
Take this, body, for the sin of the flesh!
Also thou delightest to go gay and fresh,
And in the way of damnation thou did me bring;
Therefore suffer now strokes and punishing.
Now of penance I will wade the water clear
To save me from purgatory, that sharp fire.

GOOD-DEEDS: (*standing upright and taking a step*)
I thank God, now I can walk and go,
And am delivered of my sickness and woe.
Therefore with Everyman I will go, and not spare;
His good works I will help him to declare.

KNOWLEDGE: (*as Good-Deeds moves toward Everyman*)
Now, Everyman, be merry and glad;
Your Good-Deeds cometh now; ye may not be sad;
Now is your Good-Deeds whole and sound,
Going upright upon the ground.

EVERYMAN: *(renewing his scourging)*
My heart is light, and shall be evermore;
Now will I smite faster than I did before.

GOOD-DEEDS: *(raising her right hand in blessing)*
Everyman, pilgrim, my special friend,
Blessed be thou without end;
For thee is prepared the eternal glory.
Ye have me made whole and sound,
Therefore I will bide by thee in every sound.[46]

EVERYMAN: *(giving her his book)*
Welcome, my Good-Deeds; now I hear thy voice,
I weep for very sweetness of love.

KNOWLEDGE:
Be no more sad, but ever rejoice,
God seeth thy living in his throne above;
(holding out a long white garment, the robe of contrition)
Put on this garment to thy behove,[47]
Which is wet with your tears,
Or else before God you may it miss
When you to your journey's end come shall.

EVERYMAN: *(taking the robe and examining it curiously)*
Gentle Knowledge, what do you it call?

KNOWLEDGE:
It is a garment of sorrow:
From pain it will you borrow;
(gently relieving Everyman of his scourge)
Contrition it is,
That getteth forgiveness;
It pleaseth God passing well.

GOOD-DEEDS: *(helping him on with the robe)*
Everyman, will you wear it for your heal?

EVERYMAN:
Now blessed be Jesu, Mary's Son!
For now have I on true contrition.
And let us go now without tarrying;

---

[46] Season.
[47] For your good.

Good-Deeds, have we clear our reckoning?

GOOD-DEEDS: *(indicating his book of reckoning)*

Then I trust we need not fear;

Now, friends, let us not part in twain.

KNOWLEDGE: *(holding up the scourge)*

Nay, Everyman, that will we not, certain.

GOOD-DEEDS:

Yet must thou lead with thee

Three persons of great might.

EVERYMAN:

Who should they be?

GOOD-DEEDS:

Discretion and Strength they hight,[48]

And thy Beauty may not abide behind.

KNOWLEDGE:

Also ye must call to mind

Your Five-Wits as for your counselors.

GOOD-DEEDS:

You must have them ready at all hours.

EVERYMAN:

How shall I get them hither?

KNOWLEDGE:

You must call them all together,

And they will hear you incontinent.

EVERYMAN: *(calling)*

My friends, come hither and be present:

Discretion, Strength, my Five-Wits, and Beauty.

In answer to his call, these representations of Everyman's natural attributes approach in a body. Beauty is represented by a beautiful young woman, lavishly gowned in velvets, satins with jewelled embroidery, and abundant fripperies, all subtly erotic in tone. Discretion is an older man wearing the clerical robes of a Christian scholar. Strength is a young woman, robed in white and carrying an unsheathed sword. Five-Wits wears the traditional costume of a court jester.

BEAUTY:

Hear at your will we be all ready.

---

[48] Are called.

What will ye that we should do?

GOOD-DEEDS:

That ye would with Everyman go
And help him in his pilgrimage;
Advise you, will ye with him or not in that voyage?

STRENGTH:

We will bring him all thither,
To his help and comfort, ye may believe me.

DISCRETION:

So will we go with him all together.

EVERYMAN:

Almighty God, loved thou be,
I give thee laud that I have hither brought
Strength, Discretion, Beauty, and Five-Wits; lack I
    nought;
And my Good-Deeds, with Knowledge clear,
All be in my company at my will here;
I desire no more to my business.

STRENGTH: *(raising his sword)*

And I, Strength, will by you stand in distress
Though thou would in battle fight on the ground.

FIVE-WITS: *(cutting a caper)*

And though it were through the world round,
We will not depart for sweet nor sour.

BEAUTY: *(caressing him affectionately on the cheek)*

No more will I unto death's hour,
Whatsoever thereof befall.

DISCRETION: *(with heavy solemnity)*

Everyman, advise you first of all;
Go with a good advisement and deliberation;
We all give you virtuous monition
That all shall be well.

EVERYMAN:

My friends, hearken what I will tell:
I pray God reward you in his heavenly sphere.
Now hearken, all that be here,
For I will make my testament
Here before you all present.
In alms half my good I will give with my hands twain

In the way of charity, with good intent,
And the other half still shall remain
In quiet to be returned there it ought to be.
This I do in despite of the fiend of hell
To go quite out of his peril
Ever after and this day.

KNOWLEDGE:

Everyman, hearken what I say;
Go to priesthood, I you advise,
And receive of him in any wise
The holy sacrament and ointment together;
Then shortly see ye turn again hither;
We will all abide you here.

FIVE-WITS:

Yea, Everyman, hie you that ye ready were,
There is no emperor, king, duke, nor baron
That of God hath commission
As hath the least priest in the world being:
For of the blessed sacraments pure and benign
He beareth the keys and thereof hath the cure
For man's redemption, it is ever sure;
Which God for our soul's medicine
Gave us out of his heart with great pine.[49]
Here in this transitory life, for thee and me
The blessed sacraments seven there be,
Baptism, confirmation, with priesthood good,
And the sacrament of God's precious flesh and blood,
Marriage, the holy extreme unction, and penance;
These seven be good to have in remembrance,
Gracious sacraments of high divinity.

EVERYMAN:

Fain would I receive that holy body
And meekly to my ghostly[50] father I will go.
   With bowed head, Everyman goes off.

FIVE-WITS:

Everyman, that is the best that ye can do:
God will you to salvation bring,

---

[49] Suffering.
[50] Spiritual.

For priesthood exceedeth all other thing;
To us Holy Scripture they do teach,
And converteth man from sin heaven to reach;
God hath to them more power given
Than to any angel that is in heaven;
With five words[51] he may consecrate
God's body in flesh and blood to make,
And handleth his maker between his hands;
The priest bindeth and unbindeth all bands,
Both in earth and in heaven;
Thou ministers all the sacraments seven;
Though we kissed thy feet thou were worthy;
Thou art surgeon that cureth sin deadly:
No remedy we find under God
But all only priesthood.
Everyman, God gave priests that dignity,
And setteth them in his stead among us to be;
Thus be they above angels in degree.

    KNOWLEDGE:

If priests be good, it is so surely;
But when Jesus hanged on the cross with great smart
There he gave, out of his blessed heart,
The same sacrament in great torment:
He sold them not to us, that Lord Omnipotent.
Therefore Saint Peter the apostle doth say
That Jesu's curse hath all they
Which God their Savior do buy or sell,
Or they for any money do take or tell.
Sinful priests giveth the sinners example bad;
Their children sitteth by other men's fires,[52] I have
    heard
And some haunteth women's company,
With unclean life, as lusts of lechery:
These be with sin made blind.

    FIVE-WITS:

I trust to God no such may we find;
Therefore let us priesthood honor,

---

[51] *Hoc est enim corpus meum*—"For this is my body."
[52] Their children are by other men's wives.

And follow their doctrine for our souls' succor;
We be their sheep, and they shepherds be
By whom we all be kept in surety.
Peace, for yonder I see Everyman come,
Which hath made true satisfaction.

Everyman re-enters, now holding a cross in front of him.

GOOD-DEEDS:

Methinketh it is he indeed.

EVERYMAN:

Now Jesu be our alder speed.[53]
I have received the sacrament for my redemption,
And then mine extreme unction:
Blessed be all they that counseled me to take it!
And now, friends, let us go without longer respite;
I thank God that ye have tarried so long.
Now set each of you on this rood [54] your hand,
And shortly follow me:
I go before, there I would be; God be our guide.

In spite of Everyman's tone of ringing confidence, they make no effort to touch the cross. Rather, they seem to shrink back.

STRENGTH: *(in a wavering tone which belies his words)*

Everyman, we will not from you go
Till ye have gone this voyage long.

DISCRETION: *(uncertainly)*

I, Discretion, will bide by you also.

KNOWLEDGE: *(with more confidence than the others)*

And though this pilgrimage be never so strong,
I will never part you fro:
Everyman, I will be as sure by thee
As ever I did by Judas Maccabee.[55]

EVERYMAN: *(in a quavering voice)*

Alas, I am so faint I may not stand,
My limbs under me do fold;

---

[53] Our common salvation.
[54] Cross.
[55] Leader of the great Jewish independence movement of the second century B.C.

(*He falls to his knees.*)
Friends, let us not turn again to this land,
Not for all the world's gold.
(*striking the palm of his hand on the earth*)
For into this cave must I creep
And turn to the earth and there to sleep.

BEAUTY:
What, into this grave? Alas!

EVERYMAN: (*trenchantly*)
Yea, there shall *you* consume more and less.

BEAUTY:
And what, should I smother here?

EVERYMAN: (*somberly*)
Yea, by my faith, and never more appear.
In this world live no more we shall,
But in heaven before the highest Lord of all.

BEAUTY:
I cross out all this; adieu by Saint John;
I take my cap in my lap and am gone.[56]

EVERYMAN:
What, Beauty, whither will ye?

BEAUTY:
Peace, I am deaf; I look not behind me,
Not and thou would give me all the gold in thy chest.
   Beauty goes off with a toss of her head.

EVERYMAN:
Alas, whereto may I trust?
Beauty goeth fast away hie;
She promised with me to live and die.

STRENGTH: (*as if giving the matter grave considera-tion*)
Everyman, I will thee also forsake and deny;
Thy game liketh me not at all.

EVERYMAN:
Why, then ye will forsake me all.
Sweet Strength, tarry a little space.

STRENGTH:
Nay, sir, by the rood of grace

---

[56] A proverbial expression meaning to depart quickly.

I will hie me from thee fast,
Though thou weep till thy heart brast.[57]

EVERYMAN: *(beseechingly)*

Ye would ever bide by me, ye said.

STRENGTH: *(hearteningly, as if to a child)*

Yea, I have you far enough conveyed;
Ye be old enough, I understand,
Your pilgrimage to take on hand;
I repent me that I hither came.

EVERYMAN: *(apologetically)*

Strength, you to displease I am to blame;
Will you break promise that is debt?

STRENGTH:

In faith, I care not;
Thou art but a fool to complain,
You spend your speech and waste your brain;
Go thrust thee into the ground.

Strength turns abruptly and leaves.

EVERYMAN: *(gazing gloomily after the departing figure)*

I had wend surer I should you have found.
He that trusteth in his Strength
She him deceiveth at the length.
Both Strength and Beauty forsaketh me,
Yet they promised me fair and lovingly.

DISCRETION: *(casually)*

Everyman, I will after Strength be gone,
As for me I will leave you alone.

EVERYMAN:

Why, Discretion, will ye forsake me?

DISCRETION:

Yea, in faith, I will go from thee,
For when Strength goeth before
I follow after evermore.

EVERYMAN: *(beseechingly)*

Yet, I pray thee, for the love of the Trinity,
Look in my grave once piteously.

---

[57] Burst.

DISCRETION: (*turning sharply away and going off*)
Nay, so nigh will I not come.
Farewell, every one!
  EVERYMAN: (*with growing comprehension*)
O all thing faileth, save God alone;
Beauty, Strength, and Discretion;
For when Death bloweth his blast,
They all run from me full fast.
  FIVE-WITS: (*following Discretion's departure with his eyes*)
Everyman, my leave now of thee I take;
I will follow the other, for here I thee forsake.
  EVERYMAN:
Alas! then may I wail and weep,
For I took you for my best friend.
  FIVE-WITS: (*gambolling off stage*)
I will no longer thee keep;
Now farewell, and there an end.
  EVERYMAN: (*hands raised prayerfully to heaven*)
O Jesu, help, all hath forsaken me!
  GOOD-DEEDS: (*gently placing her hand on his head*)
Nay, Everyman, I will bide with thee,
I will not forsake thee indeed;
Thou shalt find me a good friend at need.
  EVERYMAN: (*reverently raising his eyes toward her*)
Gramercy, Good-Deeds; now may I true friends see;
They have forsaken me every one;
I loved them better than my Good-Deeds alone.
Knowledge, will ye forsake me also?
  KNOWLEDGE: (*in a reassuring tone*)
Yea, Everyman, when ye to death do go:
But not yet for no manner of danger.
  EVERYMAN:
Gramercy, Knowledge, with all my heart.
  KNOWLEDGE:
Nay, yet I will not from hence depart
Till I see where ye shall be come.
  EVERYMAN: (*rising with a sense of determination*)
Methinketh, alas, that I must be gone

To make my reckoning and my debts pay,
For I see my time is nigh spent away.
Take example, all ye that this do hear or see,
How they that I loved best do forsake me,
Except my Good-Deeds that bideth truly.

GOOD-DEEDS:

All earthly things is but vanity:
Beauty, Strength, and Discretion do man forsake,
Foolish friends and kinsmen, that fair spake,
All fleeth save Good-Deeds, and that am I.

EVERYMAN: *(hands again raised in prayer)*

Have mercy on me, God most mighty;
And stand by me, thou Mother and Maid, holy Mary.

GOOD-DEEDS:

Fear not, I will speak for thee.

EVERYMAN:

Here I cry God mercy.

GOOD-DEEDS: *(gently turning Everyman to face the tomb as Death again emerges and stands beside the opening)*

Short our end, and minish our pain;[58]
Let us go and never come again.

EVERYMAN: *(slowly approaching the tomb)*

Into thy hands, Lord, my soul I commend;
Receive it, Lord, that it be not lost;
As thou me boughtest, so me defend,
And save me from the fiend's boast,
That I may appear with that blessed host
That shall be saved at the day of doom.
In manus tuas—of might's most
For ever—*commendo spiritum meum.*[59]

Death reenters the tomb. Everyman and Good-Deeds follow him into the darkness.

KNOWLEDGE: *(addressing the audience)*

Now hath he suffered that we all shall endure;
The Good-Deeds shall make all sure.
Now hath he made ending;

---

[58] Shorten our end and diminish our pain.
[59] Into thy hands I commend my spirit.

Methinketh that I hear angels sing
And make great joy and melody,
Where Everyman's soul received shall be.

An Angel, garbed in gleaming white with a glittering halo, appears where God formerly stood and gazes down at the tomb.

ANGEL:

Come, excellent elect spouse to Jesu:
Hereabove thou shalt go
Because of thy singular virtue:
Now the soul is taken the body fro;
Thy reckoning is crystal-clear.
Now shalt thou into the heavenly sphere,
Unto the which all ye shall come
That liveth well before the day of doom.

As the angel departs, a learned medieval scholar, dressed in cleric's robes, moves to the front of the stage to deliver the epilogue.

DOCTOR:

This moral men may have in mind;
Ye hearers, take it of worth, old and young,
And forsake pride, for he deceiveth you in the end,
And remember Beauty, Five-Wits, Strength, and Discretion,
They all at the last do Everyman forsake,
Save his Good-Deeds, there doth he take.
But beware, and they be small
Before God, he hath no help at all.
None excuse may be there for Everyman:
Alas, how shall he do then?
For after death amends may no man make,
For then mercy and pity do him forsake.
If his reckoning be not clear when he do come,
God will say—*ite maledicti in ignem aeternum.*[60]
And he that hath his account whole and sound,
High in heaven he shall be crowned;

---

[60] Depart, ye accursed, into the eternal fire.

Unto which place God bring us all thither
That we may live body and soul together.
Thereto help the Trinity,
Amen, say ye, for saint charity.

Johan Johan

The staging of this play calls for representation of a room in the home of Johan Johan and his wife Tyb, a street, and the door to the residence of Sir Johan. The most obvious solution would involve the construction of a room (like the late nineteenth century box set) at the rear of the stage, extending from the extreme left nearly all the way across to the right side and with a door opening on its right wall. Sir Johan's door might then open at the extreme right, and the neutral ground frontstage and between the two doors would represent the street.

Most of the action takes place in Johan Johan's combined kitchen-dining-living room. At the back is a raised hearth and a large stone fireplace where a coal fire is burning. The trestles and top of a table are stacked against the left wall near the front; behind them on the same wall are a cupboard and an open washstand with basin on top and pail beneath. Iron pots, a coal skuttle, tongs, shovel, etc. are distributed near the fireplace; a small keg of ale, a jug, earthen or pewter plates, mugs, etc. are in the cupboard.

As the play begins Johan Johan is alone in the room. He is rather short and insignificant in appearance. His loose, belted blouse which hangs to his knees, his twisted black stockings, and his worn sandals make it clear that neither money nor wifely care has been lavished on him. A mud-spattered gown is thrown over his shoulders.

JOHAN: *(addressing the audience)*
God speed you, masters, everyone!
Know ye not whither my wife is gone?
I pray God the devil take her!
For all that I do I can not make her
But she will go a gadding, very much (myche)
Like an Anthony pig,[1] with an old witch
Which leadeth her about hither and thither;
But, by Our Lady, I know not whither.
But, by God's blood, were she come home
Unto this my house, by Our Lady of Crome,
I would beat her ere that I drink.
Beat her, quod a?[2] yea, that she shall stink!
And at every stroke lay her on the ground,
And drag her by the hair about the house round.
I am even mad that I beat her not now.
But I shall reward her heartily well enough; (ynowe)
There is never a wife between heaven and hell
Which was ever beaten half so well.

Beaten, quod a? Yea, but what and she thereof die?
Then I may chance to be hanged shortly.
And when I have beaten her till she smoke
And given her many a hundred stroke,
Think ye that she will amend yet?
Nay, by Our Lady, the devil speed wit!
Therefore I will not beat her at all.

And shall I not beat her? No shall?
When she offendeth and doth amiss,
And keepeth not her house, as her duty is?
Shall I not beat her, if she do so?
Yes, by cock's[3] blood, that shall I do!
I shall beat her and thwack her, I trow,
That she shall beshit the house for very woe.

But yet I think what my neighbor will say then.
(than)

---

[1] St. Anthony, patron saint of shepherds, was frequently represented as accompanied by a pig.

[2] "Said he."

[3] A euphemism for "God's."

He will say thus: "Whom chidest thou, Johan Johan?"
"Mary!" will I say, "I chide my curst wife,
The veriest drab that ever bare life,
Which doth nothing but go and come,
And I cannot make her keep here at home."
Then I think he will say bye and bye:
"Walk her coat,[4] Johan Johan! and beat her heartily!"
But then unto him in answer shall be:
"The more I beat her, the worse is she;
And worse and worse make her I shall!"
    He will say then: "Beat her not at all."
"And why?" shall I say. "This would be known: (wyst)
Is she not mine to chastise as I list?"
    But this is another point worst of all:
The folks will mock me when they hear me brawl.
But, for all that, shall I forbear therefore
To chastise my wife ever the more
And to make her at home for to tarry?
Is not that well done? Yes, by Saint Mary!
That is a point of an honest man
For to beat his wife well now and then. (than)
    Therefore I shall beat her, have ye no dread!
And I ought to beat her till she be stark dead.
And why? By God, because it is my pleasure!
And if I should suffer her, I make you sure,
Nought should avail me, neither staff nor club; (waster)
Within a while she would be my master.
    Therefore I shall beat her, by cock's mother,
Both on the one side and on the other,
Before and behind—nought shall be her remedy— (bote)
From the top of the head to the sole of the foot. (fote)
    But, masters, for God's sake, do not entreat
For her when that she shall be beat;
But, for God's passion, let me alone
And I shall thwack her that she shall groan.
Wherefore I beseech you, and heartily you pray,
And I beseech you say me not nay,

---

4 "Tan her hide."

But that I may beat her for this once.
And I shall beat her, by cock's bones,
That she shall stink like a pole-cat!
But yet, by gog's[5] body, that need not,
For she will stink without any beating;
For every night, once she giveth me a heating,
From her issueth such a stinking smoke
That the savour thereof almost doth me choke.
But I shall beat her now, without fail;
I shall beat her top and tail,
Head, shoulders, arms, legs, and all;
I shall beat her, I trow; that I shall!
And, by gog's body, I tell you true,
I shall beat her till she be black and blue.

But where the devil trow ye she is gone?
I bet a noble[6] she is with Sir Johan.
I fear I am beguiled alway;
But yet, in faith, I hope well nay.
Yet I almost enrage that I cannot (ne can)
See the behavior of our gentlewoman.
And yet, I think, thither as she doth go,
Many an honest wife goeth thither also
For to make some pastime and sport.
But then my wife so oft doth thither resort
That I fear she will make me wear a feather.
But yet I need not for to fear neither, (nether)
For he is her gossip,[7] that is he.

But abide a while! Yet let me see!
Where the devil hath our gossipry begun?
My wife had never child, daughter nor son.

Now if I forbid her that she go no more,
Yet will she choose some other place,
And then the matter is in as ill case.

But in faith, all these words be in waste,
For I think the matter is done and past.
        (*Tyb enters and stands behind Johan, listening with*

---

[5] A euphemism for "God's"
[6] A coin of some value.
[7] A godparent of one's child.

interest. She is a large, vigorous woman, quite fashion-
ably dressed in a long gown caught up on one side at
the waist and wearing a fancy bonnet over her hair
which is braided and coiled around and on top of her
head.)

And when she cometh home she will begin to chide;
But she shall have her payment-stick by her side!
For I shall order her, for all her brawling,
That she shall repent to go caterwauling.

 TYB: *(with a throaty blast that makes Johan jump)*
Why, whom wilt thou beat, I say, thou knave?

 JOHAN: *(turning and almost cringing)*
Who? I, Tyb? None, so God me save.

 TYB: *(menacingly)*
Yes, I heard thee say thou wouldst one beat.

 JOHAN:
Marry, wife, it was stockfish[8] in Thames Street,
Which will be good meat against Lent.
Why, Tyb, what hadst thou thought that I had meant?

 TYB:
Marry, methought I heard thee bawling.
Wilt thou never leave this wauling? [9]
How the devil dost thou thyself behave?
Shall we ever have this work, thou knave?

 JOHAN: *(meekly)*
What? Wife, how sayest thou? Was it well guessed of me
That thou wouldst be come home in safety
As soon as I had kindled a fire?
Come warm thee, sweet Tyb, I thee require.

 TYB: *(suddenly clutching her stomach)*
O, Johan Johan, I am afraid, by this light,
That I shall be sore sick this night.

 JOHAN: *(aside)*
By cock's soul, now, I dare lay a swan
That she comes now straight from Sir Johan!
For ever when she hath fetched of him a lick,[10]

---

[8] Dried fish which needs to be tenderized by beating.

[9] Crying like a cat as in *caterwauling* above.

[10] Had pleasure with him.

Then she comes home and saith she is sick.

TYB: (*sharply*)
What sayest thou?

JOHAN: (*wilting*)
               Marry, I say
It is meet for a woman to go play
Abroad in the town for an hour or two.

TYB: (*as if he were fooling*)
Well, gentleman, go to, go to!

JOHAN: (*wearily*)
Well, let us have no more debate.

TYB: (*aside*)
If he do not fight, chide, and rate,
Brawl, and fare as one that were frantic,
There is nothing that is like him. (may hym lyke)

JOHAN: (*aside*)
If that the parish priest, Sir Johan,
Did not see her now and then
And give her absolution upon a bed,
For woe and pain she would soon be dead.

TYB: (*earnestly*)
For God's sake, Johan Johan, do thee not displease.
Many a time I am ill at ease.
What thinkest now, am not I somewhat sick?

JOHAN: (*aside*)
Now would to God and sweet Saint Dirik,
That thou wert in the water up to the throat,
Or in a burning oven red hot,
To see and I would pull thee out!

TYB: (*teasingly*)
Now, Johan Johan, to put thee out of doubt,
Imagine thou where that I was
Before I came home.

JOHAN: (*with heavy sarcasm*)
                  My guess, (percase)
Thou wast praying in the Church of Paul's
Upon thy knees for all Christian souls.

TYB:
Nay.

JOHAN: (*angrily*)
    Then if thou wast not so holy,
Show me where thou wast, and make no lie.
    TYB:
Truly, Johan Johan, we made a pie,
I and my gossip Margery,
And our gossip the priest, Sir Johan,
And my neighbour's youngest daughter Ann.
The priest paid for the stuff and the making,
And Margery she paid for the baking.
    JOHAN: (*aside*)
By cock's lovely wounds, that same is she
That is the most bawd hence to Coventry.
    TYB:
What say you?
    JOHAN:
                    Marry, answer me to this:
Is not Sir Johan a good man?
    TYB: (*emphatically*)
                               Yes, that he is.
    JOHAN:
Ha, Tyb, if I should not grieve thee,
I have somewhat whereof I would ask thee.
    TYB:
Well, husband, now I do believe (conject)
That thou hast me somewhat in suspect.
But, by my soul, I never go to Sir Johan
But I find him like an holy man;
For either he is saying his devotion
Or else he is going in procession.
    JOHAN: (*aside*)
Yea, round about the bed doth he go,
You two together and no more; (mo)
And for to finish the procession,
He leapeth up and thou lyest down.
    TYB:
What sayest thou?
    JOHAN:
                    Marry, I say he doth well.

For so ought a shepherd to do, as I heard tell,
For the salvation of all his fold.

    TYB: *(with gentle persuasiveness)*
Johan, Johan.

    JOHAN:
               What is it that thou would? (wolde)

    TYB:
By my soul I love thee too too!
And I shall tell thee, ere I further go,
The pie that was made, I have it now here,
And therewith I trust we shall make good cheer.

    JOHAN: *(delighted by the pie which she has produced)*
By cock's body, that is very happy!

    TYB:
But knowest who gave it?

    JOHAN:
               What the devil care I?

    TYB:
By my faith, and I shall say true, then: (than)
The devil take me and it were not Sir Johan.

    JOHAN:
O, hold the peace, wife, and swear no more!
(aside) But I beshrew both your hearts therefore.

    TYB: *(sulkily)*
Yet, peradventure, thou hast suspicion
Of that that was never thought nor done.

    JOHAN:
Tush, wife, let all such matters be.
I love thee well, though thou love not me.
But this pie doth now catch harm.
Let us set it upon the hearth to warm.

    TYB: *(placing the pie on the hearth)*
Then let us eat it as fast as we can.
But because Sir Johan is so honest a man,
I would that he should thereof eat his part.

    JOHAN:
That were reason, I thee ensure.

    TYB:
Then, since that it is thy pleasure,

I pray thee then go to him right
And pray him come sup with us tonight.

JOHAN: (*aside*)

Shall he come hither? By cock's soul, I was accursed
When that I granted to that word first!
But since I have said it I dare not say nay,
For then my wife and I should make a fray;
But when he is come, I swear by God's mother,
I would give the devil the one to carry away the other!

TYB:

What sayest?

JOHAN:

       Marry, he is my curate, I say,
My confessor, and my friend alway.
Therefore go thou and seek him bye and bye,
And till thou come again, I will keep the pie.

TYB: (*affronted*)

Shall I go for him? Nay, I shrew me then! (than)
Go thou and seek as fast as thou can,
And tell him it.

JOHAN:

       Shall I do so?
In faith, it is not meet for me to go.

TYB: (*firmly*)

But thou shalt go tell him, for all that.

JOHAN: (*grimly*)

Then shall I tell him, knowest thou what?
That thou desirest him to come make some cheer.

TYB:

Nay, that thou desirest him to come sup here.

JOHAN:

Nay, by the cross, wife, thou shalt have the worship
And the thanks of thy guest that is thy gossip.

TYB: (*aside*)

Full oft, I see, my husband will me rate
For this hither coming of our gentle curate.

JOHAN:

What sayest, Tyb? Let me hear that again.

TYB:

Marry, I perceive very plain

That thou hast Sir Johan somewhat in suspicion;
    (suspect)

But, by my soul, as far as I conjecture, (conject)

He is virtuous and full of charity.

JOHAN: (*aside*)

In faith, all the town knoweth better—that he

Is a whoremonger, a haunter of all the stews,

An hypocrite, a knave that all men refuse,

A liar, a wretch, a maker of strife—

Better than they know that thou art my good wife.

TYB:

What is that that thou hast said?

JOHAN:

Marry, I would have the table set and laid,

In this place or that, I care not whither.

TYB:

Then go to, bring the trestles hither.

JOHAN:

Abide a while, let me put off my gown!

But yet I am afraid to lay it down

For I fear it shall be soon stolen.

And yet it may lie safe enough unstolen.

It may well lie here, and I list—

(*starting to lay it on the floor*)

But, by cock's soul, here hath a dog pissed!

And if I should lay it on the hearth bare,

It might hap to be burned ere I were 'ware.

(*to one of the audience*)

Therefore I pray you take ye the pain

To keep my gown till I come again.

(*starts to hand it to a member of the audience, then
snatches it back*)

But yet he shall not have it, by my fay;

He is so near the door he might run away.

(*handing it to another member of the audience*)

But because that ye be trusty and sure,

Ye shall keep it, and it be your pleasure;

And because it is soiled at the skirt,
While ye do nothing, scrape off the dirt.
(*to Tyb*)
Lo, now am I ready to go to Sir Johan,
And bid him come as fast as he can.

   TYB: (*as Johan goes towards the door*)
Yea, do so without any tarrying.
But, I say, hark! Thou hast forgot one thing:
Set up the table, and that bye and bye.[11]
(*He obeys meekly, placing the boards on the trestles.*)
Now go thy ways.

   JOHAN:

               I go shortly;
But see your candlesticks be not out of the way.

   TYB: (*as he opens the door to leave*)
Come again and lay the table I say.
(*He returns and puts plates on the table.*)
What! Methinks ye have soon done!

   JOHAN: (*aside*)
Now I pray God that his malediction
Light on my wife and on the bald priest!

   TYB:
Now go thy ways, and hie thee! Seest?

   JOHAN: (*going toward the door again*)
I pray to Christ, if my wish be no sin,
That the priest may break his neck when he comes in.

   TYB: (*as he reaches the door*)
Now come again!

   JOHAN:
What a mischief wilt thou, fool?

   TYB:
Marry, I say, bring hither yonder stool.

   JOHAN: (*taking the stool to her*)
Now go to! A little would make me
For to say thus, "A vengeance take thee!"

   TYB:
Now go to him, and tell him plain

---

[11] Immediately.

That till thou bring him thou wilt not come again.

JOHAN: (*starting out again*)

This pie doth burn here as it doth stand.

TYB: (*as he reaches the door*)

Go wash me these two cups in my hand.

JOHAN: (*after obeying*)

I go, with "a mischief light on thy face!"

TYB: (*cheerfully*)

Go and bid him hie him apace;

And the while I shall all things amend.

JOHAN: (*hungrily eyeing the pie*)

This pie burneth here at this end.

Understandest thou?

TYB:

     Go thy ways, I say!

JOHAN: (*going toward the door again*)

I will go now, as fast as I may.

TYB: (*as he reaches the door*)

How! Come once again: I had forgot.

Look and there be any ale in the pot.

JOHAN: (*dutifully filling the pot with ale*)

Now, a vengeance and a very mischief

Light on the bald priest and on my wife,

On the pot, the ale, and on the table,

The candle, the pie, and all the rabble,

On the trestles, and on the stool!

It is much ado to please a cursed fool.

TYB: (*impatiently*)

Go thy ways now; and tarry no more,

For I am a-hungered very sore.

JOHAN: (*starting to go again*)

Marry, I go.

TYB: (*as he reaches the door*)

    But come once again yet!

Bring hither that bread, lest I forget it.

JOHAN: (*obeying*)

Indeed, it were time for to turn

The pie, for, indeed, it doth burn.

TYB: (*distractedly*)

Lord, how my husband now doth patter,
And of the pie still doth clatter.
Go now, and bid him come away;
I have bid thee an hundred times today.

JOHAN: (*at the door*)

I will not give a straw, I tell you plain,
If that the pie wax cold again—

TYB: (*furiously*)

What! Art thou not gone yet out of this place?
I had thought thou hadst been come again in the space!
But by cock's soul, and I should do these right,
I should break thy knave's head tonight.

JOHAN: (*meekly*)

Nay, then, if my wife be set a-chiding,
It is time for me to go at her bidding.
There is a proverb, which true now proveth:
"He must needs go that the devil driveth."

(*He leaves the house and crosses to the door of Sir
Johan's house where he knocks.*)

How, master curate, may I come in
At your chamber door without any sin?

*The door opens and Sir Johan greets him. The priest
is hearty and well-fed, with more than a suggestion of
roguishness about his eyes.*

SIR JOHAN:

Who is there now that would have me?
What! Johan Johan! What news with thee?

JOHAN: (*bowing*)

Marry, Sir, to tell you shortly,
My wife and I pray you heartily,
And also desire you with all our might,
That ye would come and sup with us tonight.

SIR JOHAN: (*suspiciously*)

Ye must pardon me; in faith I cannot. (ne can)

JOHAN:

Yes, I desire you, good Sir Johan,
Take pain this once. And, yet at the least,
If ye will do nought at my request,
Yet do somewhat for the love of my wife.

SIR JOHAN:

I will not go, for making of strife.
But I shall tell thee what thou shalt do:
Thou shalt tarry and sup with me ere thou go.

JOHAN:

Will ye not go then? Why so?
I pray you tell me, is there any disdain
Or any enmity between you twain?

SIR JOHAN: (*ponderously*)

In faith, to tell thee, between thee and me,
She is as wise a woman as any may be.
I know it well, for I have had the charge
Of her soul, and searched her conscience at large.
I never knew her but honest and wise,
Without any evil or any vice,
Save one fault—I know in her no more—
And because I rebuke her now and then therefor,
She is angry with me and hath me in hate.
And yet that that I do, I do it for your wealth.

JOHAN:

Now God yield it you,[12] good master curate,
And as ye do, so send you your health.
Indeed, I am bound to you a pleasure.

SIR JOHAN: (*thoughtfully*)

Yet thou thinkest amiss, peradventure,
That of her body she should not be a good woman.
But I shall tell thee what I have done, Johan,
For that matter; she and I be sometimes aloft,
And I do lie upon her many a time and oft
To prove her; yet could I never espy
That ever any did worse with her than I.

JOHAN:

Sir, that is the least care I have of nine,
Thanked be God, and your good doctrine.
But if it please you, tell me the matter
And the debate between you and her.

SIR JOHAN:

I shall tell thee, but thou must keep secret.

---

[12] God reward you for it.

JOHAN:

As for that, Sir, I shall not break faith. (let)

SIR JOHAN:

I shall tell thee now the matter plain:
She is angry with me and hath me in disdain
Because that I do her oft entice
To do some penance, after mine advice,
Because she will never leave her wauling,
But always with thee she is chiding and brawling.
And therefore, I know, she hateth my presence.

JOHAN: (*demurring*)

Nay, in good faith, saving your reverence.

SIR JOHAN: (*insistently*)

I know very well she hath me in hate.

JOHAN:

Nay, I dare swear for her, master curate.
(*aside*) But was I not a very knave!
I thought surely, so God me save,
That he had loved my wife for to deceive me.
And now he acquitteth himself; and here I see
He doth as much as he may, for his life,
To curb the debate between me and my wife.

SIR JOHAN:

If ever she did or thought me any ill,
Now I forgive her with my free will.
Therefore, Johan Johan, now get thee home
And thank thy wife, and say I will not come.

JOHAN:

Yet let me know now, good Sir Johan,
Where ye will go to supper then.

SIR JOHAN:

I care not greatly and I tell thee.
On Saturday last I and two or three
Of my friends made an appointment,
And against this night we did assent
That in a place we would sup together.
And one of them said she would bring thither
Ale and bread, and for my part, I
Said that I would give them a pie;

And there I gave them money for the making;
And another said she would pay for the baking;
And so we purpose to make good cheer
For to drive away care and thought.

JOHAN:

Then I pray you, Sir, tell me here,
Whither should all this gear be brought?

SIR JOHAN:

By my faith, and I should not lie,
It should be delivered to thy wife, the pie.

JOHAN:

By God! It is at my house standing by the fire.

SIR JOHAN: (*sternly*)

Who bespake that pie? I thee require.

JOHAN:

By my faith, and I shall not lie,
It was my wife and her gossip Margery
And your good worship called Sir Johan
And my neighbour's youngest daughter Ann;
Your worship paid for the stuff and making,
And Margery she paid for the baking.

SIR JOHAN:

If thou wilt have me now, in faith I will go.

JOHAN:

Yea, marry, I beseech your worship do so.
My wife tarrieth for none but us twain;
She thinketh long ere I come again.

SIR JOHAN: (*with Christian resignation*)

Well now, if she chide me in thy presence
I will be content and take it in patience.

JOHAN: (*blustering*)

By cock's soul, and she once chide,
Or frown, or lower, or look aside,
I shall bring you a staff, as much as I may heave.
Then beat her and spare not! I give you good leave
To chastise her for her shrewish bickering. (varyeng)

They return to Johan's house and enter.

TYB: (*greeting Johan with a pail in her hand*)

The devil take thee for thy long tarrying!

Here is not a whit of water, by my gown,
To wash our hands that we might sit down.
Go and hie as fast as a snail,
And with fair water fill me this pail.

 JOHAN: (*sighing*)
I thank our Lord of his good grace
That I cannot rest long in a place!

 TYB: (*peremptorily*)
Go, fetch water, I say, at a word,
For it is time the pie were on the board;
And go with a vengeance, and say thou art prayed.

 Johan takes the pail and starts toward the door.

 SIR JOHAN: (*going to Tyb and putting his hands on
her hips*)
Ah, good gossip! Is that well said?

 TYB:
Welcome, mine own sweetheart!
We shall make some cheer ere we depart.

 JOHAN: (*hesitating at the door*)
Cock's soul, look how he approacheth near
Unto my wife! This abateth my cheer.

 He sighs and goes out.

 SIR JOHAN: (*releasing her and laughing*)
By God, I would ye had heard the trifles,
The toys, the mocks, the fables, and the nonsense,
  (nyfyls)
That I made thy husband to believe and think!
Thou mightest as well into the earth sink,
As thou couldst forbear laughing any while.

 TYB: (*eagerly—her eyes twinkling*)
I pray thee, let me hear part of that wile.

 SIR JOHAN: (*putting an arm around her*)
Marry, I shall tell thee as fast as I can—
(*Seeing Johan about to enter, he removes his arm.*)
But peace, no more! Yonder cometh thy good man.

 JOHAN: (*bursting in*)
Cock's soul, what have we here!
As far as I saw, he drew very near
Unto my wife.

TYB: (*brusquely*)
> What, art come so soon?

Give us water to wash now; have done.

JOHAN: (*exhibiting an empty pail*)
By cock's soul, it was even now full to the brink,
But it was out again ere I could think;
Whereof I marvelled, by God Almight.
And then I looked between me and the light,
And I spied a cleft, both large and wide.
Lo, wife, here it is on the one side.

TYB: (*demandingly*)
Why dost not stop it?

JOHAN:
> Why, how shall I do it?

TYB: (*as if bored with his stupidity*)
Take a little wax.

JOHAN: (*helplessly*)
> How shall I come to it?

SIR JOHAN: (*reaching into the folds of his gown*)
Marry, here be two wax candles, I say,
Which my gossip Margery gave me yesterday.

TYB: (*disgustedly*)
Tush, let him alone; for, by the cross, (rode)
It is pity to help him or do him good.

SIR JOHAN: (*holding out the candles*)
What! Johan Johan, canst thou make no shift?
Take this wax and stop therewith the cleft. (clyfte)

JOHAN: (*taking the candles*)
This wax is as hard as any wire.

TYB:
Thou must chafe it a little at the fire.

JOHAN: (*rubbing the candles together near the fire*)
She that brought thee these wax candles twain,
She is a good companion certain!

TYB: (*to Sir Johan*)
What, was it not my gossip Margery?

SIR JOHAN:
Yes, she is a blessed woman, surely.

TYB:

Now would God I were as good as she,
For she is virtuous and full of charity.

JOHAN: *(aside)*

Now, so God help me, and by my holydom,
She is the errantest bawd between this and Rome.

TYB: *(sharply)*

What sayest?

JOHAN: *(mumbling)*

        Marry, I chafe the wax,
And I chafe it so hard that my fingers cracks.
But take up this pie that I here turn;
And it stand long, indeed, it will burn.

TYB: *(setting the pie on the table)*

Yea, but thou must chafe the wax, I say.

JOHAN: *(approaching the table)*

Bid him sit down, I thee pray—
Sit down, good Sir Johan, I you require.

TYB: *(as Sir Johan is seated)*

Go, I say, and chafe the wax by the fire
While that we sup, Sir Johan and I.

JOHAN: *(as she sits down)*

And how now! What will ye do with the pie?
Shall I not eat thereof a morsel?

TYB:

Go, and chafe the wax while thou art well!
And let us have no more prating thus.

SIR JOHAN: *(bowing his head to say grace)*
Benedicite

JOHAN: *(as if to join them at the meal)*
        Dominus.

TYB: *(vehemently)*

Now go chafe the wax, with a mischief!

JOHAN: *(apologetically)*

What? I come to bless the board, sweet wife.
It is my custom now and then. (than)
Much good do it to you, Master Sir Johan.

TYB:

Go chafe the wax, and here no longer tarry.

JOHAN: (*aside as he returns to the fireplace*)
And is not this a very purgatory:
To see folks eat, and may not eat a bite?
By cock's soul, I am a very woodcock.
This pail here, now a vengeance take it!
Now my wife giveth me a proud mock!

TYB: (*to Johan as she and Sir Johan begin to eat*)
What dost?

JOHAN: (*sulkily*)
                    Marry, I chafe the wax here,
And I imagine to make you good cheer—
(*aside*) That a vengeance take you both as ye sit,
For I know well I shall not eat a bit.
But yet, in faith, if I might eat one morsel,
I would think the matter went very well.

SIR JOHAN: (*as he and Tyb gorge themselves*)
Gossip Johan Johan, now "much good do it you!"
What cheer make you there by the fire?

JOHAN:
Master parson, I thank you now,
I fare well enough after mine own desire.

SIR JOHAN:
What dost, Johan Johan, I thee require.

JOHAN: (*wearily*)
I chafe the wax here by the fire.

TYB: (*lifting a mug*)
Here is good drink and here is good pie!

SIR JOHAN:
We fare very well, thanked be Our Lady.

TYB: (*quietly to Sir Johan*)
Look how the cuckold chafeth the wax that is hard,
And, for his life, dareth not look hitherward.

SIR JOHAN: (*to Johan*)
What doth my gossip?

JOHAN:
                    I chafe the wax—
(*aside*) And I chafe it so hard that my fingers cracks;
And also the smoke putteth out my eyes too:
I burn my face and scorch my clothes also,

And yet I dare not say one word.
And they sit laughing yonder at the board.
　　TYB: (*to Sir Johan*)
Now, by my troth, it is a pretty joke, (jape)
For a wife to make her husband her ape.
Look at Johan Johan, which maketh hard shift
To chafe the wax to stop therewith the cleft! (clyft)
　　JOHAN: (*aside*)
Yea, that a vengeance take ye both two,
Both him and thee, and thee and him also!
And that ye may choke with the same meat
At the first morsel that ye do eat.
　　TYB:
Of what thing now dost thou clatter,
Johan Johan, or whereof dost thou patter?
　　JOHAN:
I chafe the wax and make hard shift
To stop herewith of the pail the rift.
　　SIR JOHAN:
So must he do, Johan Johan, by my father's kin,
That is bound of wedlock in the yoke.
　　JOHAN: (*aside*)
Look how the bald priest crammeth in;
That would to God he might therewith choke!
　　TYB:
Now, Master Parson, pleaseth your goodness
To tell us some tale of mirth or sadness
For our pastime, in way of communication?
　　SIR JOHAN:
I am content to do it for our recreation:
And of three miracles I shall to you say.
　　JOHAN:
What, must I chafe the wax all day
And stand here, roasting by the fire?
　　SIR JOHAN:
Thou must do somewhat at thy wife's desire.
I know a man which wedded had a wife,
As fair a woman as ever bare life,
And within a sevenight after, right soon,

He went beyond sea and left her alone,
And tarried there about a seven year.
And as he came homeward he had a heavy cheer,
For it was told him that she was in heaven.
But when that he come home again was,
He found his wife, and with her children seven,
Which she had had in the mean space—
Yet had she not had so many by three
If she had not had the help of me.
Is not this a miracle, if ever were any,
That this good wife should have children so many
Here in this town while her husband should be
Beyond the sea in a far country?
    JOHAN: (*muttering to himself*)
Now in good sooth, this is a wondrous miracle!
But for your labor, I would that your tackle
Were in a scalding water well boiled. (sod)
    TYB:
Peace, I say; thou stoppest the word of God.
    SIR JOHAN:
Another miracle also I shall you say
Of a woman which that many a day
Had been wedded, and in all that season
She had no child, neither daughter nor son.
Wherefore to Saint Modwin she went on pilgrimage
And offered there a live pig, as is the usage
Of the wives that in London dwell;
And through the virtue thereof, truly to tell,
Within a month after, right shortly,
She was delivered of a child as much as I.
How say you, is not this miracle wonderous?
    JOHAN:
Yes, in good sooth, sir, it is marvelous.
But surely, after mine opinion,
That child was neither daughter nor son.
For certainly, and I be not beguiled,
She was delivered of a knave[13] child.

---

[13] *Knave* means *male*, but also *scoundrel*.

TYB:

Peace, I say, for God's passion!
Thou stoppest Sir Johan's communication.

SIR JOHAN:

The third miracle also is this:
I knew another woman besides, indeed,
Which was wedded and within five months after
She was delivered of a fair daughter,
As well formed in every member and joint,
And as perfect in every point,
As though she had gone five months full to the end.
Lo! here is five months of advantage.

JOHAN:

A wonderous miracle, so God me mend!
I would each wife that is bound in marriage
And that is wedded here within this place
Might have as quick speed in every such case.

TYB:

Forsooth, Sir Johan, yet for all that
I have seen the day that Puss, my cat,
Hath had in a year kittens eighteen.

JOHAN:

Yea, Tyb my wife, and that have I seen.
But how say you, Sir Johan, was it good, your pie?
The devil the morsel that thereof eat I.
By the good Lord, this is piteous work.
But now I see well the old proverb is true:
"The parish priest forgetteth that ever he was clerk!"
But, Sir Johan, doth not remember you
How I was your clerk and helped you mass to sing
And held the basin always at the offering?
Ye never had half so good a clerk as I!
But, notwithstanding all this, now our pie
Is eaten up, and there is not left a bit;
And you two together there do sit,
Eating and drinking at your own desire,
And I am Johan Johan, which must stand by the fire
Chafing the wax, and dare none otherwise do.

SIR JOHAN: *(impatiently to Tyb)*

And shall we always sit here still, we two?
That were too much.

TYB:

> Then rise we out of this place.

SIR JOHAN:

And kiss me then in the stead of grace.
And farewell, sweetheart and my love so dear.

JOHAN:

Cock's body, this wax it waxed cold again here.
But what! Shall I anon go to bed,
And eat nothing, neither meat nor bread?
I have not been wont to have such fare.

TYB:

Why, were ye not served there as ye are,
Chafing the wax and standing by the fire?

JOHAN:

Why, what meat gave ye me, I you require?

SIR JOHAN:

Wast thou not served, I pray thee heartily,
Both with the bread, the ale, and the pie?

JOHAN: (*bewildered*)

No, sir, I had none of that fare.

TYB: (*insistently*)

Why, were ye not served there as ye are,
Standing by the fire chafing the wax?

JOHAN: (*aside*)

Lo, here be many trifles and knacks—
By cock's soul, they think I am either drunk or mad!

TYB:

And had ye no meat, Johan Johan? no had?

JOHAN:

No, Tyb my wife, I had not a whit.

TYB:

What, not a morsel?

JOHAN: (*with determination*)

> No, not one bit.

For hunger, I trow, I shall fall in a swoon. (sowne)

SIR JOHAN:

O, that were pity, I swear by my crown.

TYB: (*solicitously*)
But is it true?

JOHAN:
                    Yea, for a surety.

TYB: (*suspiciously*)
Dost thou lie?

JOHAN:
                    No, so may I prosper! (the)

TYB:
Hast thou had nothing?

JOHAN:
                         No, not a bit.

TYB:
Hast thou not drunk?

JOHAN:
                         No, not a whit.

TYB:
Where wast thou?

JOHAN:
                    By the fire I did stand.

TYB:
What didst?

JOHAN: I chafed this wax in my hand,
Whereas I knew of wedded men the pain
That they have and yet dare not complain,
For the smoke put out my eyes two,
I burned my face and scorched my clothes also,
Mending the pail which is so rotten and old
That it will not scant together hold.
And since it is so, and since that ye twain
Would give me no meat for my sufficience,
By cock's soul, I will take no longer pain!
Ye shall do all yourself, with a very vengeance,
For me. And take thou there thy pail now,
And if thou canst mend it, let me see how.
(*He slams the pail on the floor.*)

TYB: (*in white fury*)
Ah! Whoreson knave! Hast thou broke my pail?
Thou shalt repent, by cock's lovely nail.

Reach me my distaff or my clipping shears!
I shall make the blood run about his ears.

    JOHAN: *(taking up a shovel full of coals)*

Nay, stand still, drab, I say, and come not near,
For, by cock's blood, if thou come here
Or if thou once stir toward this place,
I shall throw this shovelful of coals in thy face.

    TYB:

Ye whoreson drivel, get thee out of my door!

    JOHAN:

Nay, get thee out of my house, thou priest's whore!

    SIR JOHAN:

Thou lyest, whoreson cuckold, even to thy face!

    JOHAN:

And thou lyest, bald priest, with an evil grace!

    TYB:

And thou lyest.

    JOHAN:

               And thou lyest!

    SIR JOHAN:

                      And thou lyest again!

    JOHAN:

By cock's soul, whoreson priest, thou shalt be slain.
Thou hast eat our pie and give me nought.
By cock's blood, it shall be full dearly bought!

    TYB:

At him, Sir Johan, or else God give thee sorrow.

    JOHAN:

And have at you, whore and thief, Saint George to my
    help! (borrow)

   *Here they fight by the ears awhile, and then the priest
and the wife go out of the place.*

    JOHAN: *(to the audience)*

Ah, sirs! I have paid some of them even as I list.
They have borne many a blow with my fist.
I thank God, I have whacked them well
And driven them hence. But yet, can ye tell
Whither they be go? For, by God, I fear me
That they be gone together, he and she,

Unto his chamber; and perhaps she will,
Spite of my heart, tarry there still.
And, peradventure, there he and she
Will make me cuckold, even to anger me.
And then had I a pig in the worse pannier!
Therefore, by God, I will hie me thither
To see if they do me any villainy.
And thus, fare well this noble company!

   He goes off after his wife and Sir Johan.

The Play Called
The Four PP.

A NEW AND VERY MERRY INTERLUDE OF

A PALMER   A POTHECARY

A PARDONER   A PEDLAR

made by John Heywood

The opening line of the play implies that the
meeting of the four P's takes place in the public room
of an inn. Actually, it could occur anywhere, and since
the place is of no importance whatsoever, it is probable
that no scenery was used.

The play opens with the entrance of the Palmer, tall
and rather stately, wearing a long travelling robe and a
broad-brimmed hat. A palm-leaf is attached to his robe
in token that he has made a pilgrimage to the Holy
Land.

PALMER: (*looking around at the audience*)
Now God be here! Who keepeth this place?
Now, by my faith, I cry you mercy!
Of reason I must sue for grace,
My rudeness showeth me now so homely.[1]
Whereof your pardon asked, and won,
I sue you, as courtesy doth me kind,
To tell this which shall be begun
In order as may come best in mind.
I am a palmer, as ye see,
Which of my life much part hath spent
In many a fair and far country,

---

[1] Lacking in cultivation.

As pilgrims do of good intent.
At Jerusalem have I been
Before Christ's blessed sepulchre;
The Mount of Calvary have I seen,
A holy place, ye may be sure;
To Josephat and Olivette
On foot, God knows, I went right bare.
Many a salt tear did I sweat
Before this carcass could come there;
Yet have I been at Rome, also,
And gone the stations all arow,[2]
Saint Peter's Shrine, and many more
Than, if I told, all ye do know—
Except that there be any such
That hath been there and diligently
Hath taken heed and marked much,
Then can they speak as much as I.
Then at the Rhodes also I was,
And round about to Amyas;
At Saint Toncomber; and Saint Tronion;
At Saint Bothulph; and Saint Anne of Buckston;
On the hills of Armenia, where I see Noah's ark;
With holy Job; and Saint George in Southwark;
At Waltham, and at Walsingham;
And at the good Cross of Dagnam;
At Saint Cornelys; at Saint James in Gales;
And at Saint Winnifred's Well in Wales;
At Our Lady of Boston; at Saint Edmunds-bury;
And straight to Saint Patrick's Purgatory;
At Rydybone; and at the Blood of Hayles,
Where pilgrims' pains right much avails;
At Saint Davis; and at Saint Denis;
At Saint Matthew; and Saint Mark in Venice;
At Master John Shorne; at Canterbury;
The Great God of Katewade; at King Henry;
At Saint Saviours; at Our Lady of Southwell;
At Crome; at Wylsdome; and at Muswell;

---

[2] He has said a prayer at each of the stations of the cross in order.

At Saint Richard; and at Saint Roke;
And at Our Lady that standeth in the Oak.
To these, with other many one,
Devoutly have I prayed and gone,
Praying to them to pray for me
Unto the Blessed Trinity;
By whose prayers and my daily pain
I trust the sooner to obtain
For my salvation grace and mercy.
For, to be sure, I think surely
Who seeketh saints for Christ's sake—
And namely such as pain do take
On foot to punish their frail body—
Shall thereby merit more highly
Than by anything done by man.

The Pardoner has entered during the early part of the Palmer's recital. He is large and rotund, his round face marked with blotches from an overly rich diet. He wears a long black flowing robe, girdled at the waist with a cord, and reaching from a loose voluminous hood over his head to his sandalled feet. He carries a packet of relics and pardons which he is licensed to offer for sale. Chaucer's Pardoner is described as having "hair yellow as wax" hanging down thinly and covering his shoulders. "For amusement he wore no hood for it was packed up in his bag. He thought he rode in the latest style, dishevelled and bareheaded except for his cap. He had glistening eyes like a hare's." His bag was "crammed with pardons brought from Rome all hot."

PARDONER: (*thoroughly bored*)
And when ye have gone as far as ye can,
For all your labor and spiritual intent
Yet welcome home as wise as ye went!

PALMER: (*affronted*)
Why, sir, despise ye pilgrimage?

PARDONER: (*placatingly*)
Nay, for God, sir! Then did I rage!
I think ye right well occupied
To seek these saints on every side.

Also your pain I not dispraise it;
But yet I discommend your wit;
And, ere we go, even so shall ye,
If ye in this will answer me:
I pray you, show what the cause is
Ye went all these pilgrimages.

PALMER:

Forsooth, this life I did begin
To rid the bondage of my sin;
For which these saints, rehearsed ere this,
I have both sought and seen, indeed, (i-wys)
Beseeching them to be record
Of all my pain unto the Lord
That giveth all remission
Upon each man's contrition.
And by their good mediation,
Upon mine humble submission,
I trust to have in very deed
For my soul's health the better speed.

PARDONER:

Now is your own confession likely
To make yourself a fool quickly!
For I perceive ye would obtain
No other thing for all your pain
But only grace your soul to save.
Now, mark in this what wit ye have
To seek so far, and help so nie!
Even here at home is remedy,
For at your door myself doth dwell,
Who could have saved your soul as well
As all your wide wandering shall do,
Though ye went thrice to Jericho.
Now, since ye might have sped at home,
What have ye won by running at Rome?

PALMER:

If this be true that he have moved,[3]
Then is my wit indeed reproved!
But let us hear first what ye are.

---

[3] Propounded.

PARDONER:

Truly, I am a pardoner.

PALMER:

Truly a pardoner,—that may be true,
But a true pardoner doth not ensue!
Right seldom is it seen, or never,
That truth and pardoners dwell together;
For, be your pardons never so great,
Yet them to enlarge ye will not forbear (let)
With such lies that oftimes, Christ knows, (wot)
Ye seem to have that ye have not.
Wherefore I went myself to the thing itself (selfe thynge)
In every place, and, without feigning,
Had as much pardon there assuredly
As ye can promise me here doubtfully.
Howbeit, I think ye do but scoff.
But if ye had all the pardon ye speak of,
And no whit of pardon granted
In any place where I have haunted,
Yet of my labor I nothing repent.
God hath respect how each time is spent;
And, as in his knowledge all is regarded,
So by his goodness all is rewarded.

PARDONER:

By the first part of this last tale
It seemeth you come late from the ale!
For reason on your side so far doth fail
That ye leave reasoning and begin to rail;
Wherein ye forget your own part clearly,
For ye be as untrue as I:
And in one point ye are beyond me,
For we may lie by authority,—
And all that hath wandered so far
That no man can be their controller.
And, where ye esteem your labor so much,
I say yet again my pardons be such
That, if there were a thousand souls on a heap,
I would bring them all to heaven at a good bargain (as
good chepe)

As ye have brought yourself on pilgrimage
In the last quarter of your voyage,—
Which is far on this side heaven, by God!
There your labour and pardon is different, (od)
With small cost, and without any pain,
These pardons bringeth them to heaven plain.
Give me but a penny, or two pence,
And as soon as the soul departeth hence,
In half an hour—or three-quarters at most—
The soul is in heaven with the Holy Ghost!

During the last speech, the Pothecary has entered carrying his packet of drugs, which he prepares and sells. He wears a long gown with wide sleeves and a wide collar which meets his long black hair.

POTHECARY: (*to the Pardoner*)
Send ye any souls to heaven by water?

PARDONER: (*slightly affronted*)
If we did, sir, what does it matter?

POTHECARY:
By God, I have a dry soul should [go] thither!
I pray you let our souls go to heaven together.
So busy you twain be in soul's health,
May not a pothecary come in by stealth?
Yes, that I will, by Saint Anthony!
And, by the leave of this company,
Prove ye false knaves both, ere we go,
In part of your sayings, as this, lo:
(*to the Palmer*)
Thou by thy travail thinkest heaven to get;
(*to the Pardoner*)
And thou by pardons and relics countest no let
To send thine own soul to heaven sure,
And all other whom thou list to procure.
If I took an action,[4] then were they blank;
For like thieves, the knaves rob away my thank.
All souls in heaven having relief,
Shall they thank your crafts? Nay, thank mine, chiefly!
    (chefe)

---

[4] Legal proceedings.

No soul, ye know, entreth heaven gate
Till from the body he be separate;
And whom have ye known die honestly
Without help of the pothecary?
Nay, all that cometh to our handling—
Except ye happen to come to hanging—
That way, perchance, ye shall not need (myster)
To go to heaven without a purge! (glyster)
But, be ye sure, I would be woe
If ye should chance to beguile me so.
As good to lie with me a-night
As hang abroad in the moonlight!
There is no choice to flee my hand
But, as I said, into the noose. (bande)
Since of our souls the multitude
I send to heaven, when all is viewed,
Who should but I, then, altogether
Have thank of all their coming thither?

PARDONER:
If ye killed a thousand in an hour space,
When come they to heaven dying from state of grace?

POTHECARY:
If a thousand pardons about your necks were tied,
When come they to heaven if they never died?

PALMER:
Long life after good works, indeed,
Doth hinder man's receipt of reward, (mede)
And death before one duty done
May make us think we die too soon.
Yet better tarry a thing, than have it,
Than go too soon and vainly crave it.

PARDONER:
The longer ye dwell in communication,
The less shall you like this imagination;
For ye may perceive even at the first chop
Your tale is trapped in such a stop
That, at the least, ye seem worse than we.

POTHECARY:
By the mass, I hold us nought, all three!

Simultaneously with this remark, the Pedler enters.
He is short, compared with the others. He wears a loose,
bell-shaped hat and a simple broad-striped blouse under
a gray cape. His pack is slung on his back.

PEDLER:

By our Lady, then have I gone wrong!
And yet to be here I thought long.

POTHECARY:

Brother, ye have gone wrong no whit.
I praise your fortune and your wit
That can direct you so discreetly
To plant you in this company:
Thou a palmer, and thou a pardoner,
I a pothecary.

PEDLER:

        And I a pedler.

POTHECARY:

Now, on my faith, full well matched!
Where the devil were we four hatched?

PEDLER:

That maketh no matter, since we be matched!
I could be merry if that I catched
Some money for part of the ware in my pack.

POTHECARY:

What the devil hast thou there at thy back?

PEDLER: *(putting his pack down)*

Why, dost thou not know that every pedler
In every trifle must be a medler?
Specially in women's triflings—
Those use we chief above all things.
Which things to see, if ye be disposed,
Behold what ware here is disclosed.
(opening his pack)
This gear showeth itself in such beauty
That each man thinketh it saith, "Come, buy me!"
Look, where yourself can like to be chooser,
Yourself shall make price, though I be loser!
Is here nothing for my father Palmer?
Have ye not a wanton in a corner

For your walking to holy places?
By Christ, I have heard of as strange cases!
Who liveth in love, or love would win,
Even at this pack he must begin,
Where is right many a proper token,
Of which by name part shall be spoken:
Gloves, pins, combs, glasses unspotted,
Pomanders, hooks, and laces knotted,
Brooches, rings, and all manner beads,
Lace, round and flat, for women's heads,
Needles, thread, thimbles, shears, and all such knacks—
Where lovers be, no such things lacks—
Sypers,[5] swathing bands, ribbons, and sleeve-laces,
Girdles, knives, purses, and pincases.

POTHECARY: *(suggestively)*

Do women buy their pincases of you?

PEDLER:

Yea, that they do, I make God a-vow!

POTHECARY:

So might I thrive, then for my part,
I beshrew thy knave's naked heart
For making my wife's pincase so wide!
The pins fall out; they cannot abide.
Great pins must she have, one or other;
If she lose one, she will find another!
Wherein I find cause to complain—
New pins to her pleasure, and my pain!

PARDONER:

Sir, ye seem well versed in women's causes.
I pray you, tell me what causeth this,
That women, after their arising,
Be so long in their appareling?

PEDLER:

Forsooth, women have many problems, (lettes)
And they be masked in many nets,
As frontlets, fillets, partlets, and bracelets;
And then their bonnets and their poignets.[6]

---

[5] Materials made of cypress satin.

[6] Wrist ornaments.

By these lets and nets the let is such
That speed is small when haste is much.

POTHECARY:

Another cause why they come not forward,
Which maketh them daily to draw backward,
And yet is a thing they can not forbear—
The trimming and pinning up their gear,
Specially their fiddling with the tail-pin;
And, when they would have it pricked in,
If it chance to double in the cloth,
Then be they enraged and sweareth an oath;
Till it stand right, they will not forsake it.
Thus, though it may not, yet would they make it.
But be ye sure they do but defer it,
For, when they would make it, oftimes mar it.
But prick them and pin them as much as ye will,
And yet will they look for pinning still!
So that I dare bet you a joint
Ye shall never have them at a full point.

PEDLER:

Let women's matters pass, and mark mine!
Whatever their points be, these points be fine.
Wherefore, if ye be willing to buy,
Lay down money! Come up quickly!

PALMER:

Nay, by my troth, we be like friars:
We are but beggers; we be no buyers.

PARDONER:

Sir, ye may show your ware for your mind,
But I think ye shall not profit find.

PEDLER:

Well, though this journey bring no profit, (acquyte no
        cost)
Yet think I not my labor lost;
For, by the faith of my body,
I like full well this company.
Up shall this pack, for it is plain
I came not hither all for gain.
Who may not play one day in a week

May think his thrift is far to seek!
Devise what pastime ye think best,
And make ye sure to find me ready. (prest)

POTHECARY:

Why, be ye so universal
That you can do whatsoever ye shall?

PEDLER:

Sir, if ye wish to question me,
What I can do then shall ye see.

POTHECARY:

Then tell me this: be ye perfect in drinking?

PEDLER:

Perfect in drinking as may be wished by thinking!

POTHECARY:

Then after your drinking, how? Fall ye to sleeping?
(wynking)

PEDLER:

Sir, after drinking, while the bill is tinking,
Some heads be swimming (swynking), but mine will be
sinking,
And upon drinking mine eyes will be blinking,
For winking to drinking is always linking.

POTHECARY:

Then drink and sleep ye can well do.
But if ye were desired thereto,
I pray you, tell me, can you sing?

PEDLER:

Sir, I have some skill in singing.

POTHECARY:

But is your breath anything sweet?

PEDLER:

Whatever my breath be, my voice is meet.

POTHECARY:

That answer showeth you a right singing man!
Now what is your will, good father, then?

PALMER:

What helpeth will where is no skill?

PARDONER:

And what helpeth skill where is no will?

POTHECARY:

For will or skill, what helpeth it
Where forward knaves be lacking wit?
Leave off this subtlety; (curyosytie)
And who that list, sing after me!

*Here they sing. (Words and music are lacking in the
ms.)*

PEDLER:

This liketh me well, so may I thrive! (so mot I the)

PARDONER:

So help me God, it liketh not me!
Where company is met and well agreed,
Good pastime doth right well indeed;
But who can set in dalliance
Men set in such a variance
As we were set ere ye came in?
Which strife this man (*indicating the Palmer*) did first
    begin,
Alleging that such man as use,
For love of God, and not refuse,
On foot to go from place to place
A pilgrimage, calling for grace,
Shall in that pain with penitence
Obtain discharge of conscience—
Comparing that life for the best
Induction to our endless rest.
Upon these words our matter grew;
For, if ye could avow them true,
As good to be a gardener
As for to be a pardoner.
But when I heard him so far wide,
I then approached and replied,
Saying this: that this indulgence,
Having the foresaid penitence,
Dischargeth man of all offence
With much more profit than this pretence.
I ask but two pence at the most—
Indeed, this is not very great cost—
And from all pain, without despair—

My soul for his—keep even his chair,
And when he dieth he may be sure
To come to heaven, even at pleasure.
And more than heaven he can not get,
How far soever he wants to walk. (iet)
This is his pain more than his wit
To walk to heaven, since he may sit!
Sir, as we were in this contention,
In came this fool with his invention,
(*pointing to the Pothecary*)
Reviling us, himself avaunting,
That all the souls to heaven ascending
Are most bound to the pothecary
Because he helpeth most men to die;
Before which death he sayeth, indeed,
No soul in heaven can have his reward. (mede)

PEDLER:

What, do pothecaries kill men?

POTHECARY:

By God, men say so now and then!

PEDLER:

And I thought ye would not have missed
To make men live as long as ye wished. (lyste)

POTHECARY:

As long as we lyste? Nay, long as they can!

PEDLER:

So might we live without you then. (than)

POTHECARY:

Yea, but yet it is necessary
For to have a pothecary;
For when ye feel your conscience ready,
I can send you to heaven quickly.
Wherefore, concerning our matter here,
Above these twain I am best, clearly. (clere)
And if ye wish to take me so,
I am content you, and no more, (mo)
Shall be our judge as in this case
Which of us three shall take the best place.

PEDLER:

I neither will judge the best nor worst;
For, be ye blessed or be ye cursed,
Ye know it is no whit my sleight
To be a judge in matters of weight.
It behooveth no pedlers nor proctors[7]
To take on them judgment as doctors.
But if your minds be only set
To work for soul health, ye be well met,
For each of you somewhat doth show
That souls toward heaven by you do grow.
Then, if ye can so well agree
To continue together all three,
And all you three obey one will,
Then all your minds ye may fulfill:
As, if ye came all to one man
Who should go pilgrimage more than he can,
In that ye, Palmer, as debt,
May clearly discharge him, pardie;
(*to the Pardoner*)
And for all other sins, ones had contrition,
Your pardons giveth him full remission;
And then ye, Master Pothecary,
May send him to heaven bye and bye.

POTHECARY:

If he taste this box nigh about the prime,[8]
By the mass, he is in heaven ere evensong time!
My craft is such that I can right well
Send my friends to heaven—and myself to hell.
But, sirs, mark this man, for he is wise
Who could devise such a device;
For if we three may be as one,
Then be we Lords, everyone.[9]
Between us all could not be missed
To save the souls of whom we wished. (lyste)
But, for good order, at a word,

---

[7] University disciplinary officers.

[8] The first hour of the day.

[9] A double pun: *Lord* as *Savior* and *lord* as *nobleman*, and also
a reference to the Trinity.

Twain of us must wait on the third;
And unto that I do agree,
For both you twain shall wait on me!

PARDONER:

What chance is this that such an elf
Command two knaves beside himself?
Nay, nay, my friend, that will not be;
I am too good to wait on thee!

PALMER:

By Our Lady, and I would be loth
To wait on the better of you both!

PEDLER:

Yet be ye sure, for all this doubt,
This waiting must be brought about.
Men cannot prosper, wilfully led;
All thing decayeth where is no head.
Wherefore, doubtless, mark what I say:
To one of you three, twain must obey;
And since ye cannot agree in voice
Who shall be head, there is no choice
But to devise some kind of thing
Wherein ye all be equally cunning;
And in the same who can do best,
The other twain to make them pressed
In every thing of his intent
Wholly to be at commandment.
And now have I found one mastery
That ye can do indifferently,
And is neither selling nor buying,
But even only very lying!
And all ye three can lie as well
As can the falsest devil in hell.
And though afore ye hard me grudge
In greater matters to be your judge,
Yet in lying I have some skill;
And if I shall be judge, I will.
And, be ye sure, without flattery,
Where my conscience findeth the mastery,
There shall my judgment strict (strayt) be found,

Though I might win a thousand pound.

PALMER:

Sir, for lying, though I can do it,
Yet am I loth for to go to it.

PEDLER:	(*to the Palmer*)

Ye have not cause to fear to be bold,
For ye may be here uncontrolled.

(*to the Pardoner*)

And ye in this have good advantage,
For lying is your common usage.

(*to the Pothecary*)

And you in lying be well sped,
For all your craft doth stand in falsehood.	(falshed)

(*to all three*)

Ye need not care who shall begin,
For each of you may hope to win.
Now speak, all three, even as ye find:
Be ye agreed to follow my mind?

PALMER:

Yea, by my troth, I am content.

PARDONER:

Now, in good faith, and I assent.

POTHECARY:

If I denied, I were a noddy,
For all is mine, by God's body!

Here the Pothecary hoppeth.

PALMER:

Here were a hopper to hop for the ring!
But, sirs, this gear goeth not by hopping.

POTHECARY:

Sir, in this hopping I will hop so well
That my tongue shall hop as well as my heel;
Upon which hopping I hope, and not doubt it,
To hope so that ye shall hope without it.

PALMER:

Sir, I will neither boast nor brawl,
But take such fortune as may fall;
And if ye win this mastery,
I will obey you quietly.

And sure I think that quietness
In any man is great riches,
In any kind of company,
To rule or be ruled indifferently.

PARDONER:

By that boast thou seemest a beggar indeed.
What can thy quietness help us at need?
If we would starve, thou hast not, I think,
One penny to buy us one pot of drink.
Nay, if riches might rule the roost, (roste)
Behold what cause I have to boast!
(*opening his pack and drawing out objects as indicated*)
Lo, here be pardons half a dozen.
For spiritual (gostely) riches they have no cousin;
And, moreover, to me they bring
Sufficient succour for my liking.
And here be relics of such a kind
As in this world no man can find.
Kneel down, all three, and, when ye leave kissing,
Who list to offer shall have my blessing!
Friends, here shall ye see even anon
Of All-Hallows the blessed jaw-bone.
Kiss it heartily with good devotion!

POTHECARY: (*after kissing it*)

This kiss shall bring us much promotion.—
Fogh! by Saint Saviour, I never kissed a worse!
Ye were as good kiss All-Hallows ars!
For, by All-Hallows, methinketh
That All-Hallows' breath stinketh.

PALMER: (*severely*)

Ye judge All-Hallows' breath unknown;
If any breath stink, it is your own.

POTHECARY:

I know mine own breath from All-Hallows,
Or else it were time to kiss the gallows.

PARDONER: (*producing another relic*)

Nay, sirs, behold, here may ye see
The great-toe of the Trinity.
Who to this toe any money voweth,

And once may roll it in his mouth,
All his life after, I undertake,
He shall be rid of the toothache.

POTHECARY:

I pray you, turn that relic about!
Either the Trinity had the gout
Or else, because it is three toes in one,
God made it much as three toes alone.

PARDONER: (*exchanging the toe for another relic*)

Well, let that pass, and look upon this:
Here is a relic that doth not miss
To help the least as well as the most—
This is a buttock-bone of Pentecost!

POTHECARY:

By Christ, and yet, for all your boast,
This relic hath be-shitten the roost!

PARDONER: (*producing another relic*)

Mark well this relic: here is a whipper! [10]
My friends, unfeigned,[11] here is a slipper
Of one of the Seven Sleepers,[12] be sure.
Doubtless this kiss shall do you great pleasure,
For all these two days it shall so ease you
That none other savours shall displease you.

POTHECARY:

All these two days? Nay, all these two year!
For all the savours that may come here
Can be no worse; for at a word,
One of the Seven Sleepers trod in a turd.

PEDLER: (*to the Pothecary*)

Sir, methinketh your devotion is but small.

PARDONER:

Small? marry, methinketh he hath none at all!

POTHECARY:

What the devil care I what ye think?

---

[10] A winning exhibit.

[11] Honestly.

[12] According to legend, seven young Ephesian noblemen fled to
a cave at the time of the Decian persecution. They were walled in
and slept for two hundred years.

Shall I praise relics when they stink?
PARDONER: (*exhibiting another relic*)
Here is an eye-tooth of the Great Turk.[13]
Whose eyes be once set on this piece of work
May haply lose part of his eyesight,
But not all till he be blind outright.
POTHECARY:
Whatsoever any other man seeth,
I have no devotion to Turk's teeth;
For although I never saw a greater,
Yet methinketh I have seen many better.
PARDONER: (*pulling out a small box*)
Here is a box full of humble-bees
That stung Eve as she sat on her knees
Tasting the fruit to her forbidden.
Who kisseth the bees within this hidden
Shall have as much pardon, of right,
As for any relic he kissed this night.
PALMER: (*kissing the box*)
Sir, I will kiss them, with all my heart.
POTHECARY: (*as the Pardoner presents the box for his kiss*)
Kiss them again, and take my part,
For I am not worthy,—nay, let be!
Those bees that stung Eve shall not sting me!
PARDONER: (*exhibiting a flask*)
Good friends, I have yet here in this glass
Which on the drink at the wedding was
Of Adam and Eve undoubtedly.
If ye honor this relic devoutly,
Although ye thirst no whit the less,
Yet shall ye drink the more, doubtless.
After which drinking ye shall be as able (mete)
To stand on your head as on your feet.
POTHECARY:
Yea, marry, now I can ye thank!
In presence of this the rest be blank.

---

[13] Probably Mohammed II who conquered Constantinople in 1453.

Would God this relic had come sooner! (rather)
Kiss that relic well, good father!
Such is the pain that ye palmers take
To kiss the pardon-bowl for the drink's sake.
(*kneeling and kissing the flask*)
O holy yeast, that looketh full sour and stale,
For God's body help me to a cup of ale!
The more I behold thee, the more I thirst;
The oftener I kiss thee, more like to burst!
But since I kiss thee so devoutly,
Hear me and help me with drink till I die!
(*rising*)
What, so much praying and so little speed?

PARDONER:

Yea, for God knoweth when it is need
To send folks drink; but, by Saint Anthony,
I ween he hath sent you too much already.

POTHECARY:

If I have never the more for thee,
Then be the relics no riches to me,
Nor to thyself, except they be
More beneficial than I can see.
(*opening his packet of drugs*)
Richer is one box of treacle
Than all thy relics that do no miracle.
If thou hadst prayed but half so much to me
As I have prayed to thy relics and thee,
Nothing concerning mine occupation
But straight should have wrought in operation.
And, as in value, I pass you an ace.
(*producing another box*)
Here lyeth much riches in little space:
I have a box of rhubarb here
Which is as dainty as it is dear.
So help me God and hollydam,
Of this I would not give a dram
To the best friend I have in England's ground
Though he would give me twenty pound;
For, though the stomach do it abhor,

It purgeth you clean from the choler,
And maketh your stomach sore to squirm (walter)
That ye shall never come to the halter.

PEDLER:
Then is that medicine a sovereign thing
To preserve a man from hanging.

POTHECARY: (*exhibiting what looks like a candy-stick*)
If ye will taste but this stick that ye see,
If ever ye be hanged, never trust me!
(*producing an ointment*)
Here have I diapompholicus,
A special ointment, as doctors discuss;
For a fistula or a canker
This ointment is even shot-anchor,[14]
For this medicine helpeth one and other,
Or bringeth them in case that they need no other.
(*holding up a vial of syrup*)
Here is syrapus de Byzansis,
A little thing is enough of this,
For even the weight of one scruple
Shall make you strong as a cripple.
(*showing the rest of his wares*)
Here be others: as diosfialios,
Diagalanga, and sticados,
Blanca manna, diospoliticon,
Mercury sublime, and metridaticon,
Pelitory, and asafetida,
Cassia, and colloquintita.
These be the things that break all strife
Between man's sickness and his life.
From all pain these shall you deliver
And set you even at rest forever!
Here is a medicine—no more like the same
Which commonly is called thus by name
Alikakabus or alkakengy—
A goodly thing for dogs that be mangy.
Such be these medicines that I can
Help a dog as well as a man.

---

[14] Last hope.

Not one thing here particularly
But worketh universally—
For it doth me as much good when I sell it
As all the buyers that taste it or smell it.
Now, since my medicines be so special
And in operation so general,
And ready to work whensoever they shall,
So that in riches I am principal.
If any reward may entreat ye,
I beseech your worship be good to me,
And ye shall have a box of marmalade
So fine that ye may dig it with a spade.

PEDLER:

Sir, I thank you; but your reward
Is not the thing that I regard.
I must, and will, be indifferent.
Wherefore, proceed in your intent.

POTHECARY:

Now if I knew this wish no sin,
I would to God I might begin!

PARDONER:

I am content that thou lie first.

PALMER:

Even so am I; and say thy worst!
Now let us hear of all thy lies
The greatest lie thou mayest devise.
And in the fewest words thou can.

POTHECARY:

Forsooth, ye be an honest man.

PALMER:

There said ye much! but yet no lie.

PARDONER: (*to the Pothecary*)

Now lie ye both, by Our Lady!
Thou lyest in boast of his honesty,
And he hath lied in affirming thee.

POTHECARY:

If we both lie, and ye say true,
Then of these lies your part between two! (?—adew—
á deux?)

And if ye win, make none avaunt;
For ye are sure of one ill servant.
(*to the Palmer*)
Ye may perceive by the words he gave
He taketh your worship but for a knave.
But who told true, or lied indeed,
That will I know ere we proceed.
Sir, after that I first began
To praise you for an honest man
When ye affrmed it for no lie—
Now, by our faith, speak even truly—
Thought ye your affirmation true?

PALMER:

Yea, marry, I! for I would ye knew
I think myself an honest man.

POTHECARY:

What, thought ye in the contrary then? (than)

PARDONER:

In that I said the contrary,
I think from truth I did not vary.

POTHECARY:

And what of my words?

PARDONER:

I thought ye lied.

POTHECARY:

And so thought I, by God that died!
Now have you twain each for himself laid
That none hath lied ought, but both truesaid;
And of us twain none hath denied,
But both affirmed that I have lied:
Now since ye both your truth confess,
And that we both my lie so witness
That twain of us three in one agree,
And that the lier the winner must be,
Who could provide such evidence
As I have done in this pretence?
(*to the Pedler*)
Methinketh this matter sufficient
To cause you to give judgment,

And to give me the mastery,
For ye perceive these knaves cannot lie.

PALMER:

Though neither of us as yet had lied,
Yet what we can do is untried;
For yet we have devised nothing,
But answered you and given hearing.

PEDLER: *(nodding in agreement)*

Therefore I have devised one way
Whereby all three your minds may say:
For each of you one tale shall tell;
And which of you telleth most marvel
And most unlikely to be true,
Shall most prevail, whatever ensue.

POTHECARY:

If ye be set in marvelling,
Then shall ye hear a marvelous thing;
And though, indeed, all be not true,
Yet sure the most part shall be new:
I did a cure, no longer ago
But *Anno Domini millesimo*,[15]
On a woman, young and so fair
That never have I seen a gayer.
God save all women from that likeness!
This wanton had the falling sickness,
Which by descent came lineally,
For her mother had it naturally.
Wherefore, this woman to recure
It was more hard ye may be sure.
But though I boast my craft is such
That in such things I can do much,
How oft she fell were much to report;
But her head so giddy and her heels so short
That, with the twinkling of an eye,
Down would she fall even bye and bye.
But ere she would arise again,
I showed much practice, much to my pain;
For the tallest man within this town

---

[15] In the year 1000.

Should not with ease have broken her swoon. (sowne)
Although for life I did not doubt her,
Yet did I take more pain about her
Than I would take with my own sister.
Sir, at the last I gave her a glister:
I thrust a tampion[16] in her tool
And bade her keep it for a jewel.
But I knew it so heavy to carry
That I was sure it would not tarry;
For where gunpowder is once fired
This tampion will no longer be hard. (?—hyerd)
Which was well seen in time of this chance;
For, when I had charged this ordinance,
Suddenly, as it had thundered,
Even at a clap loosed her bumberd.
Now mark—for here beginneth the revel—
This tampion flew ten long mile level
To a fair castle of lime and stone—
For strength I know not such a one—
Which stood upon an hill full high,
At foot whereof a river ran by,
So deep, till chance had it forbidden,
Well might the Regent[17] there have ridden.
But when this tampion on this castle light,
It put the castles so far to flight
That down they came each upon other,
No stone left standing, by God's Mother!
But rolled down so fast the hill
In such a number, and so did fill,
From bottom to brim, from shore to shore,
This foresaid river, so deep before,
That who list now to walk thereto
May wade it over and wet no shoe.
So was this castle laid wide open
That every man might see the token.
But—in good hour may these words be spoken!—

---

[16] Plug.
[17] Apparently the name of a ship.

After the tampion on the walls was wrought, (wroken)
And piece by piece in pieces broken,
And she delivered with such violence
Of all her inconvenience,
I left her in good health and lust.
And so she doth continue, I trust!

PEDLER:

Sir, in your cure I can nothing tell;
But to our purpose ye have said well.

PARDONER:

Well, sir, then mark what I can say:
I have been a pardoner many a day
And done greater cures spiritually   (gostely)
Than ever he did bodily;
Namely, this one which ye shall hear,
Of one departed within this seven year—
A friend of mine, and likewise I
To her again was as friendly—
Who fell so sick so suddenly
That dead she was even bye and bye,
And never spake with priest nor clerk,
Nor had no whit of this holy work,
For I was thence; it could not be.
Yet hard I say she asked for me.
But when I bethought me how this chanced,
And that I have to heaven advanced
So many souls to me but strangers,
And could not keep my friend from dangers,
But she to die so dangerously,
For her soul health especially—
That was the thing that grieved me so
That nothing could release my woe
Till I had tried even out of hand
In what estate her soul did stand.
For which trial, short tale to make,
I took this journey for her sake—
Give ear, for here beginneth the story:
From hence I went to purgatory
And took with me this gear in my fist,

Whereby I may do there what I list.
I knocked and was let in quickly,
But, Lord, how low the souls made curtsey!
And I to every soul again
Did give a beckon them to retain,
And asked them this question then: (than)
If that the soul of such a woman
Did late among them there appear.
Whereto they said she came not here.
Then feared I much it was not well.
Alas, thought I, she is in hell!
For with her life I was so acquainted
That sure I thought she was not sainted.
With this it chanced me to sneeze;
"Christ help!" quoth a soul that lay for his fees.
"These words," quoth I, "thou shalt not lose!" (lees)
Then with these pardons of all degrees
I paid his toll and set him so quit
That straight to heaven he took his flight.
And I from thence to hell that night
To help this woman, if I might,
Not as who saith by authority,
But by the way of entreaty.
And first to the devil that kept the gate
I came and spake after this rate:
"All hail, sir devil!" and made low curtsey.
"Welcome!" quoth he, thus smilingly.
He knew me well. And I at last
Remembered him since long time past,
For, as good hap would have it chance,
This devil and I were of old acquaintance,
For oft in the play of Corpus Christi
He hath played the devil at Coventry.
By his acquaintance and my behavior
He showed to me right friendly favor.
And—to make my return the shorter—
I said to this devil: "Good master porter,
For all old love, if it lie in your power,
Help me to speak with my lord and your."

"Be sure," quoth he, "no tongue can tell
What time thou couldest have come so well,
For this day Lucifer fell—
Which is our festival in hell.
Nothing unreasonable craved this day
That shall in hell have any nay.
But yet beware thou come not in
Till time thou may thy passport win.
Wherefore stand still, and I will know (wyt)
If I can get thy safe-conduct." (condyt)
He tarried not, but shortly got it,
Under seal, and the devil's hand at it,
In ample wise, as ye shall hear.
Thus it began: "Lucifer,
By the power of God chief devil of hell,
To all the devils that there do well,
And every of them, we send greeting
Under strict charge and commanding
That they aiding and assistant be
To such a pardoner,"—and named me—
"So that he may at liberty
Pass safe without his jeopardy
Till that he be from us extinct
And clearly out of hell's precinct.
And, his pardons to keep safeguard,
We will they lie in the porter's ward.
Given in the furnace of our palace
In our high court of matters of malice,
Such a day and year of our reign."
"God save the devil!" quoth I, "for plainly (playne)
I trust this writing to be sure."
"Then put thy trust," quoth he, "in ever
Since thou art sure to take no harm."
This devil and I walked arm in arm
So far till he had brought me thither
Where all the devils of hell together
Stood in array in such apparel
As for that day there meetly fell:
Their horns well gilt, their claws full clean,

Their tails well kempt, and, as I believe, (wene)
With soothing butter their bodies anointed—
I never saw devils so well appointed.
The master devil sat in his jacket,
And all the souls were playing at racket.
None other rackets they had in hand
Save every soul a good firebrand;
Wherewith they played so prettily
That Lucifer laughed merrily,
And all the residue of the fiends
Did laugh full well together like friends.
But of my friend I saw no whit,
Nor durst not ask for her as yet.
Anon, all this rout was brought in silence,
And I by an usher brought in presence.
Then to Lucifer low as I could
I kneeled. Which he so well allowed
That thus he beckoned; and, by Saint Anthony,
He smiled on me well-favoredly,
Bending his brows, as broad as barn doors, (durres)
Shaking his ears, as rugged as burs,
Rolling his eyes as round as two bushels,
Flashing the fire out of his nostrils,
Gnashing his teeth so vaingloriously
That methought time to fall to flattery.
Wherewith I told, as I shall tell,
"O pleasant picture! O Prince of hell!
Featured in fashion abominable!
And since that it is inestimable
For me to praise thee worthily,
I leave off praise, unworthy
To give thee praise, beseeching thee
To hear my suit, and then to be
So good to grant the thing I crave.
And, to be short, this would I have:
The soul of one which hither is flitted
Delivered hence, and to me remitted.
And in this doing, though all be not quit,
Yet some part I shall deserve it,

As thus: I am a pardoner,
And over souls, as a controller,
Throughout the earth my power doth stand,
Where many a soul lyeth on my hand,
That speed in matters as I use them,
As I receive them or refuse them;
Whereby, what time thy pleasure is,
Ye shall require any part of this:
The least devil here that can come thither
Shall choose a soul and bring him hither."
"Now," quoth the devil, "we are well pleased!
What is his name thou wouldst have eased?"
"Nay," quoth I, "be it good or evil,
My coming is for a she devil."
"What callest her?" quoth he, "thou whoreson!"
"Forsooth," quoth I, "Margery Coorson."
"Now, by our honor," said Lucifer,
"No devil in hell shall withhold her!
And if thou wouldst have twenty more, (mo)
Were not for justice, they should go.
For all we devils within this den
Have more to do with two women
Than with all the charge we have beside.
Wherefore, if thou our friend will be tried,
Apply thy pardons to women so
That unto us there come no more." (mo)
To do my best I promised by oath,
Which I have kept; for, as the faith goeth,
In these days to heaven I do procure
Ten women to one man, be sure.
Then of Lucifer my leave I took
And straight unto the master cook.
I was had into the kitchen,
For Margery's office was therein.
All thing handled there discreetly—
For every soul beareth office meetly—
Which might be seen to see her sit
So busily turning of the spit;
For many a spit here hath she turned,

And many a good spit hath she burned,
And many a spit full hot hath toasted
Before the meat could be half roasted.
And, ere the meat were half roasted indeed,
I took her then from the spit for speed.
But when she saw this brought to pass,
To tell the joy wherein she was
And of all the devils for joy how they
Did roar at her delivery,
And how the chimes in hell did ring,
And how all the souls therein did sing,
And how we were brought to the gate,
And how we took our leave thereat,
Be sure lack of time suffereth not (nat)
To rehearse the twentieth part of that!
Wherefore, this tale to conclude briefly,
This woman thanked me chiefly
That she was rid of this endless death,
And so we departed on Newmarket Heath.
And if that any man do mind her,
Who list to seek her, there shall he find her!

PEDLER:

Sir, ye have sought her wondrous well;
And, where ye found her, as ye tell,
To hear the chance ye found in hell,
I find ye were in great peril. (parell)

PALMER:

His tale is all much perilous,
But part is much more marvelous,
As where he said the devils complain
That women put them to such pain
By their conditions so crooked and crabbed,
Forwardly fashioned, so wayward and rabid,
So far in division and stirring such strife,
That all the devils be wary of their life!
This in effect he told for truth;
Whereby much marvel to me ensueth,
That women in hell such shrews can be
And here so gentle, as far as I see.

Yet have I seen many a mile
And many a woman in the while—
Not one good city, town, nor borough
In Christendom but I have been through—
And this I would ye should understand:
I have seen women five hundred thousand
. . . . [18]
And oft with them have long time tarried;
Yet in all places where I have been,
Of all the women that I have seen,
I never saw, nor knew, in my conscience,
Any one woman out of patience.

POTHECARY:

By the mass, there is a great lie!

PARDONER:

I never heard a greater, by Our Lady!

PEDLER:

A greater? Nay, know ye any so great?

PALMER:

Sir, whether that I lose or get,
For my part, judgment shall be asked. (prayed)

PARDONER:

And I desire as he hath said.

POTHECARY:

Proceed, and ye shall be obeyed.

PEDLER:

Then shall not judgment be delayed.
Of all these three, if each man's tale
In Paul's Churchyard [19] were set on sale
In some man's hand that hath the skill, (sleyghte)
He should sure sell these tales by weight.
For as they weigh, so be they worth.
But which weigheth best? To that now forth:
(*to the Pothecary*)
Sir, all the tale that ye did tell
I bear in mind; (*to the Pardoner*) and yours as well;

---

[18] The line to rhyme with the following *tarried* is missing.
[19] A center for bookstalls.

And, as ye saw the matter meetly,
So lied ye both well and discreetly
Yet were your lies the least, trust me!
(*to the Pothecary*)
For if ye had said ye had made flee
Ten tampions out of ten women's tails,
Ten times ten mile, to ten castles or jails,
And fill ten rivers ten times so deep
As ten of that which your castle stones did keep;
(*to the Pardoner*)
Or if ye ten times had bodily
Fetched ten souls out of purgatory,
And ten times so many out of hell,
Yet by these ten bones (*holding up his fingers*) I could
   right well
Ten times sooner all that have believed
Than the tenth part of that he hath delivered. (meved)

   POTHECARY:

Two knaves before one lacketh two knaves of five;
Then one, and then one, and both knaves alive;
Then two, and then two, and three at a cast;
Thou knave, and thou knave, and thou knave, at last!
Nay, knave, if ye try me by number,
I will as knavishly you encumber.
Your mind is all on your private tithe,
For all in ten methinketh your wit lyeth. (lythe)
Now ten times I beseech Him that high sits
Thy wife's ten commandments may search thy five wits;
Then ten of my turds in ten of thy teeth, (teth)
And ten on thy nose which every man seeeth. (seth)
And twenty times ten this wish I would:
That thou hadst been hanged at ten year old!
For thou goest about to make me a slave.
I will thou know if I am a gentleman, knave!
(*points at the Pardoner*)
And here is another shall take my part.

   PARDONER:

Nay, first I beshrew your knave's heart
Ere I take part in your knavery!

I will speak fair, by Our Lady!
(*to the Pedler*)
Sir, I beseech your worship to be
As good as ye can be to me.

    PEDLER:

I would be glad to do you good
And him also, be he never so mad. (wood)
But doubt you not I will now do
The thing my conscience leadeth me to.
Both your tales I take for impossible,
Yet take I his farther incredible.
Not only the thing itself alloweth it,
But also the boldness thereof avoweth it.
(*to the Pothecary*)
I know not where your tale to try;
(*to the Pardoner*)
Nor yours, but in hell or purgatory;
But his boldness hath faced a lie
That may be tried even in this company,
As, if ye list, to take this order:
(*indicating the audience with a sweep of his hand*)
Among the women in this border,
Take three of the youngest and three of the oldest,
Three of the hottest and three of the coldest,
Three of the wisest and three of the shrewdest,
. . . . 20
Three of the lowest and three of the highest,
Three of the farthest and three of the nighest,
Three of the fairest and three of the maddest,
Three of the foulest and three of the saddest,
And when all these threes be had asunder,
Of each three, two, justly by number,
Shall be found shrews—except this befall,
That he hap to find them shrews all!
Himself for truth all this doth know,
And oft hath tried some of this row;
And yet he sweareth, by his conscience,
He never saw woman break patience!

------

20 The line to rhyme with *shrewdest* is missing.

Wherefore, considered with true intent,
His lie to be so evident
And to appear so evidently
That both you affirmed it a lie,
And that my conscience so deeply
So deep hath sought this thing to try,
And tried it with mind indifferent,
Thus I award, by way of judgment:
Of all the lies ye all have spent
His lie to be most excellent.

PALMER: (*modestly*)

Sir, though ye were bound of equity
To do as ye have done to me,
Yet do I thank you of your pain
And will requite some part again.

PARDONER:

Marry, sir, ye can no less do
But thank him as much as it cometh to.
And so will I do for my part:
Now a vengeance on thy knave's heart!
I never knew pedler a judge before,
Nor never will trust peddling-knave more!

(*The Pothecary makes an awkward curtsey to the Pedler.*)

What does thou here, thou whoreson noddy?

POTHECARY:

By the mass, learn to make curtsey!
Curtsey before and curtsey behind him,
And then on each side—the devil blind him!
Nay, when I have it perfectly,
Ye shall have the devil and all of curtsey!
But it is not soon learned, brother,
One knave to make curtsey to another.
Yet when I am angry, that is the worst,
I shall call my master knave at the first.

PALMER: (*haughtily*)

Then would some master perhaps clout ye!
But, as for me, ye need not doubt ye;
For I had liefer be without ye

Than have such baseness about me.

PARDONER:

So help me God, so were ye better!
What, should a begger be a strutter? (ietter)
It were no whit your honesty
To have us twain strut after ye.

POTHECARY:

Sir, be ye sure he telleth you true.
If we should serve, this would ensue:
It would be said—trust me at a word—
Two knaves made curtsey to the third.

PEDLER:

Now, by my troth, to speak my mind,
Since they be so loth to be assigned,
To let them loose I think it best,
And so shall he lie best in rest.

PALMER:

Sir, I am not on them so fond
To compel them to keep their bond.
(*to the Pothecary and the Pardoner*)
And since ye list not to wait on me,
I clearly of waiting discharge ye.

PARDONER:

Marry, sir, I heartily thank you!

POTHECARY:

And I likewise, I make God avow!

PEDLER:

Now be ye all even as ye began; (begoon)
No man hath lost nor no man hath won. (woon)
Yet in the debate wherewith ye began,
By way of advice I will speak as I can:
(*to the Palmer*)
I do perceive that pilgrimage
Is chief the thing ye have in usage;
Whereto, in effect, for love of Christ
Ye have, or should have, been enticed.
And whoso doth, with such intent,
Doth well declare his time well spent.
(*to the Pardoner*)

And so do ye in your pretence,
If ye procure thus indulgence
Unto your neighbors charitably
For love of them in God only.
All this may be right well applied
To show you both well occupied;
For, though ye walk not both one way,
Yet, walking thus, this dare I say:
That both your walks come to one end.
And so for all that do pretend,
By aid of God's grace, to pursue
Any manner kind of virtue:
As some great alms for to give,
Some in willful poverty to live,
Some to make highways and such other works,
And some to maintain priests and clerks
To sing and pray for souls departed,
These, with all other virtues well marked,
Although they be of sundry kinds,
Yet be they not used with sundry minds;
But as God only doth all these move,
So every man, only for His love,
With love and dread obediently
Worketh in these virtues uniformly.
Thus every virtue, if we list to scan,
Is pleasant to God and thankful to man;
And who that by grace of the Holy Ghost
To any one virtue is moved most,
That man, by that grace, that one apply,
And therein serve God most plentifully!
Yet not that one so far wide to perform, (wreste)
So liking the same to mislike the rest;
For whoso doeth, his work is in vain.
And even in that case I perceive you twain,
Liking your virtue in such wise
That each other's virtue you do despise.
Who walketh this way for God would find him,
The farther they seek him the farther behind him.
One kind of virtue to despise another

Is like as the sister might hang the brother.

POTHECARY:

For fear lest such perils to me might fall,
I thank God I use no virtue at all!

PEDLER:

That is of all the very worst way!
For more hard it is, as I have heard say,
To begin virtue where none is pretended
Than, where it is begun, the abuse to be mended.
Howbeit, ye be not all to begin;
One sign of virtue ye are entered in:
As this, I suppose ye did say true,
In that ye said ye use no virtue;
In the which words, I dare well report,
Ye are well beloved of all this sort, (*indicating the audience*)
By your railing here openly
At pardons and relics so lewdly.

POTHECARY:

In that I think my fault not great;
For all that he hath I know counterfeit.

PEDLER:

For his, and all other that ye know feigned,
Ye be neither counselled nor constrained
To any such thing in any such case
To give any reverence in any such place;
But where ye doubt the truth, not knowing,
Believing the best, good may be growing.
In judging the best, no harm at the least, (leste)
In judging the worst, no good at the best.
But best in these things, it seemeth to me,
To take no judgment upon ye;
But, as the Church doth judge or take them,
So do ye receive or forsake them;
And so, be sure, ye cannot err,
But may be a fruitful follower.

POTHECARY:

Go ye before, and, as I am true man,
I will follow as fast as I can.

The Pedler leaves the stage, followed by the Pothe-cary.

PARDONER:

And so will I; for he hath said so well,
Reason would we should follow his counsel.

The Pardoner goes off.

PALMER: (*addressing the audience*)

Then to our reason God give us his grace,
That we may follow with faith so firmly
His commandments, that we may purchase
His love, and so consequently
To believe his Church fast and faithfully,
So that we may, according to his promise,
Be kept out of error in any wise.
And all that hath scaped us here by negligence,
We clearly revoke and forsake it.
To pass the time in this without offence
Was the cause why the maker did make it;
And so we humbly beseech you take it;
Beseeching Our Lord to prosper you all
In the faith of his Church Universal!

He bows and makes his exit.

6 iiii

BIBLIOGRAPHY

A. C. Cawley, ed., *The Wakefield Pageants in the Towneley Cycle*. Manchester University Press, 1958.

E. K. Chambers, *English Literature at the Close of the Middle Ages*. Oxford: Clarendon Press, 1945; second impression with corrections, 1947, 1948, 1954.

——, *The Medieval Stage*, 2 vols. London: Oxford University Press, 1903; reprinted 1925, 1948.

Hardin Craig, *English Religious Drama*. Oxford: Clarendon Press, 1955.

T. W. Craik, *The Tudor Interlude, Stage, Costume, and Acting*. Leicester: University Press, 1958.

B. Hunningher, *The Origin of the Theatre*. The Hague: Martinusnijhoff; Amsterdam: E. M. Querido, 1955.

Allardyce Nicoll, *The Development of the Theatre*, 4th ed. rev. London: George G. Harrap & Co., Ltd., 1959.

Alfred W. Pollard, *English Miracle Plays, Moralities and Interludes*. Oxford: Clarendon Press (8th edition revised), 1927.

A. W. Reed, *Early Tudor Drama*. London: Methuen & Co., Ltd., 1926.

A. P. Rossiter, *English Drama from Early Times to the Elizabethans*. London: Hutchinson's University Library, 1950.

Richard Southern, *The Medieval Theatre in the Round . . . a study of the staging of the Castle of Perseverance and related matters*. London: Faber & Faber, Ltd., 1957.

John Speirs, *Medieval English Poetry, the Non-Chaucerian Tradition*. London: Faber & Faber, Ltd., 1957.

Henry W. Wells, Roger S. Loomis, eds. and trans., *Representative Medieval and Tudor Plays*. New York: Sheed and Ward, 1942.

Karl Young, *The Drama of the Medieval Church*, 2 vols. Oxford: Clarendon Press, 1933.

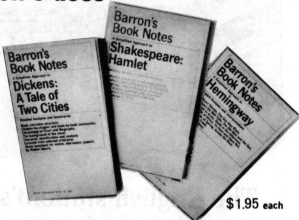

10 Steps in Writing the Research Paper

Markman and Waddell 160 pp., $4.50
The process of writing a research paper is reduced to 10 simple steps. Plus a unique section on "Plagiarism: A Step to Avoid."

The Art of Styling Sentences: 20 Patterns to Success

Wadell, Esch, and Walker
112 pp., $4.95
By imitating 20 sentence patterns and variations, students will grasp how to write with imagination, clarity, and style. Illustrated with practice material for writing more effectively.

Spelling Your Way to Success

Mersand and Griffith 224 pp., $5.95
A systematic, simplified, and progressive method of improving one's spelling without constantly having to consult a dictionary. Numerous self-tests and practice material.

Building an Effective Vocabulary

Cedric Gale 288 pp., $4.95
A thorough course in all the methods of evaluating words for richness and appropriateness to improve ability to communicate.

1001 Pitfalls in English Grammar

Vincent F. Hopper 352 pp., $5.95
The most common errors in the English language are examined, including grammar, spelling, word choice, and punctuation.

1100 Words You Need to Know

Bromberg and Gordon 220 pp., $5.95
More than 1100 words and idioms taken from the mass media and introduced in readable stories. Contains 46 daily lessons of 20 minutes each.

Essentials of English

Hopper, Foote, Gale 256 pp., $4.95
A comprehensive program in the writing skills necessary for effective communication.

Essentials of Writing

Hopper and Gale 176 pp., $5.95
A companion workbook for the material in ESSENTIALS OF ENGLISH.

Word Mastery: A Guide to the Understanding of Words

Drabkin, Bromberg 224 pp., $5.95
This fascinating book stresses word use and word development through the presentation of words in natural settings such as newspapers and magazines. With practice exercises.

How to Write Themes and Term Papers

Barbara Lenmark Ellis 160 pp., $4.95
The correct, logical approach to tackling a theme project or paper.

Words with a Flair

Bromberg and Liebb 224 pp., $5.95
A collection of 600 difficult but useful words. Includes word games and puzzles.

How to Write Themes and Term Papers

Chances are great that you will have to write many themes and term papers before four years of college are finished. Why not learn the correct way in the beginning and avoid any possible Cs or Ds. This new theme guide is one that you can understand, with common-sense advice on mastering this important task. The author traces the entire topic step-by-step from selecting the topic and deciding on the type of theme, to writing an effective conclusion.

$4.95 paper

BARRON'S EDUCATIONAL SERIES, INC.
113 Crossways Park Drive, Woodbury, N.Y. 11797

Getting Your Words Across
Murray Bromberg and Milton Katz
224 pp., $5.95
A unique new basic vocabulary book utilizing brief articles, exercises and crossword puzzles to help build word power.

A Pocket Guide to Correct Punctuation
Robert Brittain   96 pp., $2.50
Explains what each mark means, and shows how to use it with clarity and precision.

A Pocket Guide to Correct English
Michael Temple   128 pp., $2.50
A concise guide to the essentials of correct grammar and usage, spelling, punctuation, writing, and more.

A Pocket Guide to Correct Spelling
Francis Griffith   256 pp., $2.50
A handy quick-reference tool that lists 25,000 words in alphabetical order, correctly spelled and divided into syllables.

Barron's "Easy Way" Series: English Titles
Three practical guides filled with straightforward instruction and numerous examples.

English the Easy Way
Harriet Diamond and Phyllis Dutwin
224 pp., $6.95

Spelling the Easy Way
Joseph Mersand and Francis Griffith
144 pp., $6.95

Typing the Easy Way
Warren T. Schimmel and Stanley A. Lieberman
144 pp., $8.95

Handbook of Commonly Used Idioms
Maxine Tull Boatner and Jonathan Edward Gates
Update Editor Adam Makkai
224 pp., $4.95
A fascinating and useful book for people learning English as well as for "natives" who want to add color and variety to their conversations. Includes 1500 popular idioms.

You Can Succeed! The Ultimate Study Guide for Students
Eric Jensen   208 pp., $2.50
This positive guide to success in school encourages high school students to make a contract with themselves to set goals and work ambitiously toward them. Among the topics covered: Lack of Motivation—the #1 Problem, Success Habits, Attack Plan for Studying, Using Your Memory More Effectively, Word Power, How to Take Tests.

How to Beat Test Anxiety and Score Higher on Your Exams
James H. Divine and David W. Kylen   144 pp., $2.50
This reassuring book will help nervous test-takers of all ages gain skill and confidence. The authors reveal how test-taking skills can be learned; how basic preparation techniques can reduce anxiety and improve performance.
"Excellent book!" — J. Wiseman, Student Education Center, Philadelphia, Pa.

Barron's Green Guide to Better Grades in College With Less Effort
Kenneth A. Green   176 pp., $3.50
How to cope with college work is analyzed in this survival kit. Includes legitimate shortcuts to better grades with minimal hassles.

Study Tips   How to Study Effectively and Get Better Grades
William H. Armstrong   272 pp., $2.75
A guide to improving the skills necessary to earn higher grades in many subjects at many levels. Tips on how to master writing techniques, improve study habits, increase reading speed, review for exams, and more.

Study Tactics
William H. Armstrong 272 pp., $4.95
For students who want to earn higher grades, this useful guide presents an easy-to-follow plan for sound study habits. Pointers on mastering writing techniques, increasing reading speed reviewing for exams, and more are given.

The Freshman's Friend
S. J. Johnson   64 pp., $1.25
A new edition of the semi-serious, fun guide to the everyday terms and phrases used on college campuses. With alphabetically arranged entries, the book simplifies the confusion of orientation and registration and supplies valuable definitions of college lingo used by administrators and counselors, such as accelerated degree, CLEP, compensatory education, cross-disciplinary, and so forth.

How To Find What You Want In The Library

Charlotte GORDON

A concise manual that shows you how to locate the
books you want and where to go for more information.
With bibliographies and a special section on how to
uncover and assemble facts for a research paper.

$5.95

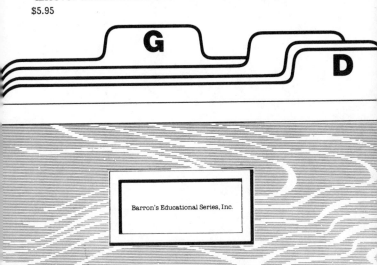

Barron's Educational Series, Inc.